Lecture Notes in Computer Science　　11512

Commenced Publication in 1973
Founding and Former Series Editors:
Gerhard Goos, Juris Hartmanis, and Jan van Leeuwen

More information about this series at http://www.springer.com/series/7408

John Miller · Eleni Stroulia ·
Kisung Lee · Liang-Jie Zhang (Eds.)

Web Services – ICWS 2019

26th International Conference
Held as Part of the Services Conference Federation, SCF 2019
San Diego, CA, USA, June 25–30, 2019
Proceedings

 Springer

Editors
John Miller
University of Georgia
Athens, GA, USA

Eleni Stroulia
University of Alberta
Edmonton, AB, Canada

Kisung Lee (iD)
Louisiana State University
Baton Rouge, LA, USA

Liang-Jie Zhang (iD)
Kingdee International Software
Group Co., Ltd.
Shenzhen, China

ISSN 0302-9743   ISSN 1611-3349 (electronic)
Lecture Notes in Computer Science
ISBN 978-3-030-23498-0   ISBN 978-3-030-23499-7 (eBook)
https://doi.org/10.1007/978-3-030-23499-7

LNCS Sublibrary: SL2 – Programming and Software Engineering

This Springer imprint is published by the registered company Springer Nature Switzerland AG
The registered company address is: Gewerbestrasse 11, 6330 Cham, Switzerland

Preface

The International Conference on Web Services (ICWS) has been a prime international forum for researchers and industry practitioners alike to exchange the latest fundamental advances in the state of the art and practice of Web-based services, identify emerging research topics, and define the future of Web-based services. All topics regarding Internet/Web services lifecycle study and management align with the theme of ICWS.

ICWS 2019 was part of the Services Conference Federation (SCF). SCF 2019 had the following ten collocated service-oriented sister conferences: 2019 International Conference on Web Services (ICWS 2019), 2019 International Conference on Cloud Computing (CLOUD 2019), 2019 International Conference on Services Computing (SCC 2019), 2019 International Congress on Big Data (BigData 2019), 2019 International Conference on AI & Mobile Services (AIMS 2019), 2019 World Congress on Services (SERVICES 2019), 2019 International Congress on Internet of Things (ICIOT 2019), 2019 International Conference on Cognitive Computing (ICCC 2019), 2019 International Conference on Edge Computing (EDGE 2019), and 2019 International Conference on Blockchain (ICBC 2019). As the founding member of SCF, the First International Conference on Web Services (ICWS) was held in June 2003 in Las Vegas, USA. The First International Conference on Web Services—Europe 2003 (ICWS-Europe 2003) was held in Germany in October 2003. ICWS-Europe 2003 was an extended event of the 2003 International Conference on Web Services (ICWS 2003) in Europe. In 2004, ICWS-Europe was changed to the European Conference on Web Services (ECOWS), which was held in Erfurt, Germany. To celebrate its 16th birthday, SCF 2018 was held successfully in Seattle, USA.

This volume presents the accepted papers for the 2019 International Conference on Web Services (ICWS 2019), held in San Diego, USA, during June 25–30, 2019. For this conference, each paper was reviewed by three independent members of the international Program Committee. After carefully evaluating their originality and quality, we accepted 12 papers in total.

We are pleased to thank the authors, whose submissions and participation made this conference possible. We also want to express our thanks to the Organizing Committee and Program Committee members, for their dedication in helping to organize the conference and in reviewing the submissions. We owe special thanks to the keynote speakers for their impressive speeches. We would like to thank Prof. Lakshmish Ramaswamy, who provided continuous support for this conference.

Finally, we would like to thank Dr. Jing Zeng for his excellent work in organizing this conference. We look forward to your great contributions as a volunteer, author, and conference participant for the fast-growing worldwide services innovations community.

May 2019   John Miller
                                                        Eleni Stroulia
                                                        Kisung Lee
                                                        Liang-Jie Zhang

Organization

General Chair

Lakshmish Ramaswamy   University of Georgia, USA

Program Chairs

John Miller   University of Georgia, USA
Eleni Stroulia   University of Alberta, Canada
Kisung Lee   Louisiana State University–Baton Rouge, USA

Services Conference Federation (SCF 2019)

SCF 2019 General Chairs

Calton Pu   Georgia Tech, USA
Wu Chou   Essenlix Corporation, USA
Ali Arsanjani   8x8 Cloud Communications, USA

SCF 2019 Program Chair

Liang-Jie Zhang   Kingdee International Software Group Co., Ltd., China

SCF 2019 Finance Chair

Min Luo   Services Society, USA

SCF 2019 Industry Exhibit and International Affairs Chair

Zhixiong Chen   Mercy College, USA

SCF 2019 Operations Committee

Huan Chen   Kingdee International Software Group Co., Ltd., China
Jing Zeng   Kingdee International Software Group Co., Ltd., China
Liping Deng   Kingdee International Software Group Co., Ltd., China
Yishuang Ning   Tsinghua University, China
Sheng He   Tsinghua University, China

SCF 2019 Steering Committee

Calton Pu (Co-chair)   Georgia Tech, USA
Liang-Jie Zhang (Co-chair) Kingdee International Software Group Co., Ltd., China

ICWS 2019 Program Committee

Ismailcem Arpinar	University of Georgia, USA
Travis Atkison	The University of Alabama, USA
Salima Benbernou	Paris Descartes University, France
Bo Cheng	Beijing University of Posts and Telecommunications, China
Wonik Choi	Inha University, South Korea
Michael Cotterell	University of Georgia, USA
Marios-Eleftherios Fokaefs	Polytechnique Montréal, Canada
Walid Gaaloul	Telecom SudParis, France
Keke Gai	Beijing Institute of Technology, China
Sheng He	Tsinghua University, China
Hamzeh Khazaei	University of Alberta, Canada
Hyuk-Yoon Kwon	Seoul National University of Science and Technology, South Korea
Ki Yong Lee	Sookmyung Women's University, South Korea
Bing Li	Wuhan University, China
Chengwen Luo	Shenzhen University, China
Massimo Mecella	Sapienza University of Roma, Italy
Yishuang Ning	Tsinghua University, China
Roy Oberhauser	Aalen University, Germany
Noseong Park	George Mason University, USA
Stephan Reiff-Marganiec	University of Leicester, UK
Young-Kyoon Suh	Kyungpook National University, South Korea
Liqiang Wang	University of Central Florida, USA
Lijie Wen	Tsinghua University, China
Lina Yao	University of New South Wales, Australia
Haibo Zhang	University of Otago, New Zealand
Rui Zhang	Chinese Academy of Sciences, China
Yang Zhou	Auburn University, USA

Contents

x   Contents

Modeling Social Influence in Mobile Messaging Apps

Songmei Yu[(✉)] and Sofya Poger

Felician University, Lodi, NJ 07644, USA
{yus, pogers}@felician.edu

Abstract. Social influence is the behavioral change of a person because of the perceived relationship with other people, organizations and society in general. With the exponential growth of online social network services especially mobile messaging apps, users around the world are logging in to messaging apps to not only chat with friends but also to connect with brands, browse merchandise, and watch content. Mobile chat apps boast a number of distinct characteristics that make their audiences particularly appealing to businesses and marketers, including their size, retention and usage rates, and user demographics. The combined user base of the top four chat apps is larger than the combined user base of the top four social networks. Therefore, it makes great sense to analyze user behavior and social influence in mobile messaging apps. In this paper, we focus on computational aspects of measuring social influence of groups formed in mobile messaging apps. We describe the special features of mobile messaging apps and present challenges. We address the challenges by proposing a temporal weighted data model to measure the group influence in messaging apps by considering their special features, with implementation and evaluation in the end.

Keywords: Social influence · Mobile messaging apps · Influence modeling

1 Introduction

Social influence refers to the behavioral change of individuals affected by others in a network. Social influence is an intuitive and well-accepted phenomenon in online social networks. The strength of social influence depends on many factors such as the strength of relationship between users in the networks (nodes), the network distance between users (edges), temporal effects (time), characteristics of networks and individuals in the network. In this paper, we build a temporal weighted data model that focuses on influence analysis in mobile messaging apps, using groups (communities) randomly formed in mobile messaging environment and individual behaviors in the groups, and describe the measures and algorithms related to group and individual characteristics analysis over a certain time period. Furthermore, we implement this model by applying it into real dataset, and evaluate its application within a given dataset.

First we survey the related work in traditional social networks. We point out the limitations of current existing models that did not give enough weight to special characteristics of mobile messaging apps, which leads to our weighted model to

© Springer Nature Switzerland AG 2019
J. Miller et al. (Eds.): ICWS 2019, LNCS 11512, pp. 1–11, 2019.
https://doi.org/10.1007/978-3-030-23499-7_1

integrate these factors into the existing techniques. Secondly, we propose the temporal weighted data model for social influence evaluation in mobile messaging apps by integrating special features. We use a bipartite graph to represent users and groups, add weights to different features of groups and users, and compute the value of influence at certain time period, as well as identify the change of this influence value over time periods. Thirdly, we discuss the applications of maximizing influence in mobile messaging apps by utilizing our proposed data model, on both group level and individual level. We implement and evaluate the model by using real data from WeChat. The paper is concluded with future work.

2 Related Work and Challenges

A social network is modeled as a graph $G = (V, E)$, where V is the set of nodes, and E is set of edges which is a subset of $V \times V$. The nodes correspond to users (people) and the edges correspond to social relationship. At the local level, social influence is a directional effect from node A to node B, and is related to the edge strength from A to B. On the global level, some nodes can have intrinsically higher influence than others due to network structures. These global influence measures are often associated with nodes and edges, which are presented as (a) Edge Measures, (b) Node Measures, and (c) Social Similarity, Influence and Actions. All of these factors were studied thoroughly [1, 2, 5, 6, 8, 10]. In this section, we will briefly discuss their limitations when applied to mobile messaging applications.

2.1 Special Features of Mobile Messaging Apps

The rise of mobile social messaging apps will increasingly threaten the influence and stickiness of conventional social networks. It is a potentially transformative trend that will see increasing numbers of app developers and business holders looking to re-orientate their social integration strategies to facilitate messaging and content sharing with communities outside of Facebook, Twitter and other more established social networks.

The leading service of this kind, WhatsApp, has in excess of 350 million active users around the world, with services such as WeChat and Line also boasting hundreds of millions of users. Traditional social networks and mobile messaging apps both provide platforms for people to connect and share content, so what distinguishes the two?

The first difference is regarding audience size, duration, and intent. A messaging app acts primarily as a one-to-one (or one-to-few) communication mechanism, and can be temporary or long-lasting. Content is intended to be private, or at least directed towards a specific group, not to the public. Whereas a social network consists of "many to many" connections, is durable, and is capable of producing network effects. Content is essentially public. Second, a user can create as many accounts as he/she wants in a traditional social network, but only one account that is based on cell phone number can be created in mobile messaging apps. Thirdly, groups/communities in traditional social network are predefined by the site administrator, and group admin account(s) are also designated by the site administrator. Those groups and admin members could last for months or years. However, in mobile messaging apps, any account can form a group at any time that attract people who are interested to join and therefore assign itself as an administrator, or dissolve a group at any time. Time is essential in mobile groups. Finally, in traditional social network, an account can join any group by just posting or replying to other posts. There is no formal way to join or quit a group. In mobile messaging apps, an account needs to be invited to join a group by the group admin, or an existing group member. On the other hand, an account needs to formally quit a group by signing out or being removed by the group admin. In this way, groups in mobile messaging apps have more control on information diffusion than traditional social networks.

2.2 Existing Work and Challenges

Social network analysis often focus on macro-level models such as degree distributions, diameter, clustering coefficient, communities, small world effect, preferential attachment, etc.; work in this area includes [1, 11]. Recently, social influence study has started to attract more attention due to the popularity of many important applications such as Twitter and Facebook. Many of the works on this area present qualitative findings about social influences [14]. Some researchers studied the influence model quantitatively, focusing on measuring the strength of topic-level social influence. However, few research work have been done on dynamic formed group level in mobile messaging systems, by analyzing behavior characteristics of group and users, which posted challenges in answering certain key questions such as (1) Which group(s) has dramatic influence change during certain time period? (2) For certain topics, which group has more influence than others among all groups relate to the same topic? (3) How to identify and connect to a particular influential user through member invitation mechanism in mobile messaging apps? Above all, the key question is how to quantify the influence in mobile messaging apps of both groups and users.

2.3 Our Contributions

Based on the unique features of mobile messaging systems, we propose a temporal weighted data model in a quantitative way that tackles the special features of mobile messaging apps. In particular, our model integrates the following factors into a mathematical model: (1) the average number of posts within a group per day during a certain period T, (2) the average number of members in a group giving its limited member size during T, (3) the ratio of number of posts to the number of members within a group during T, (4) the diversity of posting members within a group during T. *i.e.* whether the posts are coming from only one or two members or from majority members in the group. We can use the total number of members who have at least one post to measure this attribute, and (5) the interactive ratio, i.e., the ratio of original posts to replying posts from other members. This is to measure interactivity within the group. More formally, given a mobile social network for certain topic(s), we construct a social influence graph that quantitatively computes the influence level for each group during a specified time period.

3   A Temporal Weighted Data Model

3.1   Problem Formulation

In social network, bipartite networks or affiliation networks are bipartite graphs that are used to represent the members and the groups/communities they belong to. In our problem, we define the relationship between members and member-created groups as a special bipartite graph: there is an edge between a user u and a group g, if the edge is a directional edge, it means the user is a creator/admin of this associated group, else this user is just a regular member of this group. Figure 1 shows the change of group creation and member association of each group from time T_1 to time T_2. We can see the time is essential as the status of groups and associated members of each group is dynamically changing, new groups are constantly created (group D is created in T_2), some old groups could be dissolved, and members are constantly added or dismissed from each group.

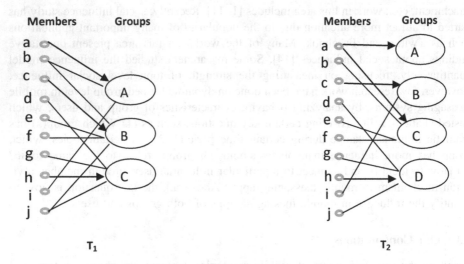

Fig. 1. The change of users/groups in the bipartite networks

The goal of social influence analysis in mobile messaging apps is to derive the *group level* social influence based on the features of topic distribution during a certain time period t, as well as the *individual level* of influence by constructing sub-graphs within a group. Weights will be considered for each factor. Here we assume each group is a topic related group, which means the topic is given for each group and all posts are related to the given topic. In this paper, we focus on the group level social influence computation.

We consider the following factors as special features associated with each group. Social influence in a mobile messaging group is primarily determined by these factors.

1. Number of posts
2. Number of members
3. Ratio of posts to members
4. Ratio of original post to replying posts from other members
5. Total number of members having a least one post

Table 1 shows the notations we use in our model:

Table 1. Notation

Symbol	Description
G	A single group
T	A time period a group G exists
N	Number of posts in G during T
M	Number of members in G during T
L	The upper limit of member size in G
O_i	Number of original posts from member i in G during T, $i \in Q$
R_{ij}	Number of replying posts from member j to member i in G during T, $i \in Q$, $j \in Q$
P	The set of posts in G during T
Q	The set of members in G
S_i	Status of a member i, $i \in Q$: $S_i = 1$ for admin, $S_i = 0$ for regular members
μ_i	The social influence of member i in G, $i \in Q$
μ_G	The social influence of G

Based on the above concepts, we can formalize the problem as follows:

Problem. Given a network $G = (P, Q, T)$, where P is set of relations (original or replying posts) within Q, Q is a set of nodes (members), and T is a specified time period that G is alive, how to (1) identify the influence level of this network G during T, (2) measure the influence level of each node in Q during T, and (3) evaluate the influence change of G and Q as T changes and therefore achieve the influence maximization at certain point.

3.2   Our Approach

The social influence analysis problem poses challenges in setting the weight for each factor associated with a mobile messaging group. For some factor, the value is dynamically changing during the time interval T. Hence setting weight for each factor to capture how it affects the social influence level of a group or a member within the group is challenging, as we are monitoring a dynamic changing entity with some factors' value are changing constantly.

Determining the Time Period T. Based on tour observation of datasets we collected from WeChat, an average life expectancy of a group is 9–12 months, from the time it is created to the time it is dissolved or it becomes quiet with no posts or very few posts posted. Of course there are exceptions that some groups are lasting for years and some groups are only alive less than 1 month. Therefore, it is essential to set up the time period based on the datasets collected.

Identifying Influence Factors. For certain factors, the value are constantly changing. For example, if we set up T as one year, it is easy to count the number of posts within a group as we can just add all posts starting from the beginning to the end of the year. However, counting number of members is a little different as some members may leave or join the group during the middle of this specific month. Since we count all posts during this year, we need to count all members accordingly during this year even some of them leave or join in the middle. Similarly, we need to count the total original posts or replying posts from each member even this member leave or join in the middle.

We identify the following factors as influence factors of a group G based on the special features of mobile messaging apps:

- Post Size N: the total number of posts in G during T
- Group Popularity M/L: the current member size in G during T over its member size upper-limit L
- Post Liveness N/M: the total number of posts over the current member size in G during T
- Post Diversity D: the diversity of G which indicates the total number of members in G during T that has at least one post
- Post Interactivity I: the total number of replying posts from member j for each original post from member i ($i \neq j$, $i \in Q$, $j \in Q$)

Determining Influence Weight Vector. Each factor is considered as one dimension/attribute of social influence for a group. Compared to others in the same dataset, a high influential group can normally attract more people to join, has more posts during a specific time period, a member will be more active to post comments and talks to each other, and the interactivity ratio will be higher too. However, these dimensions may have covariant relationship with each other, for example, a higher value of member size will produce a lower ratio of posts to members, which will affect the group influence level negatively.

We use an *Influence Weight Vector* to determine how each factor contributes to the overall influence of a group within a given dataset that composes of several similar groups. It quantifies how much positive or negative influence a factor affects the total influence level of a group. The bigger the value, the higher influence the factor contributes to the group influence level.

Definition: an *Influence Weight Vector* is a row vector V_T for a reference dataset during a specified time period T, $V_T = [W_N, W_{M/L}, W_{N/M}, W_D, W_I]$, where W_N is the weight of the factor that is the total number of posts in G during T, W_M is the weight of factor that is the number of members given its limited size (M/L_M), $W_{N/M}$ is the weight of factor that shows the ratio of total posts to total members, W_D is the weight of factor that shows the diversity of posts in G, and W_I is the weight of factor that describes the ratio of original posts from one member to replied posts from other members.

Now we describe how to compute each weight in V_T. Assume we collect a dataset which has n mobile messaging groups (G_1, G_2, ..., G_n) during T, and G_k is one of them that we are interested to measure its influence level where k = 1, 2, ..., n. We call this dataset as a reference dataset. Generally all groups in this dataset should have similar topic(s), hence it makes sense to compare their social influence levels.

$$W_N = 1 - \frac{\sum N_k/n}{N_{max}} \quad \text{where } k = 1, 2, \ldots, n. \tag{1}$$

N_k is the total number of posts within group k, $\sum N_k/n$ is the average number of group posts in reference dataset, N_{max} is the maximal number of posts that a group has in the reference dataset. We use 1- (the ratio of average number of posts to the maximal number of posts) to show the trust or importance of this factor on group influence. The rational is that if the average is close to maximum, W_N will decrease. We would think the variance of each group's post numbers is small, hence the total number of posts of each group would not be able to significantly indicate the influence level difference of each group.

$$W_{M/L} = \frac{\sum M_k/n}{L} \quad \text{where } k = 1, 2, \ldots, n. \tag{2}$$

Given the group size *L* that is set by the group admin (there could be default size for some mobile messaging apps), the ratio of current average member size in the reference dataset to the size limit shows how populated the group is. The bigger the value is, the higher the impact is. When it is 1, this factor reaches the maximum impact on the influence level.

$$W_{N/M} = \frac{\sum N_k/\sum M_k}{Max\left(\frac{N_k}{M_k}\right)} \quad \text{where } k = 1, 2, \ldots, n. \tag{3}$$

The ratio of total number of posts to the total numbers in the reference dataset shows on average how many posts each number. By dividing by the maximum value of posts per member of all groups in the dataset, this weight shows relatively how members contribute the total posts. The bigger the value is, the higher the impact is, as it shows each member on average has more posts to influence others.

$$W_D = \frac{\sum M_{ik}}{\sum M_k} \quad \text{where } i \in Q_k, k = 1, 2, \ldots n. \tag{4}$$

W_D shows how diversified the posts are in a reference dataset. $\sum M_i$ computes the total members in the dataset who has at least one post, whereas $\sum M_k$ just computes the total members in the dataset. The ratio calculates the percentage of members who do the posts. For some group(s), only one or two persons are posting, others are silent, even there are a large number of posts, it is not influential due to low diversity. The higher the value of W_D is, the more people involved in discussion, then we would think the higher the influence of this factor could be.

$$W_I = \frac{\sum Oik}{\sum Rijk} \quad \text{where } k = 1, 2, \ldots n, i \in Q_k, j \in Q_k, i \neq j \tag{5}$$

The ratio of original posts to the replying posts shows the interactivity of a chatting group, which plays an important role to determine the influence level. O_{ik} calculates the number of original posts from certain user i in group k, R_{ijk} calculates the number of replied posts from users other than i in group k. When we add all original and replying posts in the reference dataset and find out the ratio, we set up a threshold that measures the weight of interactivity. There could be a case where a lot of users post, but very few reply, which shows low response on the topic posted, therefore there is low influence in the group. The higher the threshold is, the more important the interactivity is in determining the group influence level.

Compute the Influence Level of a Group (μ_G). After we compute the influence vector V_T, we come up an algorithm to calculate the group social influence level μ_G. The bigger the value of μ_G is, the higher the social influence that this group has within a specific mobile messaging community.

Algorithm. Computing the Social Influence Level of all groups in a given reference dataset during period T. We assume the dataset has k groups which are focusing on similar topics.

Input: $G_k = (P, Q, T)$, $k = 1, 2, \ldots, n$
Output: μ_G for G_k, $k = 1, 2, \ldots, n$

1. Calculate the influence weight vector of the selected reference dataset that includes groups G_k ($k = 1, 2, \ldots, n$): $V_T = [W_N, W_{M/L}, W_{N/M}, W_D, W_I]$

2. For ($k = 1, k < n, k ++$):
     Collect resource data of each group G_k: [N, M/L, N/M, D, I]
     μ_G = [N, M/L, N/M, D, I]^T x V_{GT}
          = N x W_N + M/L x $W_{M/L}$ + N/M x $W_{N/M}$ + D x W_D + I x W_I

---

4   Model Implementation and Evaluation

We collected several groups from WeChat which have similar discussion topics, and built statistics for this bipartite network accordingly. This is our reference dataset. By analyzing these groups, we expect to find which group has higher social influence during each period, and reach a clear picture to view the influence level change of each group over time periods. Ideally, we could identify the maximized influence level at certain point for each group and use the pattern to predict the future trend if possible. This result makes great business sense to attract sponsorship, donation and advertisement for the groups.

Specifically, the dataset we collected are three groups which focus on elementary education discussion in WeChat in 2018, all of which have 500 upper limit of member size (a default WeChat group size assigned by the app). We want to compare their influence levels on the group level. We collected all needed data of each month for each group within three months, including post counts by differentiating original posts and comments, member counts, posts per each member, etc. Then we calculated the influence weight vector of this dataset, and finally calculated their social influence levels of each month accordingly.

We implemented this process using Python and reached the result as follows (Tables 2 and 3):

Table 2. Source data

	Jan 2018					Feb 2018					March 2018				
Source Data	N	M	L	D	I*	N	M	L	D	I*	N	M	L	D	I*
Group 1	356	112	500	42	120/236	702	228	500	120	122/600	1005	234	500	124	350/655
Group 2	1242	201	500	86	301/941	980	178	500	98	560/420	789	145	500	120	203/586
Group 3	1003	450	500	359	240/763	1345	456	500	400	506/839	1809	500	500	324	402/1407

*We use the number of original posts/the number of replying posts to represent group interactivity I.

Table 3. Calculated results

		Jan 2018	Feb 2018	March 2018
Dataset	Influence weight vector ** $[W_N, W_{M/L}, W_{N/M}, W_D, W_I]$	[0.14, 0.51, 0.55, 0.64, 0.34]	[0.25, 0.57, 0.64, 0.72, 0.65]	[0.34, 0.59, 0.75, 0.65, 0.36]
Group 1	Influence level μ_G. **	507.99	721.93	896.71
Group 2	Influence level μ_G. **	1000.79	1098.04	816.51
Group 3	Influence level μ_G. **	1295.99	1530.61	1631.99

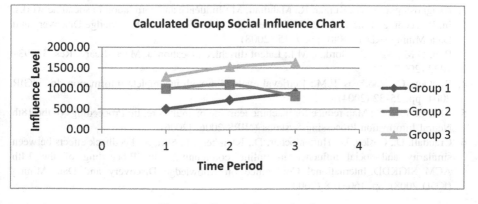

Chart 1. Group influence levels

Chart 1 shows the influence level change for each group over three periods. We can see that group 1 is getting more influential over the time periods, group 2's influential level started declining from the second period and is below group 1's level at the third period although it has much more members in the beginning, and group 3 is gradually increasing the influential level and is always on the top among three groups. We could not identify the trend for each group's social influential level as more time periods needed, but at certain point we can point out which group has more influential level than others. Also, within each group, we can identify the maximized influential point within a certain time periods.

5   Conclusions and Future Work

Social influence plays an important role in social media information dissemination. Social behavior and how consumers think have conventionally been disseminated by media such as television, radio, newspapers and magazines, but in the 21st century, social media especially mobile messaging apps have begun to replace traditional media's enduring and influential role on consumers' behavior. In mobile messaging apps, people are interested in social influence on two levels, group level and individual level. In this paper, we focus on the group level. We propose a Temporal Weighted Data Model to measure the social influence level for a special group within a set of similar groups, and find out the maximized influence level for each group during a certain period. This model is implemented and evaluated in the end.

Our future work is to build a model to measure individual social influence in each group by constructing a sub-graph within the group. Moreover, based the proposed data model, we will discuss strategies to increase the influence in mobile messaging applications for both group level and individual level.

References

1. Albert, R., Barabasi, A.L.: Statistical mechanics of complex networks. Rev. Mod. Phys. **74** (1), 47 (2002)
2. Anagnostopoulos, A., Kumar, R., Mahdian, M.: Influence and correlation in social networks. In: Proceeding of the 14th SIGKDD International Conference on Knowledge Discovery and Data Mining (KDD 2008), pp. 7–15 (2008)
3. Blei, D.M., Ng, A.Y., Jordan, M.I.: Latent dirichlet allocation. J. Mach. Learn. Res. **3**, 993–1022 (2003)
4. Buckley, C., Voorhees, E.M.: Retrieval evaluation with incomplete information. In: SIGIR 2004, pp. 25–32 (2004)
5. Chu, C.-T., et al.: Map-reduce for machine learning on multicore. In: Proceedings of the 18th Neural Information Processing Systems (NIPS 2006) (2006)
6. Crandall, D., Cosley, D., Huttenlocher, D., Kleinberg, J., Suri, S.: Feedback effects between similarity and social influence in online communities. In: Proceeding of the 14th ACM SIGKDD International Conference on Knowledge Discovery and Data Mining (KDD 2008), pp. 160–168 (2008)

7. Craswell, N., de Vries, A.P., Soboroff, I.: Overview of the TREC-2005 enterprise track. In: TREC 2005 Conference Notebook, pp. 199–205 (2005)
8. Das, A., Datar, M., Garg, A., Rajaram, S.: Google news personalization: scalable online collaborative filtering. In: Proceeding of the 16th International Conference on World Wide Web (WWW 2007) (2007)
9. Dean, J., Ghemawat, S.: MapReduce: simplified data processing on large clusters. In: Proceedings of the 6th Conference on Symposium on Operating Systems Design & Implementation (OSDI 2004), p. 10 (2004)
10. Dourisboure, Y., Geraci, F., Pellegrini, M.: Extraction and classification of dense communities in the web. In: WWW 2007, pp. 461–470 (2007)
11. Flake, G.W., Lawrence, S., Giles, C.L.: Efficient identification of web communities. In: Proceedings of the Sixth ACM SIGKDD International Conference on Knowledge Discovery and Data Mining (KDD 2000), pp. 150–160 (2000)
12. Frey, B.J., Dueck, D.: Mixture modeling by affinity propagation. In: Proceedings of the 18th Neural Information Processing Systems (NIPS 2006), pp. 379–386 (2006)
13. Mei, Q., Cai, D., Zhang, D., Zhai, C.: Topic modeling with network regularization. In: Proceedings of the 17th International World Wide Web Conference (WWW 2008), pp. 101–110 (2008)
14. Papadimitriou, S., Disco, S.J.: Distributed co-clustering with map-reduce. In: Proceedings of IEEE International Conference on Data Mining (ICDM 2008) (2008)

Pricing a Digital Services Marketplace Under Asymmetric Information

Pavel Izhutov[1,2]([⊠]) [iD] and Haim Mendelson[2] [iD]

[1] Axio Inc, Altos Platform, San Francisco and Los Altos Hills, CA, USA
[2] Stanford University, Stanford, CA, USA
{izhutov,haim}@stanford.edu

Abstract. This paper addresses the pricing problem of a digital services marketplace under asymmetric information. An example is an online learning platform such as Coursera that provides courses from service providers (in this case, universities) to learners. We focus on the matching of digital services to the consumers of these services using partially-observable consumer and service attributes. We develop the optimal pricing policies of the marketplace and show that when the distributions of unobservable valuations are exponential, the marketplace sets a single matching fee (avoiding price-discrimination across providers) which is levied on the less price-sensitive side of the marketplace.

Keywords: Online marketplaces · Digital services · Pricing · Search

1 Introduction

An increasing share of the economy is managed through platforms that leverage technology to match consumers looking for digital services with service providers. For example, an online learning marketplace such as Coursera matches learners with courses that have been developed by service providers. Such online marketplaces are enabled by the Internet, which facilitates the aggregation of information and the efficient matching of consumers and service providers.

In this paper we focus on the pricing of the matching function of a marketplace for digital services. As matching generates value to the participants, how should the marketplace be compensated for creating this value? This question is particularly timely as digital services platforms are transitioning from a customer acquisition phase, where they are free or semi-free, to a monetization phase, where they need to make money. Online learning marketplaces such as Coursera, for example, used to be entirely free. Coursera, however, is funded by venture capitalists with a profit motive, and is transitioning to a pricing regime—first for courses with certificates, then for specializations, and it will probably implement a more robust pricing scheme in the future (tellingly, Coursera's free options are increasingly hidden during the registration process). Assuming that Coursera wants to maximize profits just like any other business, how should it

© Springer Nature Switzerland AG 2019
J. Miller et al. (Eds.): ICWS 2019, LNCS 11512, pp. 12–25, 2019.
https://doi.org/10.1007/978-3-030-23499-7_2

price its services? Further, to what extent should a digital matching platform engage in price discrimination to maximize its profit?

Digital matching platforms such as Coursera maintain rich data which it can exploit when it prices its services. For example, if a student is looking for a job in the data science field, she may be willing to pay more for an advanced data science course than for a philosophy course. Should Coursera charge that student more for matching her to a data science course? When thinking about this issue, it is important to realize that some information (e.g., a customer's profile and past transaction information) is available to the digital matching platform, whereas other information remains private and is not shared by the platform (e.g., the student may be more interested in a given service provider or subject area for sentimental reasons). More formally, the value of a prospective match is driven by attributes of both consumers and service providers. Some of these attributes are private and cannot be exploited by the marketplace. Other attributes are observable and may be exploited by marketplace pricing to extract more of the value created by a match. How should the marketplace price each potential match given the observable attributes of both counterparties and the probability distributions of their unobservable attributes? And, how should it allocate its fees between consumers and service providers? These are some key research questions addressed in this paper.

We focus on digital services marketplaces with virtually unlimited supply. Our model fits such marketplaces particularly well as it addresses services that can be replicated at virtually zero cost. Our model incorporates agents' heterogeneity and asymmetric information and derive the platform's optimal pricing policies.

Pricing problems of this type are complex and are often intractable. Nevertheless, we are able to derive the optimal prices for general random (unobservable) valuations. We then specialize our results to the case where the random valuations are exponential. We find that in this case, it is optimal to charge the *same* fee for matches with *different* observable provider attributes, and this fee should be levied in its entirety on the less elastic (more price-sensitive) side of the marketplace, up to a threshold point.

In what follows, we present our model in Sect. 2, solve it in Sect. 3, and offer our concluding remarks in Sect. 4. We illustrate the application of our approach and consider structural results for a few special cases in Subsects. 3.1 and 3.2.

2   Model

A consumer a arrives at the digital services marketplace, seeking a service provider (for example, a learner may seek an appropriate course on Coursera). The consumer submits to the marketplace a request identifying the service he or she is looking for and provides other relevant information. In particular, the marketplace may manage a profile with relevant consumer information. The consumer's request remains live in the system for an exponentially-distributed period of time with mean $1/\tau_A$ and then expires.

In our model, responding service providers, whose observable characteristics can be summarized by an index b, arrive following a Poisson stream with rate $1/\tau_B$. Each arriving provider examines the consumer's known attributes (from the service request and the consumer's profile) and decides whether to respond to the request. Once the provider responds, both parties reveal their unobservable attributes to determine the actual value of a potential match. A match occurs if sufficient value is generated for both the provider and the consumer, after subtracting the marketplace fees. If this is not the case, the provider moves on and the process is repeated with subsequent suppliers until either a mutually-acceptable match is found or the consumer's request expires. We model the problem for a consumer at a time since digital services can be replicated without a supply limit. In the special case of Coursera, the provider's attributes are fully known to the marketplace and judgment is exercised only by the consumer based on her private information.

We denote a match between consumer a and a provider of type b (hereafter, "provider b") by $i = (a, b)$. Upon a successful match i, the marketplace charges consumer a a matching fee f_i^a and provider b a matching fee f_i^b. Each consumer valuation, u_i^a, is the sum of an observed valuation v_i^a and a random, unobservable valuation ϵ_i^a. Similarly, each provider valuation u_i^b is the sum of an observed valuation v_i^b and the random unobserved valuation ϵ_i^b. Consumers (providers, respectively) have an outside option value (opportunity cost) of v_0^A (v_0^B). It follows that the match will be successful if for both the consumer and the provider, the value of the match net of marketplace matching fees exceeds the value of the outside option: $u_i^a - f_i^a > v_0^A$ and $u_i^b - f_i^b > v_0^B$. The objective of the marketplace is to find the pricing policy $f_i = (f_i^a, f_i^b)$ that maximizes its expected profit.

The valuations u_i^a and u_i^b have both observable (v) and unobservable (ϵ) components: $u_i^a = v_i^a + \epsilon_i^a$, $u_i^b = v_i^b + \epsilon_i^b$. We assume that the unobserved components ($\epsilon_i^a, \epsilon_i^b$) may be correlated with distributions and arrival rates that may differ across pair types i. In what follows, we'll consider both the more general formulation and the special case of exponential random valuations. We also assume $v_i^a \leq v_0^A$, $v_i^b \leq v_0^B$ so that probabilities are well-defined for $f_i^a, f_i^b \geq 0$.

2.1 Related Literature

Research in the area of marketplace platforms is extremely broad and space limitations prevent us from reviewing this entire literature. In the economics literature, several papers study the pricing of two-sided platforms that are subject to network effects. This literature aims to find static equilibrium structures, typically assuming a linear relationship between value and number of agents (cf. [1–4]). Within that literature, some researchers study price discrimination (e.g., [5]) but they do not base prices on agents' observable attributes; rather, they offer price schedules that induce agents to reveal their private information by self-selecting into designated tiers. [6] study the effects of market thickness on the efficiency of matching in a holiday rental platform, finding that contrary to the dictum of most network effects models, increased thickness was associated with a significant decline in the matching probability due to a deadline effect. Our model does not assume the existence of network effects, and it does consider the effects of time constraints on the consumer's search. It starts from the micro level to find the optimal personalized prices based on agents' observable attributes.

Our model is also related to the task-assignment problem in the online mechanism design literature [7–10]. This literature proposes algorithms for dynamically posting prices for suppliers who bid for specific tasks. However, these papers do not derive closed-form pricing solutions because of their different objectives. In addition to their different model structures, the algorithms analyzed in these papers do not allow for price-discrimination based on observable attributes. Our approach is closer to the classic dynamic stochastic settings of [11–13]. [14] study a more complex problem where demand types are dynamically matched to supply types to maximize total reward. Like the other papers in this stream, they do not consider the informational and pricing issues studied here. Overall, our model combines timing dynamics, information asymmetry and participants' heterogeneity to find tractable results and their implications.

3   Solving the Pricing Problem

Importantly, for any pair i, the fee vector f_i affects the matching probabilities of all pairs. In particular, the higher the fees for one particular match, the more likely are other matches to be successful. This interaction among matching probabilities and fees creates a $2 \times N$-dimensional problem, where N is the number of different match types and 2 is the number of sides to be priced. However, we show below how to reduce the problem to N two-dimensional problems, which allows us to compute the solution in closed-form.

The marketplace objective function is given by

$$\sum_{i=1}^{N} E\left[v_i \middle| \text{pair } i \text{ matched} \right] Pr\left(\text{pair } i \text{ matched} \right) \equiv \sum_{i=1}^{N} v_i \phi_i,$$

where $v_i = f_i^a + f_i^b$ is the marketplace profit from a successfully matched pair i. If arrivals follow a Poisson process, then the probability ϕ_i that the pair $i = (a, b)$ is successfully matched is given by the following.

Proposition 1. *Let u_i^a be the value that the consumer a derives from being matched with provider b, and i simultaneously indexes provider b and the pair $i = (a, b)$. Similarly, u_i^b is the value that provider b derives upon being matched with the consumer a, and λ_i is the arrival rate of type-b providers (corresponding to $i = (a, b)$). Finally, let λ_{N+1} be the arrival rate of the outside option: if the outside option "arrives" before the consumer request is matched, the consumer gives up the search and exits the marketplace, leaving no revenue to the marketplace. Then the probability that the match will be successful and of type b is given by*

$$\phi_i\left(f_i^a, f_i^b\right) = \begin{cases} \dfrac{\lambda_i Pr\left(u_i^a \geq f_i^a, u_i^b \geq f_i^b\right)}{\lambda_{N+1} + \sum \lambda_j Pr\left(u_j^a \geq f_j^a, u_j^b \geq f_j^b\right)} & , \text{if } i = 1, \ldots, N \\ \dfrac{\lambda_{N+1}}{\lambda_{N+1} + \sum \lambda_j Pr\left(u_j^a \geq f_j^a, u_j^b \geq f_j^b\right)} & , \text{if } i = N+1. \end{cases} \tag{1}$$

For simplicity of exposition, we assume that prices are non-negative, although this assumption is not needed in the derivation of the optimal prices. The results below provide a way to identify optimal prices in closed form in a general marketplace setting.

Theorem 1. *Consider the optimization problem*

$$\max_{f_1, \ldots, f_N} \sum_{i=1}^{N} v_i(f_i)\phi_i(f_1, \ldots, f_N), \tag{2}$$

$$s.t. \ f_i \in \mathcal{F}_i.$$

where $v_i \equiv f_i^a + f_i^b$, $\phi_i(f_1, \ldots, f_N)$ *are given by (1), and* $P_i \equiv Pr\left(u_i^a \geq f_i^a, u_i^b \geq f_i^b\right)$ *are twice continuously-differentiable for* $i = 1, 2, \ldots, N$.

Also let $T_i^a(f_i^a) = \dfrac{\partial((f_i^a + f_i^b)P_i)/\partial f_i^a}{\partial P_i/\partial f_i^a}$ *and* $T_i^b(f_i^b) = \dfrac{\partial((f_i^a + f_i^b)P_i)/\partial f_i^b}{\partial P_i/\partial f_i^b}$. *Then, if problem (2) has an optimal solution, its value is given by the largest root of the scalar equation*

$$V = \frac{\sum_{i=1}^{N}(f_i^a(V) + f_i^b(V))\lambda_i P_i(f_i^a(V), f_i^b(V))}{\lambda_{N+1} + \sum_{i=1}^{N} \lambda_i P_i(f_i^a(V), f_i^b(V))}$$

among all potential roots V *obtained by plugging in all possible combinations* $(f_1^a(V), f_1^b(V), \ldots, f_N^a(V), f_N^b(V)$, *where* $f_i^a(V)$ *is either on the boundary of* $\mathcal{F}_i^a$ *or it solves* $T_i^a(f_i^a, f_i^b) = V$ *and* $f_i^b(V)$ *is either on the boundary of* $\mathcal{F}_i^b$ *or it solves* $T_i^b(f_i^a, f_i^b) = V$. *The vector* $(f_1^a(V^*), f_1^b(V^*), \ldots, f_N^a(V^*), f_N^b(V^*))$ *that yields the highest* V^*, *is the optimal fee vector.*

Proposition 2. *Assume that the problem (2) has an optimal solution with value* V^*. *Then for* $i = 1, 2, \ldots, N$, *each component* $f_i^* = (f_i^a, f_i^b)^*$ *of the solution* $(f_1^*, \ldots, f_N^*)$ *to problem (2) can be represented as a solution to the* i-*th subproblem*

$$max_{f_i} P_i\left(f_i^a, f_i^b\right)\left(f_i^a + f_i^b - V^*\right)$$

$$s.t. \ f_i \in \mathcal{F}_i. \tag{3}$$

That is, the optimal fee vector in each state maximizes the weighted deviation from the global optimal profit V^*.

3.1 Pricing with Exponentially-Distributed Private Valuations

We now solve for the case where the random valuations are exponentially distributed i.i.d. random variables and where the arrival rates λ_i are the same across provider types. We assume that the unobserved components, ϵ_i^a

and ϵ_i^b, come from i.i.d. exponential distributions: $\epsilon_i^a \sim Exp\left(1/v^A\right)$, $\epsilon_i^b \sim Exp\left(1/v^B\right)$. As a result, from the marketplace perspective, the matching compatibility indicators $I\left(a\ accepts\ b\right)$ and $I\left(b\ accepts\ a\right)$ become random variables. In particular, the probability of b being acceptable to a is $Pr\left(a\ accepts\ b\right) = Pr\left(u_i^a \geq f_i^a + v_0^A\right) = Pr\left(v_i^a + \epsilon_i^a > f_i^a + v_0^A\right) = exp\left(\frac{v_i^a - f_i^a - v_0^A}{v^A}\right)$. Similarly, the probability of b willing to serve a is $Pr\left(b\ accepts\ a\right) = Pr\left(u_i^b \geq f_i^b + v_0^B\right) = Pr\left(v_i^b + \epsilon_i^b \geq f_i^b + v_0^B\right) = exp\left(\frac{v_i^b - f_i^b - v_0^B}{v^B}\right)$.

To solve the pricing problem, we first derive the matching probabilities. Applying Proposition 1 to the exponential case, we get

Corollary 1. *Given the information available to all participants (and, in particular, the marketplace), the probability that the request results in a match $i = (a, b)$, is given by*

$$\phi_i = Pr\left(b\ serves\ a\right) = \phi \frac{\beta_i e^{-\alpha f_i}}{\sum_j \beta_j e^{-\alpha f_j}} = \frac{\beta_i e^{-\alpha f_i}}{\sum_j \beta_j e^{-\alpha f_j} + \frac{1}{k}}, \tag{4}$$

where $\alpha \equiv \left(\alpha^A, \alpha^B\right)$, $f_i \equiv \left(f_i^a, f_i^b\right)$, $\alpha f_i \equiv \alpha^A f_i^a + \alpha^B f_i^b$.

We interpret $\alpha^A \equiv \frac{1}{v^A}$ as the price sensitivity of demand and $\alpha^B \equiv \frac{1}{v^B}$ as the price sensitivity of supply.

In the exponential case, the profit that the marketplace generates from each request is given by

$$\sum_{i=1}^N \left(f_i^b + f_i^a\right) \phi_i = \sum_{i=1}^N \left(f_i^b + f_i^a\right) \frac{\beta_i e^{-\alpha^A f_i^a - \alpha^B f_i^b}}{\sum_j \beta_j e^{-\alpha^A f_j^a - \alpha^B f_j^b} + \frac{1}{k}}.$$

Thus, the reward in state i is given by

$$v_i\left(f_i^a, f_i^b\right) = \begin{cases} \left(f_i^b + f_i^a\right) & \text{if } i = 1, \ldots, N \\ 0 & \text{if } i = N + 1 \end{cases},$$

and the matching demand function is given by

$$\begin{cases} P_i\left(f_i^a, f_i^b\right) = \beta_i e^{-\alpha^A f_i^a - \alpha^B f_i^b} & \text{if } i = 1, \ldots, N \\ P_{N+1} = \frac{1}{k} & \text{if } i = N + 1 \end{cases}$$

The profit maximization problem of the marketplace is thus

$$\max_{\left(f_i^a, f_i^b\right)} \sum_{i=1}^N \left(v_i P_i / \sum_{j=1}^{N+1} P_j\right)$$

$$s.t.\ \left(f_i^a, f_i^b\right) \geq \left(v_i^a - v_0^A, v_i^b - v_0^B\right).$$

The solution is given by the following Proposition.

Proposition 3. *The pricing policy maximizing marketplace profit is as follows:*

(a) *If* $\alpha^A > \alpha^B$, *then*

$$\begin{cases} f_i^{b*} = v^B \left[1 + W_0 \left(e^{-\alpha^A v_0^A - \alpha^B v_0^B - 1} \frac{\tau_A}{\tau_B} \sum_j e^{\alpha^A v_j^a + \alpha^B v_j^b - (\alpha^A - \alpha^B) f_j^{a*}} \right) \right] - f_i^{a*} \\ f_i^{a*} = v_i^a - v_0^A \end{cases}$$

(b) *If* $\alpha^B > \alpha^A$, *the result is symmetric to (a), i.e.,*

$$\begin{cases} f_i^{a*} = v^A \left[1 + W_0 \left(e^{-\alpha^A v_0^A - \alpha^B v_0^B - 1} \frac{\tau_A}{\tau_B} \sum_j e^{\alpha^A v_j^a + \alpha^B v_j^b - (\alpha^B - \alpha^A) f_j^{b*}} \right) \right] - f_i^{b*} \\ f_i^{b*} = v_i^b - v_0^B \end{cases}$$

(c) *If* $\alpha^A = \alpha^B$,

$$\begin{cases} f_i^{b*} + f_i^{a*} = v^A \left(1 + W_0 \left(e^{-\alpha^A v_0^A - \alpha^B v_0^B - 1} \frac{\tau_A}{\tau_B} \sum_j e^{\alpha^A v_j^a + \alpha^B v_j^b} \right) \right) \\ \\ f_i^{b*} \geq v_i^b - v_0^B, \ f_i^{a*} \geq v_i^a - v_0^A \end{cases}$$

(d) *the optimal total price* $f_i^{a*} + f_i^{b*}$ *is the same for each matched pair.*
$W_0 (\cdot)$ *is the Lambert function [15] which is the solution to the equation*

$$z = W \left(z e^z \right), \ z \geq -1.$$

Part (d) of Proposition 3 is surprising: even though the marketplace is able to price-discriminate among providers (and matched pairs) based on the particular information it observes about them, it charges the same price to all. This does not mean, of course, that it does not take advantage of that information at all. In fact, an increase in valuations within a particular pair will increase the fees charged to all pairs. Further, the optimal price depends on the observable consumer attributes. What the marketplace does not do is differentiate among providers (and corresponding pairs) based on the differences in observed valuations. This result follows from the memoryless property of the exponential distribution: the expected ex-ante value of a match is given by $E \left[V + \epsilon \middle| V + \epsilon > v_0 + f \right] = E\epsilon + v_0 + f$, which is *independent* of the observable component V.

Intuitively, the optimal price structure is driven by the probability distribution of the random valuation components. The observable component of the valuations affects the matching probabilities: the higher the valuation, the higher the probability of a match. Our finding means that the marketplace is better off engaging in quantity (or probability) differentiation (higher expected probability of a match for higher valuations) than in price discrimination.

Another important result is that the fee split between the provider and the consumer depends only on their respective price sensitivities and is always obtained at an extreme point: the side with the greater price sensitivity is charged the lowest price needed to attract any participants to the marketplace. In particular, when prices are non-negative, the less price-sensitive side of the market pays the entire marketplace fee while the other side pays nothing.

3.2 Generalizations

To what extent do our structural results for the exponential case generalize to other distributions? The following Corollary shows that prices remain the same across provider matches as long as the matching demand functions $P_i \left(f_i^a, f_i^b \right)$ are proportional across the different providers.

Corollary 2. *If the matching demand functions $P_i \left(f_i^a, f_i^b \right)$ are proportional to each other for a subset of types I, i.e.,*

$$P_i \left(f_i^a, f_i^b \right) = C_i P \left(f_i^a, f_i^b \right), \ i \in I,$$

then the optimal fees charged by the marketplace to different pairs within the set I are the same.

This result directly follows from Proposition 2, as the optimization subproblems solved for each match $i \in I$ are the same (if there are multiple optima, one of them will have the same fees).

Next consider the allocation of the total marketplace fee between the consumer and the provider. Using our aggregate matching demand formulation, the price sensitivity of the consumer (provider, respectively) to its marketplace fee is $\frac{\partial P_i}{\partial f_i^a}$ ($\frac{\partial P_i}{\partial f_i^b}$, respectively). Transforming our variables to $\left(f_i^a, f_i^\Sigma \right)$, where $f_i^\Sigma \equiv f_i^a + f_i^b$, in each subproblem i, the partial derivative of the objective function with respect to f_i^a is $\left(f_i^\Sigma - V^* \right) \left(\frac{\partial P_i}{\partial f_i^a} - \frac{\partial P_i}{\partial f_i^b} \right)$, and at the optimum, $V^* < \left(f_i^\Sigma \right)^*$. Thus, the fee split is determined by the sign of $\left(\frac{\partial P_i}{\partial f_i^a} - \frac{\partial P_i}{\partial f_i^b} \right)$. In particular, if $\left(-\frac{\partial P_i}{\partial f_i^a} > -\frac{\partial P_i}{\partial f_i^b} \right)$ for all $\left(f_i^a, f_i^b \right) \in \mathcal{F}_i$, then the entire fee should be paid by the supplier and the consumer pays nothing, and if $\left(-\frac{\partial P_i}{\partial f_i^a} < -\frac{\partial P_i}{\partial f_i^b} \right)$ for all $\left(f_i^a, f_i^b \right) \in \mathcal{F}_i$, then the entire fee is paid by the consumer and the provider pays nothing. This directly generalizes the results we obtained in the exponential case. A similar analysis may be performed using the underlying preferences of marketplace participants. Here,

$$P_i \left(f_i^a, f_i^b \right) \equiv Pr \left(v_i^a + \epsilon_i^a \geq v_0^A + f_i^a, v_i^b + \epsilon_i^b \geq v_0^B + f_i^b \right)$$

For subproblem i, in transformed coordinates $\left(f_i^a, f_i^\Sigma \right)$, the partial derivative of the objective function with respect to f_i^a is $\left(f_i^\Sigma - V^* \right) \left(\frac{\partial P_i}{\partial f_i^a} - \frac{\partial P_i}{\partial f_i^b} \right)$. Thus, similar to the above analysis, the fee split is determined by the sign of

$\left(\frac{\partial P_i}{\partial f_i^a} - \frac{\partial P_i}{\partial f_i^b} \right)$: if $\left(-\frac{\partial P_i}{\partial f_i^a} > -\frac{\partial P_i}{\partial f_i^b} \right)$ for all $\left(f_i^a, f_i^b \right) \in \mathcal{F}_i$, then the entire market-place fee is paid by the supplier, and if $\left(-\frac{\partial P_i}{\partial f_i^a} < -\frac{\partial P_i}{\partial f_i^b} \right)$ for all $\left(f_i^a, f_i^b \right) \in \mathcal{F}_i$, the entire marketplace fee is paid by the consumer[1].

Since we allowed for different matching demand functions for different matches, it is of course possible that unlike the more restrictive exponential case, one provider will be uniformly *more* price sensitive than the consumer whereas another will be uniformly *less* price sensitive than the consumer. In this case, the former provider will pay zero whereas the latter will pay the entire marketplace fee.

Our formulation also allows for more general fee splits. For example, if the matching demand functions are log-linear of the form $P_i \left(f_i^a, f_i^b \right) = C_i \left(A - f_i^a \right)^\alpha \left(B - f_i^b \right)^\beta$ for $f_i^a \in [0, A], f_i^b \in [0, B]$, then $\frac{\partial P_i}{\partial f_i^a} = -\alpha C_i \left(A - f_i^a \right)^{\alpha-1} \left(B - f_i^b \right)^\beta$ and $\frac{\partial P_i}{\partial f_i^b} = -\beta C_i \left(A - f_i^a \right)^\alpha \left(B - f_i^b \right)^{\beta-1}$, implying that $\frac{A - (f_i^a)^*}{B - (f_i^b)^*} = \frac{\alpha}{\beta}$. Thus, the optimal fees are the same for all i (Proposition 2), and their ratio is inversely related to their elasticity coefficients, consistent with our intuition.

4   Concluding Remarks

The Internet has spawned new forms of economic activity and gave rise to the development and growth of online services marketplaces which in turn created new research challenges for both academics and practitioners. This paper derives optimal pricing policies for a matching marketplace platform for digital services. We show that with exponentially-distributed random participants' valuations, it is optimal to charge a constant total fee across provider matches, and this fee should be levied on the less elastic side of the market up to a threshold. For a marketplace such as Coursera, this means that the profit-maximizing matching fee would be constant across providers. Further, if learners are more price-sensitive than providers, Coursera would charge its entire matching fee to its content providers.

Our results shed light on how marketplaces for digital services may be compensated for their matching function, and it will be useful to consider them in conjunction with more elaborate specifications of particular vertical marketplaces.

---

[1] If the fees can be negative, the more price-sensitive side of the market will pay the lowest possible fee, and the less price-sensitive side will pay the highest possible fee.

5   Proofs

Proof of Proposition 1
The successful requests of type $i = (a, b)$ arrive as a marked Poisson process with the arrival rate $\lambda_i Pr(u_i^a \geq f_i^a, u_i^b \geq f_i^b)$, where $u_i^a \geq f_i^a, u_i^b \geq f_i^b$ is the condition that "marks" the match between the consumer and supplier successful. The outside option and the successful requests of other types arrive with the Poisson rates of λ_{N+1} and $\sum_{-i} \lambda_j Pr(u_j^a \geq f_j^a, u_j^b \geq f_j^b)$. As long as the first arrival occurs from the first stream, i.e., the one with the rate of $\lambda_i Pr(u_i^a \geq f_i^a, u_i^b \geq f_i^b)$, the request will be served by the provider of type i.

The probability of such an event is given by $Pr(t_i \leq min(t_{-i}, t_{N+1}))$, where t_i is the arrival time of the successful match of type i, t_{-i} – the arrival time of the successful match of any type other than i and t_{N+1} is the arrival time of the outside option. Since all the arrival streams are Poisson, and, hence, the respective arrival times are exponentially distributed, including $min(t_{-i}, t_{N+1})$, therefore

$$
\phi_i \left(f_i^a, f_i^b \right) = \begin{cases} \dfrac{\lambda_i Pr(u_i^a \geq f_i^a, u_i^b \geq f_i^b)}{\lambda_{N+1} + \sum \lambda_j Pr(u_i^a \geq f_i^a, u_i^b \geq f_i^b)} & , \text{ if } i = 1, \dots, N \\[2ex] \dfrac{\lambda_{N+1}}{\lambda_{N+1} + \sum \lambda_j Pr(u_i^a \geq f_i^a, u_i^b \geq f_i^b)} & , \text{ if } i = N+1 \end{cases}
$$

Proof of Theorem 1:
The first-order condition w.r.t. f_i^a is given by

$$
\frac{\frac{\partial}{\partial f_i^a} \left((f_i^a + f_i^b) \lambda_i P_i \right) \left(\lambda_{N+1} + \sum_{i=1}^N \lambda_i P_i \right) - \frac{\partial}{\partial f_i^a} (\lambda_i P_i) \sum_{i=1}^N \left((f_i^a + f_i^b) \lambda_i P_i \right)}{\left(\lambda_{N+1} + \sum_{i=1}^N \lambda_i P_i \right)^2} = 0,
$$

which implies

$$
\frac{\partial}{\partial f_i^a} \left((f_i^a + f_i^b) \lambda_i P_i \right) = \frac{\sum_{i=1}^N (\lambda_i P_i)(f_i^a + f_i^b)}{\left(\lambda_{N+1} + \sum_{i=1}^N \lambda_i P_i \right)} \frac{\partial}{\partial f_i^a} (\lambda_i P_i) = V^* \frac{\partial}{\partial f_i^a} (\lambda_i P_i),
$$

where $V^* = V(f_1, \dots, f_N)$ is the optimal profit.

Repeating the above with respect to f_i^b yields

$$
\begin{cases} \frac{\partial}{\partial f_i^a} \left((f_i^a + f_i^b) P_i \right) = V^* \frac{\partial}{\partial f_i^a} P_i, \\ \frac{\partial}{\partial f_i^b} \left((f_i^a + f_i^b) P_i \right) = V^* \frac{\partial}{\partial f_i^b} P_i, \end{cases} \tag{5}
$$

Let $f^* = (f_1^*, \dots, f_N^*)$ denote the optimal fee vector, then $(f_i^a(V^*))^*$, $(f_i^b(V^*))^*$ either solves the respective equation in (5) or is on the boundary of $\mathcal{F}_i$. As a result, there is a set of candidates $\{f^j(V)\}$ for an optimal fee vector f^*. For each j we plug $f^j(V)$ in the expression for the objective $V = \frac{\sum_{i=1}^N (f_i^a(V) + f_i^b(V)) \lambda_i P_i(f_i^j(V))}{\lambda_{N+1} + \sum_{i=1}^N \lambda_i P_i(f_i^j(V))}$ and solve for V. Then we arrive at the set of values $\{V^j\}$ corresponding to optimal action candidates $\{f^j(V)\}$. Obviously, the largest value $V^* \equiv V^{j^*} = \max_j V^j$ is the optimal profit value, and, hence, the corresponding vector $f^{j^*}(V^{j^*})$ is the optimal fee vector.

Proof of Proposition 2:
If f_i^* is the solution to (3), then for all f_i

$$(v_i^* - V^*)\, h_i^* \ge (v_i - V^*)\, h_i, \tag{6}$$

where for $i = 1 \ldots N$, $v_i^* = \left(f_i^a + f_i^b\right)^*$, $h_i^* = \lambda_i P_i(f_i^*)$, $v_i = f_i^a + f_i^b$, $h_i = \lambda_i P_i(f_i)$ and $v_{N+1} = 0$, $h_{N+1} = \lambda_{N+1}$.

Plugging in

$$V^* = \frac{v_i^* h_i^* + (VH)_{-i}^*}{h_i^* + H_{-i}^*},$$

where $(VH)_{-i} = \sum_{-i} v_j h_j$, $H_{-i} = \sum_{-i} h_j$, into (6) we get

$$\left(v_i^* - \frac{v_i^* h_i^* + (VH)_{-i}^*}{h_i^* + H_{-i}^*}\right) h_i^* \ge \left(v_i - \frac{v_i^* h_i^* + (VH)_{-i}^*}{h_i^* + H_{-i}^*}\right) h_i$$

Rearranging this expression yields

$$\left(\frac{v_i^* h_i^* + (VH)_{-i}^*\, h_i^*}{h_i^* + H_{-i}^*}\right) \ge \frac{v_i h_i^* h_i + v_i H_{-i}^* h_i - v_i^* h_i^* h_i + (VH)_{-i}^*\, h_i}{h_i^* + H_{-i}^*}$$

$$(v_i^* - v_i)\, h_i^* h_i + \left(v_i^* H_{-i}^* - (VH)_{-i}^*\right) h_i^* - \left(v_i H_{-i}^* - (VH)_{-i}^*\right) h_i \ge 0$$

$$\left(v_i^* h_i^* + (VH)_{-i}^*\right) \left(h_i + H_{-i}^*\right) \ge \left(v_i h_i + (VH)_{-i}^*\right) \left(h_i^* + H_{-i}^*\right)$$

$$\frac{\left(v_i^* h_i^* + (VH)_{-i}^*\right)}{h_i^* + H_{-i}^*} \ge \frac{\left(v_i h_i + (VH)_{-i}^*\right)}{h_i + H_{-i}^*}.$$

Thus, f_i^* is the optimal solution for (2) as well.

Proof of Proposition 3
We solve the problem in four steps.

Step 1: show that the optimal value V^* exists and is finite. The existence and finiteness of V^* follow from three facts: *(a)* the value function is linear in the marketplace fees, whereas *(b)* the matching probabilities decline exponentially with the marketplace fees, and *(c)* the marketplace can achieve zero revenue by rejecting all suppliers. It follows that there is an optimal solution with a finite, positive V^*.

The optimal prices are in a bounded set for the following reason. since V^* is finite, the gradient of the objective function with respect to at the optimal fee vector f^* is given by

$$\frac{\frac{\partial}{\partial f_i^a} h_i}{\sum_j h_j} \left[T\left(\begin{bmatrix} f_i^a \\ f_i^b \end{bmatrix} \right) - V^* \right] = \frac{\frac{\partial}{\partial f_i^a} h_i}{\sum_j h_j} \left[f_i^a + f_i^b - \begin{bmatrix} 1/\alpha^A \\ 1/\alpha^B \end{bmatrix} - V^* \right],$$

where $h_i = \lambda_i P_i$ for $i = 1, \ldots, N$.

Since $\frac{\frac{\partial}{\partial f_i^a} h_i}{\sum_j h_j} < 0$ uniformly, $\frac{\partial V}{\partial f_i^a} < 0$ for large enough f_i^a. Similarly, $\frac{\partial V}{\partial f_i^b} < 0$ for large enough f_i^b. Thus, the optimal prices are contained in a bounded set.

Step 2: decompose the global objective. By Proposition 2, we can decompose the problem into N optimization problems, one for each match i, $i = 1, 2, \ldots, N$:

$$max_{f_i} P_i \left(f_i \right) \left(v_i \left(f_i \right) - V^* \right)$$
$$s.t. \ \left(f_i^a, f_i^b \right) \geq \left(v_i^a - v_0^A, v_i^b - v_0^B \right),$$

which yields the following first-order conditions:

$$f_i^a + f_i^b - \begin{bmatrix} 1/\alpha^A \\ 1/\alpha^B \end{bmatrix} = \begin{bmatrix} V^* \\ V^* \end{bmatrix}.$$

Step 3: filter the set of solution candidates. There are two candidate points for the consumer-side fee f_i^a – one interior solution $V^* + 1/\alpha^A - f_i^b$ and one corner solution $\left(v_i^a - v_0^A \right)$. Similarly, there are 2 corresponding candidates for the supply-side fee f_i^b: $V^* + 1/\alpha^B - f_i^a$ and $\left(v_i^b - v_0^B \right)$. Thus, the optimal candidate fees $\left(f_i^a, f_i^b \right)$ for state i constitute all four pairwise combinations of these individual candidates. Then, we have the following candidate pair types: $\left(v_i^a - v_0^A, v_i^b - v_0^B \right)$, $\left(V^* + 1/\alpha^A - f_i^b, V^* + 1/\alpha^B - f_i^a \right)$, $\left(v_i^a - v_0^A, V^* + 1/\alpha^B - \left(v_i^a - v_0^A \right) \right)$, and $\left(V^* + 1/\alpha^A - \left(v_i^b - v_0^B \right), v_i^b - v_0^B \right)$.

Rather than enumerate the results, we can eliminate some of the candidates upfront. For instance, both partial derivatives at $\left(v_i^a - v_0^A, v_i^b - v_0^B \right)$ are positive, hence this candidate be eliminated. The second candidate

$$\begin{bmatrix} f_i^a \\ f_i^b \end{bmatrix} = \begin{bmatrix} V^* + 1/\alpha^A - f_i^b \\ V^* + 1/\alpha^B - f_i^a \end{bmatrix}$$

can be eliminated if $\alpha^A \neq \alpha^B$. In fact, we can rewrite the expression as

$$\begin{bmatrix} f_i^a + f_i^b \\ f_i^a + f_i^b \end{bmatrix} = \begin{bmatrix} V^* + 1/\alpha^A \\ V^* + 1/\alpha^B \end{bmatrix},$$

which becomes inconsistent if $\alpha^A \neq \alpha^B$. Thus, if the price sensitivities are different, then we necessarily have a corner solution. Further, a variation in the fees $\left(\Delta f_i^a, \Delta f_i^b \right) = \left(\epsilon, -\epsilon \right)$, where $\epsilon > 0$, is profitable if $\alpha^B > \alpha^A$, that is, such variation increases the objective function value. Hence, if $\alpha^B > \alpha^A$, then the corner solution $\left(v_i^a - v_0^A, \; V^* + 1/\alpha^B - \left(v_i^a - v_0^A\right)\right)$ cannot be optimal since it permits the above variation. As a result, when $\alpha^A \neq \alpha^B$ we are left with only one solution candidate, namely,

$$\left(f_i^a, f_i^b\right) = \begin{cases} \left(v_i^a - v_0^A, \; V^* + 1/\alpha^B - \left(v_i^a - v_0^A\right)\right) & \alpha^A > \alpha^B \\ \left(V^* + 1/\alpha^A - \left(v_i^b - v_0^B\right), \; v_i^b - v_0^B\right) & \alpha^A < \alpha^B \end{cases} . \tag{7}$$

Finally, if $\alpha^A = \alpha^B$, the total price must be equal to $V^* + 1/\alpha^A$, and it may be allocated arbitrarily between the consumer and the service provider.

Step 4: plug the solution candidates into the equation for V^*. Plugging $\left(f_i^a, f_i^b\right)$ into the equation $V^* = \sum_{i=1}^{N+1} v_i \left(f_i^a, f_i^b\right) \frac{P_i\left(f_i^a, f_i^b\right)}{\frac{1}{k} + \sum_j P_i\left(f_i^a, f_i^b\right)}$, then solving for V^* and plugging it back into the expression (7) completes the solution. The exact formula is given in the statement of the proposition.

Frequently, the elimination of certain candidate solutions may come from additional constraints imposed by the nature or operating rules of the marketplace. For instance, for some platforms, charging the consumer (e.g., Yelp) or consumer and supplier (e.g., Stackoverflow) may be inappropriate, while the feasible price region for another side (e.g., advertisers) is unconstrained. In that case, constraints of the form of $f_i^a = 0$ or $f_i^b = 0$ may automatically eliminate a number of solution candidates.

References

1. Caillaud, B., Jullien, B.: Chicken & Egg: competition among intermediation service providers. The RAND J. Econ. **34**(2), 309–328 (2003)
2. Rochet, J.-C., Tirole, J.: Two-sided markets: a progress report. RAND J. Econ. **37**(3), 645–667 (2006)
3. Armstrong, M.: Competition in two-sided markets. RAND J. Econ. **37**(3), 668–691 (2006)
4. Weyl, E.G.: A price theory of multi-sided platforms. Am. Econ. Rev. **100**(4), 1642–1672 (2010)
5. Damiano, E., Li, H.: Price discrimination and efficient matching. Econ. Theory **30**(2), 243–263 (2007)
6. Li, J., Netessine, S.: Market Thickness and Matching (In)efficiency: Evidence from a Quasi-Experiment. Working Paper (2017)
7. Blum, A., Kumar, V., Rudra, A., Wu, F.: Online learning in online auctions. Theor. Comput. Sci. **324**(2–3 SPEC. ISS.), 137–146 (2004)
8. Babaioff, M., Dughmi, S., Kleinberg, R., Slivkins, A.: Dynamic pricing with limited supply. In: Proceedings of the 13th ACM Conference on Electronic Commerce - EC 2012, vol. 3, no. 1, p. 74 (2012)
9. Badanidiyuru, A., Kleinberg, R., Singer, Y.: Learning on a budget. In: Proceedings of the 13th ACM Conference on Electronic Commerce - EC 2012, vol. 1, no. 212, p. 128 (2012)
10. Singla, A., Krause, A.: Truthful incentives in crowdsourcing tasks using regret minimization mechanisms. In: WWW 2013 Proceedings of the 22nd International Conference on World Wide Web, pp. 1167–1177 (2013)

11. Keilson, J.: A simple algorithm for contract acceptance. Opsearch **7**, 157–166 (1970)
12. Lippman, S.A., Ross, S.M.: The streetwalker's dilemma: a job shop model. SIAM J. Appl. Math. **20**(3), 336–342 (1971)
13. Mendelson, H., Whang, S.: Optimal incentive-compatible priority pricing for the M/M/1 queue. Oper. Res. **38**(5), 870–883 (1990)
14. Hu, M., Zhou, Y.: Dynamic Matching in a Two-Sided Market. Working Paper (2015)
15. Corless, R.M., Gonnet, G.H., Hare, D.E.G., Jeffrey, D.J., Knuth, D.E.: On the lambert W function. Adv. Comput. Math. **5**, 329–359 (1996)

Profit Maximization and Time Minimization Admission Control and Resource Scheduling for Cloud-Based Big Data Analytics-as-a-Service Platforms

Yali Zhao[1]([✉]), Rodrigo N. Calheiros[2], Athanasios V. Vasilakos[3], James Bailey[1], and Richard O. Sinnott[1]

[1] The University of Melbourne, Melbourne, Australia
yalizhao.alice@gmail.com,
{baileyj,rsinnott}@unimelb.edu.au
[2] Western Sydney University, Sydney, Australia
r.calheiros@westernsydney.edu.au
[3] Lulea University of Technology, Lulea, Sweden
athanasios.vasilakos@ltu.se

Abstract. Big data analytics typically requires large amounts of resources to process ever-increasing data volumes. This can be time consuming and result in considerable expenses. Analytics-as-a-Service (AaaS) platforms provide a way to tackle expensive resource costs and lengthy data processing times by leveraging automatic resource management with a pay-per-use service delivery model. This paper explores optimization of resource management algorithms for AaaS platforms to automatically and elastically provision cloud resources to execute queries with Service Level Agreement (SLA) guarantees. We present admission control and cloud resource scheduling algorithms that serve multiple objectives including profit maximization for AaaS platform providers and query time minimization for users. Moreover, to enable queries that require timely responses and/or have constrained budgets, we apply data sampling-based admission control and resource scheduling where accuracy can be traded-off for reduced costs and quicker responses when necessary. We conduct extensive experimental evaluations for the algorithm performances compared to state-of-the-art algorithms. Experiment results show that our proposed algorithms perform significantly better in increasing query admission rates, consuming less resources and hence reducing costs, and ultimately provide a more flexible resource management solution for fast, cost-effective, and reliable big data processing.

Keywords: Optimization · Service level agreement · Analytics-as-a-service · Admission control · Resource scheduling · Data sampling · Big data · Cloud computing

© Springer Nature Switzerland AG 2019
J. Miller et al. (Eds.): ICWS 2019, LNCS 11512, pp. 26–47, 2019.
https://doi.org/10.1007/978-3-030-23499-7_3

1 Introduction

Big data becomes an emerging trend that many organizations and companies are currently facing. A tremendous amount of data is being produced at an ever-accelerating rate from a myriad of sources such as IoT sensors, smart mobile devices, social media platforms amongst many other sources covering all aspects of society including health, commerce, government, and education. The need for advanced technologies to tackle data production, processing, and storage is clear. However, big data can only create values through the help of data analytics technologies to extract insights from such big datasets. It is fair to say that the success of many organizations, companies, and individuals lies heavily on big data analytics solutions.

Big data typically refers to massive volumes of structured, semi-structured, un-structured or real time data that exceed the processing and management capacities of traditional techniques [1]. Big data analytics is usually associated with cloud computing technologies. Cloud computing [2] provides a computing paradigm to dynamically provision resources for big data analytics solutions based on varying numbers of requests from users. As the data volumes increase to levels that exceed the storage and processing capabilities of individual computers, clouds allow to automatically and elastically provision cloud resources such as virtual machines (VMs) on-the-fly to process datasets for timely decision making as required by users and businesses. Cloud resources are typically provisioned in a pay-per-use model that enables users to only pay for the used resources. As such, big data analytics for small enterprises and individuals is possible, as they do not need to acquire expensive hardware and software directly or deal with the overheads with the management of such infrastructures.

AaaS platforms provide a way to tackle expensive resource costs and avoid long query times by leveraging automatic resource management capabilities. AaaS service delivery should ideally minimize the complexity of the resource management requirements for in depth knowledge of Big Data Analytics Applications (BDAAs) by users. It allows users from various domains to process big data with reduced times and cheaper costs based on SLA agreements between AaaS users and providers. In order to allow AaaS platforms to deliver SLA guaranteed AaaS for high user satisfactions, efficient and automatic resource scheduling is essential [3]. Resource scheduling is a core function of the AaaS platform and a central component to coordinate all the other AaaS platform components to deliver performance-oriented AaaS solutions. Our motivation in this paper is to provide optimal resource scheduling algorithms that can, on the one hand maximize the profits of AaaS providers, while on the other hand deliver AaaS to users within controllable budgets, factoring in deadline and accuracy guarantees for timely and reliable decision making.

A number of related research works [3, 11–25] have explored resource management in different perspectives and scenarios with support of various techniques in cloud environments. However, none of these works consider data sampling-based admission control and cloud resource scheduling algorithms to deliver AaaS with budget, accuracy, and deadline guarantees to support cost-efficient, reliable, and fast decision making. Resource scheduling of AaaS platforms faces several research challenges. Firstly, elastic and automatic resource provisioning is required to deal with dynamic online queries. Such requests can be stochastic in nature and have varying demands on the underlying cloud resources. Secondly, to support queries on very large datasets that cannot be processed under limited budgets or deadlines where accuracy can be traded-off for approximate processing [4], data sampling-based scheduling can be used. Thirdly, effective admission control should be applied to only admit queries satisfying Quality of Service (QoS) requirements that meet given SLAs. Finally, profit maximization and time minimization scheduling under various constraints represent a non-trivial multi-objective optimization problem, especially for complex BDAAs. This requires accurate modelling and formulation of the optimization problem.

To tackle the above challenges, the major **contribution** of our work is providing efficient and effective admission control and resource scheduling algorithms to elastically and automatically provision cloud resources to schedule queries that serve the objectives of profit maximization for AaaS providers and query time minimizations for users while guaranteeing SLAs. The proposed algorithms apply data sampling-based admission and scheduling methods for big data processing under tight budget or deadline constraints. We formulate the resource management problem and implement the proposed admission and scheduling algorithms in the AaaS framework. To evaluate the performance of the proposed algorithms, we conduct extensive experiments. Experiment evaluations show that the proposed admission control and resource scheduling algorithms outperform the state-of-the-art algorithms in admitting more queries, creating higher profits, generating less resource costs with efficient resource configurations, and provide timely AaaS solutions with accuracy guarantees for reliable decision making under controllable budgets and tight deadlines.

2   Problem Statement

User submit queries $Querys = \{Query_1, \ldots, Query_M\}$ to a given AaaS platform. A query can be a scan query such as select patient name from patient table where patient age is greater than 30, or a more complex query such as a deep learning algorithm used to process large medical datasets to analyze the key factors that lead to diabetes. These queries request specific $BDAAs = \{BDAA_1, \ldots, BDAA_P\}$ that utilize a set of cloud resources $Resources = \{Resource_1, \ldots, Resource_N\}$ and generating resource $Costs = \{Cost_1, \ldots, Cost_N\}$. An example $BDAA$ can be a medicare application. A resource can be cloud containers, storage, single or clusters of VMs.

$Query = \{QoS, CR, BDAA, CH, AC, DE\}$. QoS requirements of a query request contain budget: the maximum costs to run a query; deadline: the latest time to deliver query result, accuracy: the confidence interval of the query result. CR is the cloud resources needed to run a query. $BDAA$ details a specific BDAA requested for big data analytics. CH details the big data characteristics, such as the data distribution, data size, data type, accuracy requirement, and data locality. AC indicates whether the accuracy can be traded-off for reduced times and cheaper costs by applying effective data sampling methods. DE represents task dependency requirements including execution logic and sequence. Big data is assumed to be pre-stored in cloud datacenters, where users pay data transfer and storage costs and hence the costs are not included in the cost models.

$BDAA = \{AT, P\}$. AT denotes the BDAA type and P is the BDAA profile. This includes mappings of the application cost, resource times required by queries including the processing and sampling time, and the resource configurations needed for queries. Obtaining application profiles of heterogeneous BDAAs typically requires expertise varied by different application domains. Therefore, reliable BDAA profiles are assumed to be maintained by third-party BDAA providers.

$Resource = \{RT, REC, NR, CC\}$. RT indicates the cloud resource type such as single or cluster of CPU optimized VMs. REC shows the cloud resource capacity including CPU, storage, memory. NR is the number of cloud resources needed to execute a query request. CC represents the cloud resource cost.

$Cost = \{RC, BC, PC, AC, PR\}$. RC is the overall cloud resource costs of the AaaS platform. BC represents the BDAA cost, which is assumed charged by BDAA providers as a constant value. PC represents the penalty cost that AaaS platforms need to pay users for SLA violation. AC represents the overall AaaS Cost (AC) that AaaS platforms charge users for utilizing AaaS, and PR represents the overall profits created by AaaS platforms. A fixed AaaS cost is assumed charged by AaaS platforms for a specific query based on its requirements of QoS, BDAA, and resource demands, and hence AC is a constant value.

The profit optimization problem to maximize the profits of the AaaS platform while minimizing the query times under various constraints is an NP-complete decision problem. The problem can be polynomially transformed to a mixed Integer Linear Programming (ILP) [5] problem with optimization formulation and modeling. We utilize the ILP modeling to formulate the multi-objective scheduling problem. AC and BC are constant values based on the cost models and PC is zero if AaaS is delivered with SLA guarantees. The profit of the AaaS platform is calculated by $PR = AC - RC - BC - PC$. Maximization of PR is transformed to minimize RC and deliver AaaS with minimized times subject to various constraints. We formulate the multi-objective Z based on a combination of individual optimization Objective X and Objective Y.

Objective $X = minimize\ (\sum_{j=1}^{n} C_j * t_j)$, where j denotes a resource; n represents a resource set; t_j is the number of resource required for j; C_j is the unit cloud resource cost of j. Objective X targets to minimize the RC, calculated as the product of the purchased time t_j and the unit cost C_j of all cloud resources.

Objective $Y = minimize\ (\sum_{i=1}^{m} s_i)$, where i is a query i; m represents a set of queries, and s_i represent the query start time of i. Objective Y targets at finding an optimal solution of the resource scheduling to minimize the resource costs with optimized configuration to execute queries at its earliest times. This allows all queries starting earliest times to minimize t_j to save resource costs and improve the query performances with quickest responses.

Objective Z $= minimize\ (F_0 * \sum_{j \in n} (C_j * t_j) + \sum_{i \in m} s_i)$ is a combination of X and Y that aims to minimize RC while choosing a time-minimized scheduling plan, subject to optimization constraints (1)–(37). This combination contributes to a standard lexicographic problem [6]. The importance leading to the profit optimal scheduling solutions of individual objectives is $X > Y$. Coefficient $F_0 = max(Y) - min(Y) + 1$ is assigned to X to ensure the aggregated optimization with minimized individual objectives is consistent to the original optimization problem where changes of Objective X dominates all the changes in Objective Y.

Query Resource Capacity Constraints guarantee that the overall cloud resource times needed to process the complete datasets on resource j should be within the available time remained on resource j, (1), where x_{ij} is a variable with binary value that represents if query i is assigned to run on j; R_{ij} is the cloud resource time needed by i to process the complete dataset using resource j; t_j is the resource time of j that is to be purchased. For a given resource, T_j represents the remained resource time of j that is purchased in the previous schedule. For resources that is newly created, T_j is negative to deduct the resource creation time of j from t_j. When i executes on j, $x_{ij} = 1$; otherwise, $x_{ij} = 0$ shown in (2).

$$\sum_{i \in m, j \in n} (R_{ij} * x_{ij}) \leq t_j + T_j \tag{1}$$

$$x_{ij} = \begin{cases} 1, & i \text{ is assigned to execute on } j \\ 0, & \text{otherwise} \end{cases}, \forall i \in m; j \in n \tag{2}$$

Query Execution Sequence Constraints (3) ensure the unique query execution sequence as required by the optimal scheduling. b_{ik} is defined as a binary variable that defines the query execution sequence of i and k. If query i is scheduled to execute before k, $b_{ik} = 1$; otherwise, $b_{ik} = 0$.

$$b_{ik} + b_{ki} \leq 1, \forall i, k \in m \tag{3}$$

Query Dependency Constraints define query dependencies, $b_{ik} = 1$ when i is a dependent task requiring the execution results of k or a child task that can only start after k defined by (4). Query dependency constraints enable the definition of simple to complex task dependencies including bag of tasks, enterprise workflows, and scientific dataflows. For queries requiring data sampling for approximate processing, where data sampling and processing tasks are processed independently, query processing on sampled datasets can only start after data sampling finishes, as shown in (5).

$$b_{ki} = 1, \text{ if } i \text{ is a child/dependent task of } k, \forall i, k \in m \tag{4}$$

$$b_{ki} = 1, \text{ if } i \text{ processes data sample of } k, \forall i, k \in m \tag{5}$$

Query Deadline Constraints ensure scheduling solutions are generated before query deadlines for SLA guarantee purposes, as shown in Constraints (6)–(11). Constraint (6) guarantee the unique query execution sequence of i and k that allows either b_{ik} or b_{ki} to be 1. Task i must execute either before or after task k when they are assigned to the same resource j as guaranteed by (7). Non-linear relationship (12) is transformed to linear relationship (7) through linearization, which guarantees if both i and k are scheduled to execute on j, $b_{ik} = 1, b_{ki} = 0$ when i is executed before k, or $b_{ik} = 0, b_{ki} = 1$ when i is executed after k. Big M method is utilized to derive Constraint (8) from non-linear constraint (13) to guarantee i should end before k starts if

$b_{ik} = 1$. F_1 serves as a sufficient large constant that satisfies (14) [3]. Constraint (9) ensure query i finishes before its deadline D_i when executes on j at starting time s_i, derived from (15), which is non-linear constraint where F_2 serves as a sufficient large constant that satisfies (16). Non-linear relationship (17) is used to derive (10). F_3 serves as a sufficient large constant value that satisfies (18) to guarantee i finishes earlier than the purchased time of j to process the full dataset. The purchased time is accumulated from previous End of Purchased Time, EPT_j, and newly purchased time as t_j. Constraint (11) is generated based on the non-linear constraint (19). F_4 guarantees i starts at Earliest Available Time, EAT_j, of j, which satisfies (20) as a sufficient small constant. For an already created j with executing tasks, EAT_j represents the query finish time of j; otherwise, EAT_j represents the current clock time. If j has not been created, EAT_j is the sum of creation time and clock time of resource j.

$$b_{ik} = \begin{cases} 1, & i \text{ is executed before } k \\ 0, & \text{otherwise} \end{cases}, \forall i, k \in m \tag{6}$$

$$b_{ik} + b_{ki} - x_{ij} - x_{kj} \geq -1, \forall i, k \in m; \; j \in n \tag{7}$$

$$s_i - s_k + F_1 * b_{ik} \leq F_1 - R_{ij}, \forall i, k \in m; \; j \in n \tag{8}$$

$$s_i + F_2 * x_{ij} \leq F_2 + D_i - R_{ij}, \forall i \in m, j \in n \tag{9}$$

$$s_i - t_j + F_3 * x_{ij} \leq F_3 - R_{ij} + EPT_j, \forall i \in m, j \in n \tag{10}$$

$$s_i + x_{ij} * F_4 \geq F_4 + EAT_j, \forall i \in m, j \in n \tag{11}$$

$$\left. \begin{array}{r} x_{ij} = 1 \\ x_{kj} = 1 \end{array} \right\} \overset{either}{\Rightarrow} \begin{cases} b_{ik} = 1, b_{ki} = 0 \\ b_{ik} = 0, b_{ki} = 1 \end{cases}, \forall i, k \in m, j \in n \tag{12}$$

$$b_{ik} = 1 \Rightarrow s_i + R_{ij} \leq s_k, \forall i, k \in m, j \in n \tag{13}$$

$$F_1 \geq \max(s_i + R_{ij} - s_k) + 1, \forall i, k \in m, j \in n \tag{14}$$

$$s_i * x_{ij} + R_{ij} \leq D_i, \forall i \in m, j \in n \tag{15}$$

$$F_2 \geq \max (s_i + R_{ij} - D_i) + 1, \forall i \in m, j \in n \tag{16}$$

$$x_{ij} = 1 \Rightarrow s_i + R_{ij} \leq t_j + EPT_j, \forall i \in m, j \in n \tag{17}$$

$$F_3 \geq \max (s_i - t_j + R_{ij} - EPT_j) + 1, \forall i \in m, j \in n \tag{18}$$

$$x_{ij} = 1 \Rightarrow s_i \geq EAT_j, \forall i \in m, j \in n \tag{19}$$

$$F_4 \leq \min (s_i - EAT_j) - 1, \forall i \in m, j \in n \tag{20}$$

Data Sampling-based Query Budget Constraints guarantee that the resource cost to execute i on j is within the budget of B_i. If the entire dataset of query is to be processed in full, as shown in (21), C_{ij} represents the execution cost of query i on j that is within B_i. Otherwise, the accuracy of query may have to be sacrificed due to time and budget constraints, as shown in (22). SC_{ij} is the cost to sample and execute i on the data samples on j. This should be less than the budget of the query as B_i. Constraint (24) ensure if the cost of j exceeds the B_i j will be eliminated from the resource pool to enable the ILP solver to reduce the solution space and improve the algorithm performance.

$$C_{ij} * x_{ij} \leq B_i, \forall i \in m, j \in n \tag{21}$$

$$SC_{ij} * x_{ij} \leq B_i, \forall i \in m, j \in n \tag{22}$$

$$x_{ij} = 0, \; if \; j \; cannot \; satisfy \; deadline \; of \; i, \; \forall i \in m; \; j \in n \tag{23}$$

$$x_{ij} = 0, \; if \; j \; cannot \; satisfy \; budget \; of \; i, \; \forall i \in m; \; j \in n \tag{24}$$

Query Scheduling Times Constraints (25) guarantee the scheduling times of a query by specifying x_{ij} as 1 so that i is guaranteed to be scheduled to one cloud resource for execution in order to satisfy SLAs defined with users.

$$\sum_{i \in m, j \in n} x_{ij} = 1 \tag{25}$$

Data Locality Constraints ensure that queries can only execute on resources where datasets can be accessed. The aim is to avoid lengthy big data transfer times and expensive big data transfer costs, as shown in (26). If a resource j has no access to the large datasets to be processed by i, $x_{ij} = 0$ guarantees i is not scheduled to j for SLA guarantees. While $x_{ij} = 1$ is set where the scheduling is required for the optimal scheduling solution.

$$x_{ij} = 0, \; if \; j \; has \; no \; access \; to \; data \; of \; i, \; \forall i \in m, \; j \in n \tag{26}$$

Data Sampling-based Query Resource Constraints, as shown in (27), ensure that the sum of data sampling time to obtain samples and the processing time to execute task on samples using j can be satisfied by available time of j. ST_{ij} represents the required Sampling Time (ST) to sample large dataset and process query i using j.

$$\sum_{i \in m, j \in n} \left(ST_{ij} * x_{ij} \right) \leq t_j + T_j \tag{27}$$

Query Accuracy Constraints determine the available resource configurations needed to execute queries without violating query deadlines and budgets. The accuracy of queries determines the data sample size and associated resources to execute the data sample. Increased accuracy requires that a larger data size will be selected and more computing resources will be consumed to process the larger sample. Resource j with a configuration not satisfying the accuracy requirements of queries will be eliminated from the selectable resource pool, as shown in Constraint (28), to enable the ILP solver to obtain the optimized solution in a reduced search space.

$$x_{ij} = 0, \; \text{if } j \text{ cannot satisfy accuracy of } i, \; \forall i \in m; j \in n \tag{28}$$

Data Sampling-based Query Deadline Constraints (29) guarantee if $b_{ik} = 1$, i should finish sampling data and executing query on data sample no later than the start time of query k. Non-linear constraint (32) is used to generates (29) with F_5 satisfies (33) as a sufficient large constant. Constraint (30) ensure if i executes on j at s_i, they should finish sampling and execution no later than D_i. Non-linear constraint (34) is used to generate (30) with F_6 as a constant that is sufficient large satisfies (35). Non-linear relationship (36) is used to generate (31) with F_7 satisfies (37) as a sufficient large constant. This restricts if i executes on j, the data sampling and processing time of i should not exceeds the purchased resource time of j as the sum of EPT_j and t_j.

$$s_i - s_k + F_5 * b_{ik} \leq F_5 - ST_{ij}, \forall i, k \in m; j \in n \tag{29}$$

$$s_i + F_6 * x_{ij} \leq F_6 + D_i - ST_{ij}, \forall i \in m, j \in n \tag{30}$$

$$s_i - t_j + F_7 * x_{ij} \leq F_7 - ST_{ij} + EPT_j, \forall i \in m, j \in n \tag{31}$$

$$b_{ik} = 1 \Rightarrow s_i + ST_{ij} \leq s_k, \forall i, k \in m, j \in n \tag{32}$$

$$F_5 \geq \max (s_i + ST_{ij} - s_k) + 1, \forall i, k \in m, j \in n \tag{33}$$

$$s_i * x_{ij} + ST_{ij} \leq D_i, \forall i \in m, j \in n \tag{34}$$

$$F_6 \geq max(s_i + ST_{ij} - D_i) + 1, \forall i \in m, j \in n \tag{35}$$

$$x_{ij} = 1 \Rightarrow s_i + ST_{ij} \leq t_j + EPT_j, \forall i \in m, j \in n \tag{36}$$

$$F_7 \geq max(s_i - t_j + ST_{ij} - EPT_j) + 1, \forall i \in m, j \in n \tag{37}$$

3 Admission Control and Resource Scheduling

Big data analytics faces the challenges of tight budgets and/or deadlines, where queries cannot always be fully admitted whilst satisfying all QoS requirements with SLA guarantees during AaaS delivery. To tackle such research challenges, data sampling-based optimization algorithms are proposed that process data samples and return AaaS solutions in a faster manner with significantly reduced resource costs and enhanced profits.

3.1 Admission Control

Queries are submitted online to the AaaS platform from various domain users. The admission controller iteratively admits each query. The pseudo code of the admission control algorithm is shown in Algorithm 1. The admission controller first checks if BDAA is available and the associated dataset is accessible. If so, it further estimates if

---

Algorithm 1: Query Admission Control Algorithm

Input: big data analytics requests/ queries, BDAAs, cloud resources, resource configurations
Output: query acceptance or rejection decisions
1: **for** every submitted query ∈ submitted big data analytics requests
2:     requested BDAA by the query ← broker/search the BDAA registry
3:     **if** the BDAA is brokerable/available && big data can be accessed
4:         configurations ← search the resource registry for all configurations
5:         **if** configurations > 0
6:             **for** every configuration ∈ all available resource configurations
7:                 ET ← estimate the execution time on the resource configuration
8:                 EC ← estimate the query cost on the resource configuration
9:                 **if** EC < budget && ET < deadline
10:                    admQueries ← query admission as fullQuery
11:                **end if**
12:                **else if** the query request allows sacrificing accuracy for reduced times and costs
13:                    apprQueries ←get queries support approximate processing
14:                    **for** every query request in the apprQueries
15:                        SC ← estimate the cloud resource cost of data sampling
16:                        ST ← estimate the required time of data sampling
17:                        DPC ← estimate the cloud resource cost to process data samples
18:                        PT ← estimate the time to process data samples
19:                        QA ← estimate data accuracy to process data samples
20:                        **if** SC + DPC < budget && ST + PT < deadline && A > accuracy
21:                            admQueries ← query admission as apprQuery
22:                            avaiResources ← update the available cloud resources
23:                        **end if**
24:                    **end for**
25:                **end if**
26:         **end for**
27:         **if the query request is not successfully admitted**
28:             reject the data analytics request with rejection details
29:         **end if**
30:     **end if**
31:**end for**

---

the QoS requirements of budget, deadline, and accuracy can be satisfied by any existing cloud resource configuration in the AaaS platform or whether it can be brokered from third party resource providers. It searches all resource configurations in the registry of cloud resources. The admission controller calculates the Estimated Cost (EC) and Estimated Time (ET) for each configuration to execute a query satisfying the given QoS requirements. If such configuration is found, the admission controller admits the query as *fullQuery* and adds the query to the admission queue (Lines 1–11).

If the admission controller cannot admit a query with tight budgets and/or deadlines, approximate processing of the query is considered only if the results are meaningful without affecting reliable decision making. The admission controller estimates if QoS requirements can be satisfied through the support of data sampling considering the overall query cost that is calculated as the sum of the Sampling Cost (SC) and the Data Processing Cost (DPC). The overall query time is calculated as the sum of data Sampling Time (ST) and Processing Times (PT). Furthermore, the admission controller estimates whether the query Accuracy (A) can be fulfilled by processing the data samples on given resource configuration (Lines 12–19).

BDAA profiles provisioned by third-party providers contain information of the BDAA costs, the required resource times including sampling times and query times, as well as the resource configurations for different query requests. BDAA application profiles are the bases for the AaaS platform to make accurate estimation of query processing time, accuracy, and cost for admission and scheduling decisions. BDAA costs for the same BDAA can be different for different versions, e.g. sequential processing versions usually costs less than parallel processing versions.

Based on the application profiles, we can obtain the query processing times for given resource configurations, the accuracy on given resource configurations, and the BDAA costs to decide whether QoS requirements of queries can be fulfilled. This is achieved by using estimation method in the following way: for a given query, based on the accuracy requirement, profiles satisfying accuracy can be preliminarily selected. After considering budget requirements, all of the profiles that are still possible to be selected to execute a given query within user specified budgets are selected. The admission controller further calculates the overall costs including BDAA costs and resource costs for available BDAA profiles to satisfy the budget constraints of queries.

For a given query that supports approximate processing, if all QoS requirements can be satisfied by at least one cloud resource configuration, such a query is acceptable and executable as *apprQuery* and the SLAs are established by the SLA manager; otherwise, the query has to be rejected to avoid significant penalty costs caused by SLA violations. Afterwards, the AaaS platform utilizes optimization algorithm to make scheduling decisions to maximize the profits while minimizing query response times in the AaaS platform. After the data sampling-based admission control, rejection reasons are given to users to subsequently modify query specifications for potential resubmission (Lines 20–31).

Admitted queries can be assigned to existing resources for execution if the current resources have sufficient capacity; otherwise, new cloud resources are created to execute the query following the SLA agreements. The optimal query assignment and resource provision decisions are ultimately provided by the resource scheduler for profit maximization and query time minimization.

3.2 Resource Scheduling

To provide timely, reliable, and cost-effective scheduling solutions for the AaaS platform, a data SAmpling-based Profit Optimization (SAPO) scheduling algorithm is put forward. SAPO offers scheduling with SLA aware and data sampling-based methods to provision resources to query processing on data samples to meet QoS requirements of budget, deadline, and accuracy. The pseudo code of the SAPO resource scheduling algorithm is shown in Algorithm 2.

SAPO allows data analytics results to be returned in a time-efficient and reliable manner with controllable resource costs that can benefit users with limited budgets and with timely decision making requirements where accuracy bounds is necessary for reliable decision making. Resource scheduling is the core function of the AaaS platform required to coordinate all the other components to deliver satisfactory services to users through the SAPO algorithm.

The AaaS service delivery scenario starts when users submit queries to the AaaS platform. Each query requests for specific BDAA to analyze the data. For a BDAA, the SAPO scheduler first obtains information from all queries and resources supporting the

BDAA, along with the up-to-date information on the resource configurations from the AaaS platform as the input to the scheduler.

The SAPO scheduler calls the admission controller to admit query requests. Queries are admitted by the admission controller in the following two scenarios. **Scenario 1**: sufficient budgets as well as deadlines are given by users to execute the queries that can meet SLA guarantees on AaaS delivery based on processing the full datasets, named as *fullQueries*. **Scenario 2**: tight deadlines and/or limited budgets are given by users. In this way, processing the entire dataset is not permitted. If accuracy of queries can be traded-off where effective approximate processing is supported for reliable data analytics results, data sampling is used to approximately process smaller sampled datasets to tackle the time and cost challenges with reliable accuracy bounds presented to users, such queries are named as *apprQueries*. SAPO schedules queries by applying the *SAPOOptimization* method that adopts and implements the formulation of the optimization scheduling problem by applying the ILP programming model with Objective Z subjecting to a range of optimization scheduling constraints (1)–(37).

For queries that cannot be executed in full by processing the entire datasets under tight budgets and/or deadlines, the admission controller attempts to admit *apprQueries*. If the sampling technique can deliver satisfactory AaaS services, such *apprQueries* are admitted to the AaaS platform. The SAPO scheduler then generates *anaQueries* from all admitted analytics tasks. The scheduler then provisions *heuCloudResources* applying the *selectSampledResHeuristic* method. Furthermore, the SAPO scheduler utilizes the proposed *SAPOOptimization* algorithm by applying the ILP programming model to create profit-maximization and cost-minimization scheduling solutions (Lines 1–12).

If the generated optimization solutions are feasible that is returned before system-defined scheduling timeout, the optimal solution is then utilized to guide query execution and resource provisioning in the AaaS platform (Lines 13–16). If no scheduling solution is generated before the timeout setting of the optimization algorithm, a heuristic approach named as *DTHeuristic* is used to generate alternative heuristic solutions to avoid SLA violations caused by the failure of query execution. After the scheduling solution is created for the current schedule, the SAPO scheduler triggers auto-scaling to downgrade the capacity by terminating active cloud resources that are idle to save costs at checkpoints by the *scaleDown* method (Lines 17–23).

The *SAPOOptimization* method (Lines 24–30) first obtains the current platform information regarding the queries, resources, and BDAAs that are used as the input to the ILP solver. SAPO defines and implements the optimization objectives and constraints. SAPO enables the objective function to maximize the profits and minimize query responses for the AaaS platform. SAPO is subject to various constraints (1)–(37) based on the mixed ILP formulation of the optimization problem. SAPO support data sampling and SLA aware resource scheduling solutions that are designed to tackle the resource scheduling challenges for fast, reliable, and cost-effective optimization solutions to improve the performance and quality of service delivery by the AaaS platform.

The *DTHeuristic* method (Lines 31–33) applies a maximum delay time-based heuristic algorithm to map *admQueries* to *exeCloudResources* and executes queries at the earliest available start time on the selected cloud resources.

Algorithm 2: SAPO Cloud Resource Scheduling Algorithm

Input: user submitted big data analytics requests, cloud configurations, all available BDAAs, cloud resources.
Output: optimized | heuristic resource scheduling solution.
1: **for** each requested BDAA ∈ all available BDAAs
2:     admQueries ← admissionControl (queries, resourceConfigurations, BDAA)
3:     fullProcessingTasks ← obtain all fullQueries from admitted queries
4:     apprQueries ← obtain all approximate queries from admitted queries
5:     **for** every query request in apprQueries
6:         dataSamplingTasks ← create data sampling tasks
7:     **end for**
8:     anaQueries ← fullProcessingTasks + dataSamplingTasks
9:     **if** (anaQueries > 0)
10:        resources ← obtain all existing cloud resources running BDAA
11:        heuCloudResources ← **selectSampledResourceHeuristic** (resources, configurations, anaQueries, BDAA)
12:        optimalSolution ← **SAPOOptimization** (anaQueries, BDAAs, heuCloudResources)
13:        **if** a feasible solution is obtained before timeout setting
14:            apply the optimal solution to provision resources for query execution
15:        **end if**
16:        **else**
17:            heuristicSolution ← **DTHeuristic** (heuCloudResources, anaQueries, BDAA)
18:            apply the heuristic solution to run queries
19:        **end else**
20:        activeResources ← update existing active resources running BDAA
21:        scaleDown (activeResources)
22:    **end if**
23: **end for**
24: **Procedure: SAPOOptimization** (anaQueries, heuCloudResources, BDAA)
25:    getUpdateToDateInfo (anaQueries, heuCloudResources, BDAA)
26:    defineOptimizationScheduleObjectives (**Objective Z**)
27:    defineOptimizationScheduleConstraints (**Constraints (1)-(37)**)
28:    defineOptimizationTimeOut (schedulingTimeout)
29:    solveOptimizationScheduleProblem ()
30:    optimalSolution ← getOptimizationScheduleSolution ()
31: **Procedure: DTHeuristic** (admQueries, heuCloudResources, BDAA)
32:    sort admQueries based on maximum delay time
33:    schedule admQueries to resources with minimized earliest start time
34: **Procedure: selectSampledResHeuristic** (resources, BDAAs, configurations, admQueries)
35:    avaiCloudResources ← obtain all available cloud resources
36:    exeCloudResources ← obtain resources from avaiCloudResources
37:    newCloudResources ← generate new resources to execute queries
38:    heuCloudResources ← exeCloudResources + newCloudResources

---

The *selectSampledResourceHeuristic* method (Lines 34–38) significantly reduces the Algorithm Running Time (ART) of *SAPOOptimization* by reducing the problem search space to efficiently generate data sampling-based optimized resource scheduling solutions. The method first selects *avaiCloudResources* as the available cloud resources selected from the existing cloud resources. It then selects cloud resources with the capacity to execute at least a *fullQuery* or an *apprQuery* satisfying its QoS requirements utilizing *avaiCloudResources* that is defined as *exeCloudResources*. The *selectResourceHeuristic* further generates new resources to execute the submitted queries if the platform does not have sufficient resource capacity to execute newly submitted query requests. The method finally generates *heuCloudResources* as the summation of *exeCloudResources* and *newCloudResources* that are then input to the *SAPOOptimization* method. The *heuCloudResources* is able to provision sufficient resources that enable *SAPOOptimization* to find feasible solutions to schedule queries satisfying SLAs. The *heuCloudResources* method provisions sufficient resources with capacity close to the optimal configuration created by *SAPOOptimization*. The aim is to reduce the search space to enable *SAPOOptimization* to return optimal solutions in a timely, reliable, cost-effective way.

We compare the performance of SAPO to a Profit Optimization (PO) scheduling algorithm. PO [3] serves as a suitable comparison algorithm as it serves the same objective as SAPO to maximize the profits for the AaaS platform while providing AaaS with minimized queries times for users. Moreover, PO also builds on ILP-based formulation and provides optimal resource scheduling solutions in the AaaS platform. PO applies SLA-based scheduling mechanisms that are able to deliver optimal solutions subject to different constraints, which are: resource capacities, budget requirements, deadline requirements, task execution times and sequences, task dependencies, and data locality constraints [3]. Since PO is not able to support sampling-based scheduling solutions to process big data under constraints of tight deadlines and budgets, it has the limitations in only admitting and scheduling queries with sufficient budgets and deadlines. Thus, PO is not able to tackle big data challenges incurring expensive costs or lengthy processing times where fast, cost-effective, and reliable AaaS is required by decision making in BDAA domains such as banking and stock market. To face such challenges, SAPO serves as the ideal optimization resource scheduling algorithm that is able to deliver optimal solutions not only support big data analytics scenarios enabled by PO but also support big data analytics within tight deadline and limited budget constraints by applying data sampling-based scheduling for timely, cost-efficient, and reliable AaaS solutions in the cloud computing environments.

4   Performance Evaluation

We conducted experimental evaluations to analyze the efficiency of the profit maximization and cost minimization algorithms including SLA guarantees, query admission control, cost saving, resource configuration, profit enhancement, accuracy analysis, and ART analysis.

Experiment Setup: We built the AaaS framework using Cloudsim [7] and utilize IBM CPlex 5.5 as the optimization ILP solver [8]. We conducted experiments for real time and periodic cloud resource scheduling with different Scheduling Intervals (SIs).

Resource Configuration: 4 datacenters are simulated. Each datacenter consists of 500 nodes while each node contains 400 CPU, 10 PB storage, 30 TB memory, and bandwidth of 10 GB/s. Six types of VMs are considered as memory optimized Amazon EC2 VMs: r4.large, r4.xlarge, r4.2xlarge, r4.4xlarge, r4.8xlarge, and r4.16xlarge [9]. A resource can be a CPU core, a single or a cluster of VMs. The unit for memory, storage, cost, and SI is GiB, GB, dollar, minute accordingly.

Data Analytics Workload utilizes Big Data Benchmark [10] and BlinkDB data sampling workload [11]. The big data benchmark provides query response times and

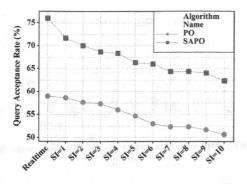
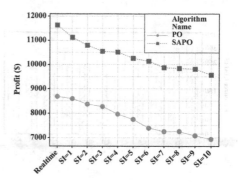

Fig. 1. Admission rates of SAPO and PO.   **Fig. 2.** Profits of SAPO and PO.

the cloud resource configurations using Amazon EC2 VMs to execute on big data analytic frameworks with detailed data size, data location, and data type of datasets. The BlinkDB technique samples the original datasets for sampling processing of the data. The BlinkDB workload provides the resource times, configurations to sample big data with query times and error bounds on accuracies. Based on the big data benchmark and BlinkDB, the times for data sampling and query processing on various configurations using BDAAs are modeled.

Query Information: *Submission time* is generated using one-minute mean Poisson arrival interval. *Query type* has 4 types including scan, join, aggregation, and user defined function. BDAAs has 3 types including Hive on Hadoop as BDAA 1, Hive on Spark without caching as BDAA 2, and Hive on Spark with caching as BDAA 3. *Resource time* contains the resource requirements of queries. Two types of deadline and budgets are considered: tight, which are generated with a Normal Distribution of (3, 1.4), and loose, which are generated with a Normal Distribution of (8, 3). *Accuracy* is generated-based on the BlinkDB sampling workload which details the guaranteed accuracy with given response times and cloud resource costs to execute the approximate queries with error bounds of results. 5 types of accuracy are considered that are 100%, 99%, 95%, 90%, and 85%.

1. Admission Control and SLA Guarantees: To evaluate the algorithm performance of efficient and effective admission control, we conduct experiments for real time and periodic scheduling where SI is in the range of [1, 10]. We compare the algorithm performance of SAPO compared to PO with results shown in Fig. 1. We can see that the SAPO is able to admit more queries for processing for both real time and periodic resource scheduling with an increased query admission rate in the interval of [12%, 17%]. Higher admission rate for processing queries can creates higher profits, increase user satisfactory levels, and enlarge markets by processing more data analytics requests, and hence is highly preferred. Moreover, results also show that all admitted queries by SAPO and PO are processed with SLA guarantees, which proves the effectiveness of the admission control.

2. Profit Enhancement: We evaluate the profit enhancement advantages of SAPO for real time and periodic scheduling scenarios, as shown in Fig. 2. Results show that SAPO creates significantly higher profit than PO for all scheduling scenarios. The

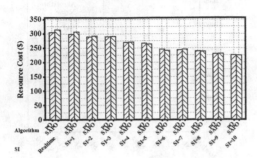
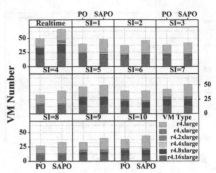
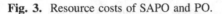

Fig. 3. Resource costs of SAPO and PO.   **Fig. 4.** Resource configurations of SAPO and PO.

increased profit interval is [27.5%, 38.6%]. The enhanced profits come from higher query admission rates and reduced resource consumption from data sampling-based query processing. The profits show a decreasing trend for both SAPO and PO due to the rejection of queries with tight deadlines for periodic SIs. Real time scheduling is not realistic for all online resources since it would generate unnecessarily large computing usage and hence periodic scheduling approaches are supported to schedule queries that arrive during specified SIs. We find SI = 1 is the most suitable periodic SI that can, on the one hand admit more queries, while on the other hand it reduces frequent scheduling computations, which is important for higher admission rates and higher profit enhancements. We further analyze the data processing methods of SAPO and PO and provide details of the data processing methods. We find that the SAPO algorithm supports both full data processing and sampling-based processing of the datasets while the PO scheduling algorithm only supports full data processing. The percentage of queries that are processed using data sampling methods for the SAPO algorithms are in the interval of [16.6%, 22.4%], which shows an increased query rate that benefits creating higher profits for SAPO.

3. *Cost Savings*: Resource cost is another key performance indicator for algorithm performance. As shown in Fig. 3, we can see that the resource costs of both SAPO and PO are similar. The increased cost rates of SAPO compared to PO are in the interval of [−0.02%, −0.3%]. Under the condition that SAPO admits [12%, 17%] more queries and creates higher profits of [27.5%, 38.6%], such similar resource consumptions and costs clearly indicate the performance advantages of SAPO in cost saving. SAPO is able to reduce costs and increase profits through better optimal decision making. SAPO allows to better utilize resources on larger number of queries with a more comprehensive optimization solution.

4. *Resource Configuration*: The resource configurations of SAPO and PO for real time and periodic scheduling are shown in Fig. 4. There is a trend whereby r4.large and r4.16xlarge are more frequently utilized by both SAPO and PO. This is consistent with the query workload property whereby the workload is generated with query deadlines and budgets in two categories: tight and loose. For tight deadlines, r4.16xlarge can offer higher processing capacity to meet deadline requirements while r4.large can reduce unit

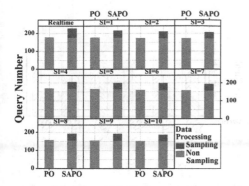

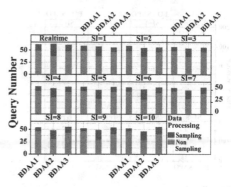

Fig. 5. Query number of data sampling and non sampling processing of SAPO and PO.

Fig. 6. Query number of sampling and non sampling processing for each BDAA.

resource waste for tight budgets when VMs are idle, hence both r4.large and r4.16xlarge are utilized more frequently. We can also see that the SAPO algorithm has an overall higher number of VMs utilization due to the higher number of admitted queries that require more cloud resources to provide the required computing power for the query workload. We notice the decrease in resource consumption trend for both PO and SAPO due to the decreased query admission rates and hence decreased resource requirements. Decreased resource consumption also comes from the higher number of queries to be scheduled in increased SIs with resultant improvements in resource utilizations.

5. *Data Processing Method Analysis*: We further analyze the data processing methods of SAPO and PO for better understanding of the performance advantages of SAPO. We obtain the data processing methods of all queries for both SAPO and PO. Results show that the SAPO algorithm supports both full data processing and data sampling-based processing of the datasets while the PO scheduling algorithm only supports full data processing for all BDAAs, as shown in Fig. 5. The percentage of queries that are processed using data sampling methods for the SAPO algorithms are in the interval of [16.6%, 22.4%], which shows that increased query rates create higher profits for SAPO.

After the overall analysis of the algorithm performance for all BDAAs, we further analyze the algorithm performance of SAPO for each BDAA. The number of queries processed by different BDAAs for SAPO and the details of the data processing method are shown in Fig. 6. The number of queries with approximate processing is shown in Fig. 7. We can see that although admitted queries that support approximate processing are in the interval [80.4%, 81.2%] in Fig. 8, SAPO only applies sampling-based scheduling on queries when the QoS requirements cannot be fulfilled to prioritize highly accurate query processing needed for reliable decision making. As a result, approximately processed queries are in the interval [16.5%, 22.4%]. SAPO prioritizes the processing of the entire datasets to provide full accuracy of data analytics results to help users make better strategies and decisions while it deprioritizes the profit gaining

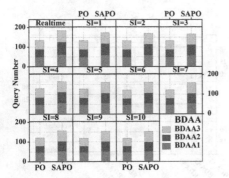

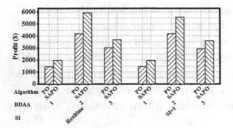

Fig. 7. Approximate query processing number for each BDAA.

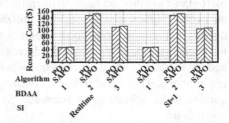

Fig. 8. Query acceptance number for BDAAs.

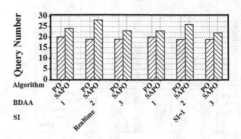

Fig. 9. Profits of SAPO and PO for different BDAAs.

Fig. 10. Resource costs of BDAAs of SAPO and PO for real time and SI = 1

created by approximate processing. SAPO aims to help the AaaS platform to achieve the best performance for higher user satisfaction and enlarge market share by higher quality AaaS delivery.

6. BDAA Analysis: After the algorithm performance analysis for the entire query workload processed by all BDAAs, we further detail the performance evaluation results for each BDAA to show the performance advantages of SAPO. The results show that SAPO outperforms PO for each BDAA with real time scheduling and periodic scheduling using real time scheduling and SI = 1 as examples. The results also show that SAPO is able to admit more queries for both real time and SI = 1 with an increased query acceptance rate in the interval of [15.8%, 42.4%] for BDAA 1-3. The profits created by the SAPO algorithm for BDAA 1-3 are [22.4%, 41.7%] significantly higher than PO as shown in Fig. 9. Moreover, we further analyze the resource costs for SAPO in Fig. 10. With all above performance advantage for query admission and profit enhancement, the resource cost of SAPO is only [0.01%, 0.03%] higher than the PO algorithms for BDAA 1-3, resulting in a significant performance advantage and cost saving. The results also show that SAPO is able to significantly outperform PO for the entire query workload with higher admission rates, higher profits, and lower resource costs. Experimental evaluations also show SAPO significantly outperforms PO for each BDAA for both real time and periodic scheduling.

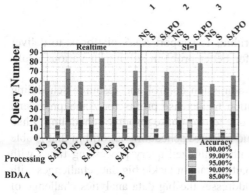

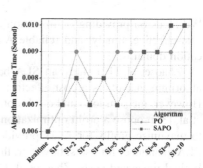

Fig. 11. Accuracy analysis

Fig. 12. ART analysis.

7. Accuracy Analysis: We further analyze the accuracy of queries for different query processing methods with results shown in Fig. 11. We can see that for data Sampling (S)-based processing, Non-Sampling (NS)-based processing, and SAPO processing queries with both S and NS-based methods, the number of queries processed with different accuracy requirements varies for different BDAAs. All of the accuracy requirements of the queries are fulfilled with 100% SLA guarantees for both SAPO and PO algorithms. For NS-based processing, we notice that though the query percentage with full accuracy requirements is in the interval of [17%, 36%], NS-based processing method of SAPO does not support approximate processing but only supports full processing of queries. Furthermore, for SAPO, despite [75%, 86%] queries supporting approximate processing, SAPO only process [14%, 30%] of queries with the data sampling-based processing method. The reason is that SAPO prioritizes fully accurate query processing for better decision making though approximate query processing thereby creating higher profits and reducing resource costs. SAPO aims to help the AaaS platform to improve the quality of AaaS delivery for efficient and reliable problem solving and decision making for users in various application domains.

8. ART Analysis: The average ART of SAPO and PO algorithms for real time and periodic scheduling are shown in Fig. 12. The results show an overall increasing trend for ART as more queries are scheduled and more optimization constraints need to be applied for more complex optimization problems with larger inputs and hence a larger solution space. Both SAPO and PO can deliver resource scheduling solutions within 6–10 ms that illustrates the efficiency of the scheduling algorithms. As such, ART does not limit the SAPO scheduling algorithm in delivering effective and efficient resource scheduling solutions. In order to prevent an unexpected large number of queries arriving so that the solution space and input scale exceed the capacity of the opti-mization algorithms to deliver solutions within SIs, heuristic algorithms are applied as backup solutions. These are able to make near optimal scheduling solutions to guar-antee SLAs for the AaaS delivery. The backup heuristics enable the AaaS platform to provide comprehensive scheduling solutions for unexpectedly large query arrivals to mitigate risks and support AaaS delivery with SLA guarantees.

5 Related Work

We focus on providing optimization algorithms to support AaaS platforms to deliver cost-effective, timely, and reliable AaaS for better problem solving in various application domains.

Zhao et al. [12] study an SLA-based admission control and resource scheduling algorithm that offers a cost-effective solution to increase profits for AaaS providers. However, the solution can be sub-optimal due to two-phase resource scheduling. Zhao et al. [3] propose a profit optimization cloud resource scheduling algorithm that is able to maximize profits for AaaS providers with minimized query processing times with SLA guarantees for users, however, this solution cannot tackle big data challenges with limited times and costs. Zhao et al. [13] addresses the big data analytics challenge of resource scheduling under limited deadlines and budgets where accuracy can be traded-off by applying data splitting-based query admission control and profit optimization cloud resource scheduling algorithms. The approach trades-off accuracy for reduced costs and quicker times while guaranteeing budget and deadline requirements of queries, however, it does not provide accuracy guarantees during AaaS delivery that are essential to support reliable and accurate decision making.

There are related works that diverse the BDAAs for the AaaS platforms. Agarwal et al. [11] propose BlinkDB to approximately process large datasets for reliable results with response time error bounds. Zhang et al. [14] build an ND-based solution to split large medical data in clouds providing faster responses with reduced costs and higher flexibility. Tordini et al. [15] process sequencing datasets of complex workflows applying data splitting techniques while maintaining high accuracy.

Mian et al. [16] apply heuristics to provision resources for data analytics workloads with effective resource configuration in a public cloud, however, they sacrifice SLAs to reduce resource costs. This is different from our SLA guarantee purpose as satisfactory AaaS delivery is the fundamental for user satisfaction. Wang et al. [17] support data-aware scheduling for efficient load balancing, however, they do not consider QoS, SLA guarantee, or cost optimization. Xia et al. [18] support a fair and collaborative way to place big data into distributed datacenters, however, they do not consider QoS, SLAs, or indeed AaaS delivery.

Garg et al. [19] manage resources for general cloud applications instead of big data analytics applications. Gu et al. [20] support cost-minimized big data analytics in distributed datacenters, however, does not support cost-optimization and SLA guarantees. Zheng et al. [21] proposed a variety of algorithms to schedule big data workflows on clouds to minimize the costs under deadlines. However, they do not provide automatic scheduling, nor consider budget constraints or consider admission control satisfying SLAs. Dai et al. [22] propose a multi-objective resource allocation approach for big data applications to obtain optimal deployment of VMs in clouds. However, they neither consider admission control nor tackle the time challenges for big data processing.

Zhou et al. [23] propose a declarative optimization engine to provision cloud resources for workflows utilizing available GPU power for timely solutions. They neither consider QoS requirements nor SLA guarantees. Mao et al. [24] propose an auto-scaling mechanism for traditional workflow scheduling to satisfy task deadlines while minimizing financial costs. However, their approach does not target big data analytics or consider budget or accuracy requirements of requests. Chen et al. [25] propose a utility model-based scheduling mechanism for cloud service provider to optimize profits or user satisfaction. However, they do not consider budget, deadline, accuracy as the key QoS factors of tasks. They trade-off customer satisfaction while we aim to maximize user satisfaction by providing high quality AaaS satisfying query QoS requirements.

The novelty of our research work is proposing data sampling-based admission control and cloud resource scheduling algorithms with SLA guarantees on budget and deadline requirements to support big data analytics solutions under limited times and tight budgets. Moreover, we provide accuracy bounds for big data analytics results to support reliable and accurate decisions. Our proposed algorithms are able to provide profit optimized and time minimized AaaS solutions for fast, cost-effective, and reliable problem solving and decision making in various BDAA domains, which cannot be supported by the above related works.

6 Conclusion and Future Works

Admission control and resource scheduling serve as the key functions to maximize profits and minimize query response times for AaaS platforms to deliver SLA-guaranteed AaaS to various domains of users. We proposed timely, cost-efficient, and reliable query admission control and resource scheduling solutions by modeling, for-mulating, and implementing the data sampling-based multi-objective optimization solutions. Experimental evaluation shows the admission control and scheduling algo-rithms significantly increase admission rates, increase profits, and reduce resource costs with efficient resource configurations for the entire the query workloads and for dif-ferent BDAAs under real time and periodic scheduling scenarios compared to the state-of-the-art algorithms. Furthermore, our proposed algorithms significantly benefit big data analytics under tight deadlines and limited budgets by supporting fully accurate query processing as well as sampling-based query processing that enable users to obtain cost and time effective big data solutions with accuracy guaranteed AaaS for timely, cost-efficient, and reliable decision making.

As part of the future research works, we will continue investigating and proposing automatic and efficient optimization algorithms to tackle big data analytics challenges under various QoS requirements. We will keep working on proposing effective and efficient sampling and splitting-based optimization algorithms to help AaaS platforms to deliver satisfactory AaaS to various domains of users offering faster query response times and reduced cloud resource costs without compromising the reliability of big data analytics solutions.

References

1. Assunção, M.D., Calheiros, R.N., Bianchi, S., Netto, M.A., Buyya, R.: Big data computing and clouds: trends and future directions. J. Parallel Distrib. Comput. **79**, 3–15 (2015)
2. Hashem, I.A.T., Yaqoob, I., Anuar, N.B., Mokhtar, S., Gani, A., Khan, U.: The rise of 'big data' on cloud computing: review and open research issues. Inf. Syst. **47**, 98–115 (2014)
3. Zhao, Y., Calheiros, R.N., Bailey, J., Sinnott, R.: SLA-based profit optimization for resource management of big data analytics-as-a-service platforms in cloud computing environments. In: Proceedings of the IEEE International Conference on Big Data, pp. 432–441 (2016)
4. Chaudhuri, S., Das, G., Narasayya, V.: Optimized stratified sampling for approximate query processing. ACM Trans. Database Syst. (TODS) **32**(2), 9 (2007)
5. Benayoun, R., De Montgolfier, J., Tergny, J., Laritchev, O.: Linear programming with multiple objective functions: step method (STEM). Math. Program. **1**, 366–375 (1971)
6. Isermann, H.: Linear lexicographic optimization. OR Spektrum **4**, 223–228 (1982)
7. Calheiros, R.N., Ranjan, R., Beloglazov, A., De Rose, C.A., Buyya, R.: CloudSim: a toolkit for modeling and simulation of cloud computing environments and evaluation of resource provisioning algorithms. Softw. Pract. Exp. **41**(1), 23–50 (2011)
8. IBM ILOG CPLEX Optimization Studio. https://www.ibm.com/developerworks/downloads/ws/ilogcplex/. Accessed 03 Dec 2018
9. Amazon EC2. http://aws.amazon.com/ec2/instance-types/. Accessed 03 Dec 2018
10. Big Data Benchmark. https://amplab.cs.berkeley.edu/benchmark/. Accessed 12 Dec 2018
11. Agarwal, S., Mozafari, B., Panda, A., Milner, H., Madden, S., Stoica, I.: BlinkDB: queries with bounded errors and bounded response times on very large data. In: Proceedings of the 8th ACM European Conference on Computer Systems, p. 29 (2013)
12. Zhao, Y., Calheiros, R.N., Gange, G., Ramamohanarao, K., Buyya, R.: SLA-based resource scheduling for big data analytics as a service in cloud computing environments. In: Proceedings of the 44th IEEE International Conference on Parallel Processing, pp. 510–519 (2015)
13. Zhao, Y., Calheiros, R.N., Gange, G., Bailey, J., Sinnott, R.: SLA-based profit optimization for resource scheduling of big data analytics-as-a-service in cloud computing environments. IEEE Trans. Cloud Comput. 1–18 (2018)
14. Zhang, H., Zhao, Y., Pang, C., He, J.: Splitting large medical data sets based on normal distribution in cloud environment. IEEE Trans. Cloud Comput. (99), 1 (2015, in press)
15. Tordini, F., Aldinucci, M., Viviani, P., Merelli, I., Lio, P.: Scientific workflows on clouds with heterogeneous and preemptible instances. In: Proceedings of the International Conference on Parallel Computing, pp. 605–614 (2017)
16. Mian, R., Martin, P., Vazquez-Poletti, J.: Provisioning data analytic workloads in a cloud. Future Gener. Comput. Syst. **29**(6), 1452–1458 (2013)
17. Wang, K., Zhou, X., Li, T., Zhao, D., Lang, M., Raicu, I.: Optimizing load balancing and data-locality with data-aware scheduling. In: Proceedings of the 2014 IEEE International Conference on Big Data, pp. 119–128 (2015)
18. Xia, Q., Xu, Z., Liang, W., Zomaya, A.Y.: Collaboration-and fairness-aware big data management in distributed clouds. IEEE Trans. Parallel Distrib. Syst. **27**(7), 1941–1953 (2015)
19. Garg, S.K., Toosi, A.N., Gopalaiyengar, S.K., Buyya, R.: SLA-based virtual machine management for heterogeneous workloads in a cloud datacenter. J. Netw. Comput. Appl. **45**, 108–120 (2014)
20. Gu, L., Zeng, D., Li, P., Guo, S.: Cost minimization for big data processing in geo-distributed data centers. IEEE Trans. Emerg. Top. Comput. **2**(3), 314–323 (2014)

21. Zheng, W., Qin, Y., Bugingo, E., Zhang, D., Chen, J.: Cost optimization for deadline-aware scheduling of big data processing jobs on clouds. Future Gener. Comput. Syst. **82**, 244–255 (2018)
22. Dai, W., Qiu, L., Wu, A., Qiu, M.: Cloud infrastructure resource allocation for big data applications. IEEE Trans. Big Data **4**(3), 313–324 (2018)
23. Zhou, A.C., He, B., Cheng, X., Lau, C.T.: A declarative optimization engine for resource provisioning of scientific workflows in IaaS clouds. In: Proceedings of the 24th International Symposium on High Performance Parallel Distributed Computing, pp. 223–234 (2015)
24. Mao, M., Humphrey, M.: Auto-scaling to minimize cost and meet application deadlines in cloud workflows. In: Proceedings of 2011 International Conference for High Performance Computing, Networking, Storage and Analysis, Seatle, WA, pp. 1–12 (2011)
25. Chen, J., Wang, C., Zhou, B.B., Sun, L., Lee, Y.C., Zomaya, A.Y.: Tradeoffs between profit and customer satisfaction for service provisioning in the cloud. In: Proceedings of the 20th International Symposium on High Performance Distributed Computing, pp. 229–238 (2011)

A User Constraint Awareness Approach for QoS-Based Service Composition

Zhihui Wu, Piyuan Lin$^{(\boxtimes)}$, Peijie Huang, Huachong Peng, Yihui He, and Junan Chen

South China Agricultural University, Guangzhou, China
pyuanlin@scau.edu.cn

Abstract. Web service composition adopts functional features including the inputs and outputs, and non-functional features including quality of service (QoS), conditional structure constraints, user preferences, and trusts to compose homogeneous or heterogeneous services together in order to create value-added services. However, in some complex practical application scenarios, the web services with the same function can provide the generous differentiated contents, and there is no approach to focus on the user's constraints on the content provided by the web services. In this paper, we focus on handling three composition dimensions simultaneously including functional features, QoS and the user's constraints on the contents provided by the web services. Therefore, an improved genetic algorithm to obtain an optimal solution for this task is applied. In addition, we also take it into consideration that the over-constrained problem caused by implicit conflicting constraints and improve a constraint correction approach to solve this problem with less cost of consistency checks. Experimental results using the real datasets about travel demonstrate the effectiveness of our approach in creating the fully functional and quality-optimized solutions, on the premise that the users constraints on the content are satisfied.

Keywords: User constraint awareness · Web service composition · Over-constrained problems · Genetic algorithm · Constraint correction

1 Introduction

Nowadays, Service-Oriented Computing (SOC) has been widely employed in many fields and plays an important role in practical applications. Considering the complexity of user requirements, web service composition is an effective and available solution by composing homogenous or heterogeneous services together in order to create value-added services that meet user requirements [1]. Thus, promoting automated web service composition by considering functional and non-functional features has attracted the attention of researchers [2].

The complexity of web service composition lies in the number of distinct dimensions it must simultaneously account for [3]. On the first dimension, services must be combined so that their inputs and outputs are properly linked. In other words, the output produced by a given service can be used as an input to the next service in the combination, ultimately resulting in the desired overall output. On the second dimension, the composition must

© Springer Nature Switzerland AG 2019
J. Miller et al. (Eds.): ICWS 2019, LNCS 11512, pp. 48–62, 2019.
https://doi.org/10.1007/978-3-030-23499-7_4

meet any specified user constraint or preference. A constraint is defined as the user restriction that must be met to make the composited solution valid. On the third dimension, considering the quality of service (QoS) and service trust, the resulting combination must achieve the best overall QoS in terms of time, cost, reliability, etc.

Thus, several techniques have been proposed to address this composition problem, which are QoS-based approaches [4–8], constraint/preference-based approaches [1, 3, 9, 10], and trust-based approaches [1, 11] in the literature. Initially, QoS-based approaches are committed to building functional and quality-optimized applications based on non-functional features. Secondly, considering the degree of user preference for non-functional features (QoS) and user constraint, constraint/preference-based approaches focus on providing personalized web service compositions to users. Thirdly, trust-based approaches further recognize the importance of involving trust in web service composition in generating trustworthy web service compositions. These above works can effectively meet user complex requirements and generate the most suitable service compositions. Despite these advantages, one limitation of existing works is they only consider structure constraints (e.g. the user can specify logical branching) and neglect the user's constraints on the content provided by the web service. For example, a typical composite service is illustrated in Fig. 1 where a user in Canton plans a trip to attend an international conference held in Beijing. It consists of three parts: (1) train/flight services from Canton to Beijing; (2) booking a hotel closer to conference venue; (3) transportation used during the conference period.

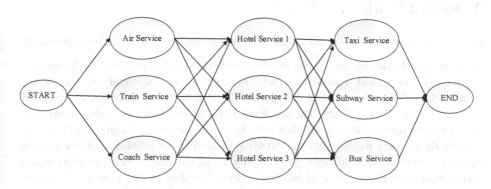

Fig. 1. A typical composite service for a user's trip to attend a conference

We assume that the tuple <Air Service, Hotel Service 1, Taxi Service> is the best solution whose overall quality of service is maximum. However, the user's expected cost does not exceed 1,500 RMB. Obviously, the price of round-trip tickets from Canton to Beijing exceeds the budget. Additionally, Users can express more constraints on the content, such as train type, seat type, hotel price, hotel grade, etc. Hence, implicit conflicting constraints given by the user lead to no solution in this problem. For example, the user's expected cost is less than 1,500 RMB and the expected transportation is by airplane. In this paper, we aim to resolve this problem by integrating the user's constraints on the content provided by the web service into an optimization model.

We apply the genetic algorithm to obtain an optimal solution in which each service can return some contents that meet the user's corresponding constraints. To address the over-constrained problem, the interactive constraint satisfaction problem (ICSP) is used [12]. The experimental results on the real data set demonstrate the efficiency and effectiveness of our method in comparison with other counterparts. In short, we shade light on a new way to promote web service composition by integrating the user's constraints on the content provided by the web service.

In summary, the major contributions of this paper are:

(1) We take it into consideration that the user's constraints on the content provided by the web services in order to express user requirement more completely.
(2) We formulate the service composition as a combined optimization problem that aims to satisfy the user's constraints and achieve the best overall QoS.
(3) We improve a constraint correction approach for solving over-constrained on user requirements.

The remainder of this paper is organized as follows: Sect. 2 gives an overview of related research. Section 3 defines the combined optimization problem addressed in this paper. Section 4 presents the improved genetic algorithm and constraint correction approach. Section 5 showed that where our method can achieve superior performance. Finally, Sect. 6 concludes our present work and outlines future research directions.

2   Related Work

In this section, we discuss previous work related to the two aspects of our approach.

Web Service Composition. In the existing researches, many research works on web service discovery and composition rely on syntax and semantics-based service matchmaking [13]. The effective method is to formulate the web service composition problems as network optimization problems [14]. Service network (SN) approaches have been put forward to deal with this issue in a cost-effective and agile way [15]. And various AI planning methods are used to solve these network problems for discovering optimal solutions with different goals. Wang et al. combined both qualitative and quantitative preferences as well as service trust together in the process of service composition and discovered the best solution by genetic algorithm and simulated annealing algorithm [1]; Rodriguez-Mier et al. used the hybrid local-global search to extract the optimal QoS with the minimum number of services [4]; Wang et al. proposed a dynamic web service composition method based on automatic hierarchical reinforcement learning (HRL) that addresses the problem of low efficiency in web service composition based on traditional reinforcement learning (RL) when applied to large scale services [5]. And Wang et al. proposed a new service composition solution based on deep reinforcement learning (DRL) for adaptive and large-scale service composition problems [6]; Labbaci et al. proposed a deep learning approach for long-term QoS-based service composition [8]; Zhao et al. used the multi-objective reinforcement learning (MORL) algorithm to make trade-offs among user preferences and recommend a collection of services to achieve the highest objective [9]. Broadly, the above approaches can be classified into three categories, namely QoS-, constraints/preference- and trust-based approaches [1], which choose the optimal web service combination according to QoS, user preference and service trust. Different from the researches discussed above, we pay attention to the service composition problem in application scenarios such as in a tour where the user's constraints on the content provided by the web service are important and non-ignorable.

User Constraints Problem. User constraints that determine the complexity of the problem are the root cause for cumbersome burdens of users. Silva et al. presented a genetic programming approach that addresses the web service composition problems including conditional constraints. But these conditional constraints are branching constraints [3]. Najar et al. focused on predicting the user's future intention based on his/her context, in order to offer him the most suitable service considering his/her incoming constraints [16]. But this approach is based on the assumption that, even in a dynamic and frequently changing pervasive information system, common situations can be found. Zhao et al. mined user intents using natural language processing techniques [17]. However, in practical application scenarios, users constraints sometimes are too tight. Therefore, there are maybe over-constrained problems that lead to no solution. ICSP corrects over-constrained problems by computing maximal satisfiable subset (MSS) or minimal correction subset (MCS) of users' constraints, which ensure that the original constraints are retained as much as possible under the circumstance that there is at least one solution [18]. Alessandro et al. proposed a novel approach to speeding up MCS enumeration over conjunctive normal form propositional formulas by caching of so-called premise sets seen during the enumeration process [19]. And Nina et al. proposed a new algorithm named FLINT for extracting minimal unsatisfiable cores and correction sets simultaneously [20]. But these works are not applicable to our task by considering that in our context different user preferences for constraints need the optimal MSS/MCS, not all MSS/MCS enumeration. Therefore, the algorithms proposed by Li et al. are more suitable, who generate the optimal MSS by taking into account different user preferences for constraints [18].

3   Problem Description

The objective of web service composition is to create a new, composite service that accomplishes a given task. A user sends a composition request that is automatically processed by a system that then returns an application assembled using a set of atomic services. In the web service composition, an atomic web service can be represented as $S = (input, output, QoS(q_1, \ldots, q_n))$, where n is the number of QoS attributes considered. Services are selected from a service repository $SR = \{S_1, \ldots, S_m\}$ (where m is the number of services in the repository) and combined according to the specifications of a composition request $R = (input, output)$ in order to produce a solution with the desired overall outputs. In certain cases, however, the customer may have specific constraints $C = \{C_1, \ldots, C_g\}$ on the content returned by the web service (where g is the number of constraints). For example, the customer's preferred class of airline ticket is likely to depend on his/her current budget: if the customer has enough money to pay for the book, then he/she would like to book the first-class cabin. However, if no first class tickets available in the flight service A. In this case, the flight service A is not a good choice. Specifically, we divide the constraints into 2 parts: the local constraints and the global constraints. The local constraints apply only to a single service, like the hotel price. And the global constraints work on the web services combination, such as the expected total cost. On the premise that the user's constraints on the content returned by the web service are satisfied, the objective is to produce a composition solution with the highest possible quality, which is optimized by calculating the weighted sum of a set of objective functions $f_1, \ldots, f_n$, corresponding to the different QoS attributes considered.

In our work, three popularly considered attributes [21] have been considered: availability (A), the probability of a service immediately responding to a request; reliability (R), the probability that the response produced by the service is accurate; time (T), the overall execution time for responding a request. Besides, we apply the number of solutions provided by a composition which satisfies the user constraints as a new QoS index, named N.

The overall QoS for a composition is determined by two aspects: the QoS values of the single services within it and the structure of the workflow, which are based on existing composition languages [22]. In our work, two constructs, sequence and parallel [21] are considered.

(1) Sequence construct. The services in this construct are chained together so that the outputs of the preceding service can fulfill the inputs of the next one, as shown in Fig. 2. The overall A and R probabilities are calculated by multiplying the individual values associated with each service in the construct, and the overall T is calculated by adding up the individual values. And N is calculated by the following methods. Firstly, considering the local constraints, the overall N is calculated by multiplying the number of the content provided by each service in the construct. Therefore, n_k must be greater than 0. Next, we will remove some solutions that do not meet the global constraints. Finally, we will normalize N to [0, 1] by the maximum and minimum normalization.

(2) Parallel construct. As seen in Fig. 3, the parallel constructs allow the services to be executed in parallel, which means that their inputs are independent, so their outputs are also independent. While A, R, and N are still calculated in the same way as the sequence construct, T is obtained by the longest service execution time in the construct.

4   Design of Proposed Approach

4.1   Overview of the Framework

Figure 4 shows the overview of our framework. At a high level, the three components of our proposed approach are the service network graph, the genetic programming for generating an optimal solution, and the over-constrained problems solver.

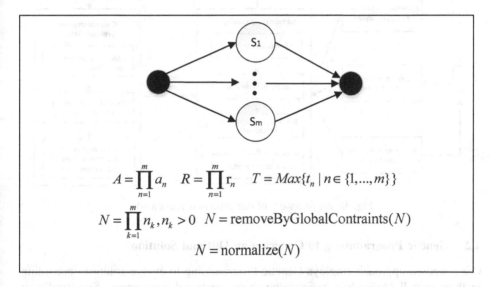

Fig. 2. Sequence construct and formulae for calculating its traditional QoS properties [21].

$$A = \prod_{n=1}^{m} a_n \quad R = \prod_{n=1}^{m} \mathrm{r}_n \quad T = \sum_{n=1}^{m} t_n$$

$$N = \prod_{k=1}^{m} n_k, n_k > 0 \quad N = \text{removeByGlobalContraints}(N)$$

$$N = \text{normalize}(N)$$

Fig. 3. Parallel construct and formulae for calculating its traditional QoS properties [21].

The process begins when the user provides a composition request R and the expression of user constraints. First, we use the composition request R to identify the service layers and extract related service network graph. In this graph, the single web service is represented by the big orange circle when the small cyan circle represents the input/output of a service or the parameters of composition request R. Then, the expression of user constraints is considered when generating the solution with the optimal overall QoS for the service composition task. However, if there is no solution due to too tight constraints, the over-constrained problems solver will detect conflicts among user constraints and computing maximal relaxation of user original constraints based on user's preference on constraints. Thus, the user original constraints are updated by the new constraints and applied when generating the optimal solution for the service composition task again. Finally, the optimal solution that meets the user original/new constraints is returned to users.

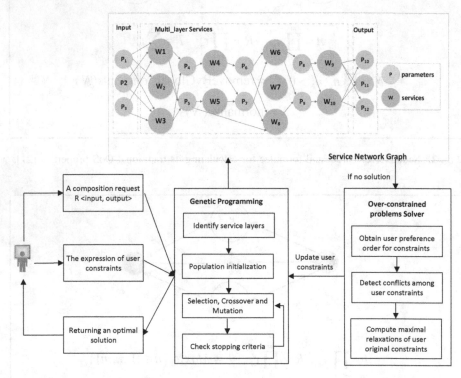

Fig. 4. An overview of our proposed framework.

4.2   Genetic Programming to Generate an Optimal Solution

Our proposed approach employs Genetic Programming to evolve solutions according to their overall QoS while maintaining their functional correctness. Specifically, it consists of three important parts: the identification of service layers, the population initialization and the genetic operators.

Identification of Service Layers. Before the composition process takes place, it is necessary to determine which layer each candidate service belongs to. This is done to prevent cycles from forming during the solution decoding process when using a backward graph-building algorithm. The identification process is detailed in [23]. The overall idea is to iteratively classify services in sets, each time finding a new set of services (i.e. new layer) whose inputs can be entirely fulfilled by the previously found services.

Fitness Function. The fitness function is used to measure the overall quality of a candidate composition. The traditional function is to calculating the weighted sum of the several overall composition QoS attributes [24]. In this paper, we apply the number of solutions provided by a composition satisfied by the user constraints as a new QoS attributes, named S. Therefore, our fitness function must take this new QoS attribute into account, as the following equation shown:

$$fitness_i = W_1(1 - A_i) + W_2(1 - R_i) + W_3T_i + W_4(1 - N_i) \tag{1}$$

where $\sum_{i=0}^{4} w_i = 1$. The value of the function is in the range of 0 to 1, and the smaller the better. The A, R, T and S values for each candidate composition are computed by the formula shown in Figs. 2 and 3. And S describes the number of solutions and are normalized by using the smallest (Min) and largest (Max) respective values, as the Eq. 2 shown. N_{orig} is the number of solutions provided by the service composition under the user constraints before normalization. Especially, the smallest value of N is 0 corresponding to over-constraints problems and the largest value of N is corresponding to the unconstrained problem and determined by the dataset.

$$N = normalize(N) = \frac{N_{orig} - N_{min}}{N_{max} - N_{min}} \tag{2}$$

Population Initialization. As opposed to generating a composition candidate purely based on a set of available inputs and another of desired outputs, when handing user constraints on the content returned by the web service it is necessary to ensure that selected web services can return content that meets user constraints. Thus, when facing a web service, we first check the consistency between user constraints and the web service. If false, remove it directly. Otherwise, the fitness value will be considered. When choosing the web service in the zeroth layer, a random strategy is adapted to select the service from a set of services that satisfy user constraints. Then, we use a greedy strategy to select services on the remaining layers. Specifically, we traverse all the available services in this layer and then calculate the fitness of the current service composition. After selecting n service combinations with the lowest fitness as candidates, the roulette strategy is adopted to randomly select one from candidates.

Crossover and Mutation. The crossover operator employed in the evolutionary process exchanges node fragments from two individuals with common service nodes. If the generated offsprings are satisfied with the user constraints, they are retained, otherwise, the parents are retained. In the mutation operation, we first traverse all the service nodes on the current service composition and check the consistency between user constraints and the web service and calculates the fitness of each available service on the layer where the service node is located. If the user constraints are satisfied and the fitness is higher than the original fitness, the original service node is replaced with the new node.

4.3   Solving Over-Constrained Problems

The main cause of the over-constrained problems is that the user constraints are too tight in the actual application scenarios. An effective way to solve this problems is that the user should modify or remove some constraints. However, user is not familiar with the main cause of the over-constraint problem. In other word, users do not know which constraints resulted to the over-constrained problems. Therefore, it may occur that the over-constrained problems still exist even though the users have modified or removed certain irrelevant constraints. In order to ensure that the original constraints of users are not changed as much as possible and accelerate user planning by reducing retrieval burdens, the interactive constraint satisfaction problem (ICSP) is adopted to describe and solve the over-constrained problems in this paper.

ICSP has many applications in Artificial Intelligence. Its interactive applications often require suggestions from a system to help a user solve the problem. It was developed from a constraint satisfaction problem (CSP) [25]. ICSP consists of four fundamental components denoted as $(X, D, U \cup B)$. X is a set of n variables $X = \{x_1, x_2,..., x_n\}$, D is a set of domains $D = \{dom(x_1), dom(x_2),..., dom(x_n)\}$ where $dom(x_i)$ is a finite set of possible values for variable x_i, B is the set of background constraints which are generated from the technical characteristics of the problem and cannot be modified and U is the set of user constraints which represent users constraints and can be modified [18]. There are two main strategies for ICSP to solve over-constrained problems: Junker U computed the minimal and preferred conflicts for solving over-constrained problems [26] and Li et al. proposed two algorithms to generate Corrective Explanations by computing maximal relaxations called CORRECTIVER-ELAXREDUCED (CER) and CORRECTIVERELAXDC (CEDC) respectively [18]. And the CEDC algorithm performs best in reducing consistency checks when generating corrective explanations. In this paper, we have improved the algorithm CEDC to make it outperformed than other algorithms.

Compared to CEDC, the improved CEDC, named Imp_CEDC which uses an extra space to record the consistency status of previously checked constraints. This strategy effectively reduces duplicate checks and therefore the number of consistency checks is less than CER. We used the Imp_CEDC algorithm to compute maximal relaxations of user constraints when facing the over-constrained problems. At the same time, Imp_CEDC takes it into account that different user preferences for constraints. Therefore, Imp_CEDC will preserve the user preferred constraints as much as possible.

The method Imp_CEDC is depicted in Fig. 5. Users give a set of user constraints U which result in over-constrained problems. The algorithm first checks if the RECORD contains the consistency state of the current constraint U. If true, then skip the method Consistent. U is divided into $\Delta1$ and $\Delta2$ by Imp_CEDC. Then, it calculates the relaxation of $\Delta1$ and $\Delta2$ respectively, and ultimately combines them to obtain the relaxation of U. The method named Split is to divide the user's constraint set into two equal parts. And the method named Consistent is aimed to check the consistency of a set C of constraints. Based on the current constraints, it returns true if at least one solution can be generated.

---

global RECORD

Algorithm: Imp_CEDC (R, U, B)

Input: The current relaxation R; the ordered set of constraints being tested in this invocation U; and the set of background constraints B.

Output: A maximal relaxation of U.

if R ∪ U in RECORD.keys **then**

      status = RECORD [(R ∪ U)]

else

      RECORD [(R ∪ U)] = Consistent (R ∪ U ∪ B)

      status = RECORD [(R ∪ U)]

end if

if status **then**

    return R ∪ U

else if len(U) > 1 **then**

      Let($\Delta 1, \Delta 2$)← Split (U) ,

      R = Imp_CEDC (R, $\Delta 1$, B),

      R = Imp_CEDC (R, $\Delta 2$, B)

end if

return R

Fig. 5. Imp_CEDC Algorithm.

5 Experiments

5.1 Datasets

To evaluate the performance of our proposed approach, we applied it to real datasets about travel crawled from Ctirp, 12306, Nuomi, Elong, etc. This datasets are composed of the information of transportation, restaurants, hotels, and attractions. In this experiment, we assume that a user in Guangzhou is planning a day trip to Hangzhou. Therefore, there are three types of transport tool from Guangzhou to Hangzhou: coach, trains and airplanes. In addition, based on some attributes of the content like seat type, a user can have dozens of choices for transportation. Then, we have collected 635 restaurants information, 2164 hotels information and 436 attractions information. They have a variety of different attributes, including price, user rating, location, style, tags, etc.

5.2   Experiment Results

The QoS-based Composition Tasks. In order to show the efficiency of the proposed algorithm, we compare our proposed algorithm with the state-of-the-art algorithms named GP, proposed by Silva et al. [3]. In this experiments, we generate K web services with the inputs, outputs, and additional QoS attributes automatically whose type belongs to one of the transportation, restaurant, hotel, and interest. And we randomly assign the contents to these services. The range of K is 100–1000. Experiment results are shown in Figs. 6 and 7. Figures 6 and 7 display the mean best fitness values and the mean best numbers of solutions separately when running the QoS-based composition tasks over 20 runs with the horizontal ordinate showing the number of web services.

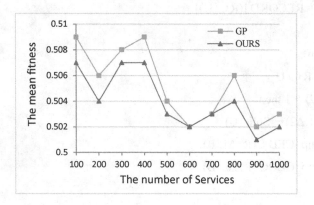

Fig. 6. Mean for the fitness of each approach.

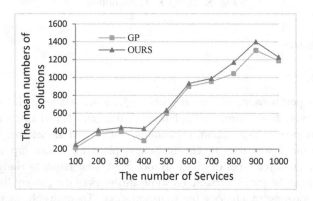

Fig. 7. Mean for the numbers of solutions of each approach.

Solving Over-constrained Problems. In this experiment, to verify the effectiveness of the approach to solve over-constrained problems, firstly, we created dozens of user constraints sets, each of which leads to over-constrained problems. Specifically, M user constraints on the contents are generated randomly, and the range of M is 3-10 in our experiment. And we assume that, users will correct some of the constraints by cumulatively removing constraints just based on their own preference for the constraints when facing the over-constraint problem in practice. Therefore, we simulated user's actual operation only using the user's preference for constraints as the strategy of removing the requirements, called User_TRY approach. The Figs. 8 and 9 contain the results for running the over-constrained tasks, and the effectiveness is compared among our algorithm Imp_CEDC, the algorithm CEDC and User_TRY. The average number of remaining constraints is shown in Fig. 7 while Fig. 8 showing the mean number of consistency checks and their abscissas both represent the number of user original constraints.

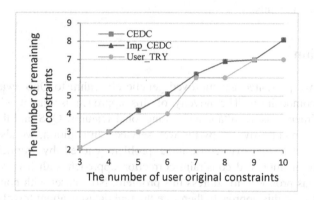

Fig. 8. Mean for the number of remaining constraints of each approach.

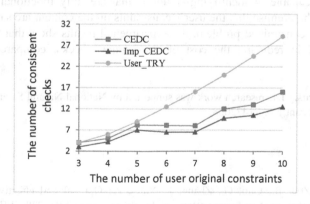

Fig. 9. Mean for the number of consistency checks of each approach.

Discussions. For the QoS-based composition tasks, we assume that these fitness values are quite close to the global optimal solution for each task, though the exact optimal values are not known. The fitness of GP and ours are calculated using the same function, and the results shown in Fig. 6 indicate that our algorithm performs better with the better fitness than GP on each dataset. In terms of the mean numbers of solutions, we can see that more solutions are generated by our algorithm compared to GP from Fig. 7.

When solving the over-constrained problems, it is observed that as the number of user original constraints grows, the number of user constraints to be remained are equal between CEDC and Imp_CEDC from the Fig. 8. However, Fig. 9 shows that the number of consistency checks of Imp_CEDC is less than CEDC. In other words, Imp_CEDC can give users the same suggestions at less cost and faster speed than CEDC. In addition, we can observe that when the number of user original constraints is small, the user can find the conflicts among their constraints with less number of trial. But with the number of user original constraints grows, the cost for users to correct their original constraints without any system suggestion became increasingly expensive, that shown by the higher number of consistency checks and the lower number of remained user constraints.

6   Conclusion

In this paper, we presented an improved genetic algorithm to QoS-aware automated Web service composition. The novelty of this approach is that it addresses three composition dimensions simultaneously: functional features, QoS and the user's constraints on the content provided by the web services. In addition, we also took it into consideration which the over-constrained problem caused by implicit conflicting constraints and an improved constraint correction approach with less cost of consistency checks was proposed to address this problem. No dataset with conditional tasks was available to test this approach, therefore the real datasets about travel crawled from the Internet were extended and used for this purpose. Results showed that the proposed approach was capable of identifying solutions that are fully functional and quality-optimized, on the premise that the user's constraints on the content are satisfied. While facing the over-constrained problem, the experimental results show that the efficiency of our method in reducing the cost of consistency checks, compared with other counterparts.

Acknowledgments. The research work was supported by National Natural Science Foundation of China under Grant No. 71472068.

References

1. Wang, H., Zou, B., Guo, G., Zhang, J., Yang, Z.: Optimal and effective web service composition with trust and user preference. In: Proceedings of the 22th IEEE International Conference on Web Services (ICWS 2015), pp. 329–336 (2015)
2. Lamparter, S., Ankolekar, A., Studer, R., Grimm, S.: Preference-based selection of highly configurable web services. In: Proceedings of the 16th International Conference on World Wide Web, pp. 1013–1022 (2007)
3. da Silva, A., Ma, H., Zhang, M.: A GP approach to QoS-aware web service composition including conditional constraints. In: Proceedings of the 2015 IEEE Congress on Evolutionary Computation (CEC 2015), pp. 2113–2120 (2015)

4. Rodriguez-Mier, P., Mucientes, M., Lama, M.: A hybrid local-global optimization strategy for QoS-aware service composition. In: Proceedings of the 22th IEEE International Conference on Web Services (ICWS 2015), pp. 735–738 (2015)
5. Wang, H., Huang, G., Yu, Q.: Automatic hierarchical reinforcement learning for efficient large-scale service composition. In: Proceedings of the 23th IEEE International Conference on Web Services (ICWS 2016), pp. 57–64 (2016)
6. Wang, H., Gu, M., Yu, Q., Fei, H., Li, J., Tao, Y.: Large-scale and adaptive service composition using deep reinforcement learning. In: Maximilien, M., Vallecillo, A., Wang, J., Oriol, M. (eds.) ICSOC 2017. LNCS, vol. 10601, pp. 383–391. Springer, Cham (2017). https://doi.org/10.1007/978-3-319-69035-3_27
7. Wang, H., Chen, X., Wu, Q., Yu, Q., Zheng, Z., Bouguettaya, A.: Integrating on-policy reinforcement learning with multi-agent techniques for adaptive service composition. In: Franch, X., Ghose, Aditya K., Lewis, Grace A., Bhiri, S. (eds.) ICSOC 2014. LNCS, vol. 8831, pp. 154–168. Springer, Heidelberg (2014). https://doi.org/10.1007/978-3-662-45391-9_11
8. Labbaci, H., Medjahed, B., Aklouf, Y.: A deep learning approach for long term qos-compliant service composition. In: Maximilien, M., Vallecillo, A., Wang, J., Oriol, M. (eds.) ICSOC 2017. LNCS, vol. 10601, pp. 287–294. Springer, Cham (2017). https://doi.org/10.1007/978-3-319-69035-3_20
9. Zhao, Y., Wang, S., Zou, Y., Ng, J., Ng, T.: Automatically learning user preferences for personalized service composition. In: Proceedings of the 24th IEEE International Conference on Web Services (ICWS 2017), pp. 776–783 (2017)
10. Mistry, S., Bouguettaya, A., Dong, H., Erradi, A.: Probabilistic qualitative preference matching in long-term iaas composition. In: Maximilien, M., Vallecillo, A., Wang, J., Oriol, M. (eds.) ICSOC 2017. LNCS, vol. 10601, pp. 256–271. Springer, Cham (2017). https://doi.org/10.1007/978-3-319-69035-3_18
11. Paradesi, S., Doshi, P., Swaika, S.: Integrating behavioral trust in web service compositions. In: Proceedings of the 16th IEEE International Conference on Web Services (ICWS 2009), pp. 453–460 (2009)
12. Freuder, E., Mackworth, A.: Constraint satisfaction: an emerging paradigm. Found. Artif. Intell. **2**, 13–27 (2006)
13. Zhang, J., et al.: A bloom filter-powered technique supporting scalable semantic service discovery in service networks. In: Proceedings of the 23th IEEE International Conference on Web Services (ICWS 2016), pp. 81–90 (2016)
14. Oh, S., Lee, D., Kumara, S.: Effective web service composition in diverse and large-scale service networks. IEEE Trans. Serv. Comput. **1**, 15–32 (2008)
15. Wang, S., Wang, Z., Xu, X.: Mining bilateral patterns as priori knowledge for efficient service composition. In: Proceedings of the 23th IEEE International Conference on Web Services (ICWS 2016), pp. 65–72 (2016)
16. Najar, S., Pinheiro, M.K., Souveyet, C.: A context-aware intentional service prediction mechanism in PIS. In: Proceedings of the 21th IEEE International Conference on Web Services (ICWS 2014), pp. 662–669 (2014)
17. Zhao, Y., Wang, S., Zou, Y., Ng, J., Ng, T.: Mining user intents to compose services for end-users. In: Proceedings of the 23th IEEE International Conference on Web Services (ICWS 2016), pp. 348–355 (2016)
18. Li, H., Shen, H., Li, Z., Guo, J.: Reducing consistency checks in generating corrective explanations for interactive constraint satisfaction. Knowl.-Based Syst. **43**, 103–111 (2013)
19. Alessandro, P., Carlos, M., Matti, J., Joao, M.: Premise set caching for enumerating minimal correction subsets. In: Proceedings of the 32nd National Conference on Artificial Intelligence (AAAI 2018), pp. 6633–6640 (2018)

20. Nina, N., Nikolaj, B., Maria-Cristina, M., Mooly S.: Core-guided minimal correction set and core enumeration. In: Proceedings of the 27th International Joint Conference on Artificial Intelligence (IJCAI 2018), pp. 1353–1361 (2018)

21. Al-Masri, E., Mahmoud, Q.H.: QoS-based discovery and ranking of web services. In: Proceedings of the 16th International Conference on Computer Communications and Networks (ICCCN 2007), pp. 529–534 (2007)

22. Wohed, P., van der Aalst, W., Dumas, M., ter Hofstede, A.: Analysis of web services composition languages: the case of BPEL4WS. In: Proceedings of the 22th International Conference on Conceptual Modeling (ER 2003), pp. 200–215 (2003)

23. da Silva, A., Mei, Y., Ma, H., Zhang, M.: A memetic algorithm-based indirect approach to web service composition. In: Proceedings of the 2016 IEEE Congress on Evolutionary Computation (CEC 2016), pp. 3385–3392 (2016)

24. da Silva, A., Hui, M., Zhang, M.: A graph-based particle swarm optimisation approach to QoS-aware web service composition and selection. In: Proceedings of the 2014 IEEE Congress on Evolutionary Computation (CEC 2014), pp. 3127–3134 (2014)

25. Jannach, D., Zanker, M., Fuchs, M.: Constraint-based recommendation in tourism: a multiperspective case study. Inf. Technol. Tourism **11**, 139–155 (2009)

26. Junker, U.: QUICKXPLAIN: preferred explanations and relaxations for over-constrained problems. In: Proceedings of the 19th National Conference on Artificial Intelligence (AAAI 2004), pp. 167–172 (2004)

AnomalyDetect: An Online Distance-Based Anomaly Detection Algorithm

Wunjun Huo[1], Wei Wang[1,2(✉)], and Wen Li[1]

[1] Department of Computer Science and Engineering, Tongji University,
Shanghai, China
willtongji@gmail.com
[2] School of Data Science and Engineering, East China Normal University,
Shanghai, China

Abstract. Anomaly detection is a key challenge in data mining, which refers to finding patterns in data that do not conform to expected behavior. It has a wide range of applications in many fields as diverse as finance, medicine, industry, and the Internet. In particular, intelligent operation has made great progress in recent years and has an urgent need for this technology. In this paper, we study the problem of anomaly detection in the context of intelligent operation and find the practical need for high-accuracy, online and universal anomaly detection algorithms in time series database. Based on the existing algorithms, we propose an innovative online distance-based anomaly detection algorithm. K-means and time-space trade-off mechanism are used to reduce the time complexity. Through the experiments on Yahoo! Web-scope S5 dataset we show that our algorithm can detect anomalies accurately. The comparative study of several anomaly detectors verifies the effectiveness and generality of the proposed algorithm.

Keywords: Anomaly detection · Time series · Online algorithm ·
Euclidean distance · Intelligent operation

1 Introduction

Time series refers to a set of random variables arranged in chronological order. We can record the value of a random event in time order to obtain a time series sequence. Time series data appears in every aspect of today's life as diverse as finance, medicine, industry, and the Internet. For example, time series can be the daily settlement price of each stock, the monthly deposit balance of a customer, and the number of heart beats per minute of a patient. Finding the rules among these time series has great application prospects. In general, the research on time series includes prediction, pattern mining, clustering, classification, anomaly detection, etc. In the financial field, time series prediction can be applied in stock price forecasting. Prediction and classification can help banks to determine customer credit rating. In the medical field, pattern mining and anomaly detection can help doctors find abnormal situations in patient monitoring data quickly and make timely process.

© Springer Nature Switzerland AG 2019
J. Miller et al. (Eds.): ICWS 2019, LNCS 11512, pp. 63–79, 2019.
https://doi.org/10.1007/978-3-030-23499-7_5

In intelligent operation, a series of time series data can be obtained by real-time monitoring and recording on various hardware and software indicators. Some abnormal behaviors such as hardware and software failures, malicious attacks, etc. are directly reflected in these time series databases, forming abnormal data. One of the duties of the operation staff is to monitor these indicators in real time, and make timely repair when abnormalities occur. The key to intelligent operation is using anomaly detection algorithms to monitor the abnormal situation in the time series database of operation field automatically. Therefore, the detection of abnormal data in time series data becomes a key technology in intelligent operation. In this context, we analyze the existing algorithms, combine the characteristics and requirements of intelligent operation, and propose an innovative online anomaly detection algorithm.

Anomaly detection in time series refers to finding a point or a sequence, which do not conform to their expected behavior. In real cases, the abnormal points or sequences generally represent abnormal situations: illegal transaction, abnormal heartbeat, cyber malicious attacks, etc. There are many algorithms for anomaly detection in time series. The idea of most algorithms is to find the laws of normal time series data, when the current observation point or sequence is too different from the normal law, it will be regarded as abnormal.

However, in the field of intelligent operation [27], the data generated from hardware and software is streaming data. Hardware and software have a great variety of indicators, so the amount of data is large. What's more, the time series fluctuates frequently and irregularly. When the abnormal behavior occurs, the abnormal types of these data are also different. Therefore, combined with the characteristics of the operation data and the requirements of the operation scene, an appropriate anomaly detection algorithm is of great significance to the landing of intelligent operation.

The online distance-based anomaly detection algorithm proposed in this paper has several advantages to meet the requirements of intelligent operation. First, it applies the sliding window mechanism to calculate the anomaly of each point online. Second, although the orders of magnitude of different time series may be of large difference, the distributing fitting method can use the quantiles to determine the anomalies efficiently. Third, online algorithms often require a fast detection method, we take an innovative mechanism in this paper to reduce time complexity.

The rest of this paper is organized as follows: in Sect. 2, we give the main background definitions used in our proposed algorithm and review the related academic work. Section 3 gives the total steps and details of the innovative online anomaly detection algorithm proposed in this paper. Section 4 shows the performance result of the algorithm on the specific datasets. We give a summary and outlook in Sect. 5.

2   Problem Description and Related Work

This section specifies the relevant background knowledge of the anomaly detection algorithm, describes the specific problems to be solved in this paper, and introduces the related research work.

2.1 Definition and Description

A time series generally refers to a sequence in which a random variable is arranged in chronological order. The time series can be defined as follows.

Definition 1. *Time Series.* We use a set of random variables arranged in chronological order, i.e. $X_1, X_2, \cdots, X_t, \cdots$, to represent the time series of a random event, $\{X_t, t \in T\}$ in short. We use $x_1, x_2, \cdots, x_n$ or $\{x_t, t = 1, 2, \cdots, n\}$ to represent the ordered observations of the random sequence, called the observation sequence with length n.

An abnormal point often refers to a data point that differs greatly from the surrounding points in a time series. An abnormal sequence refers to several continuous points in a period behave differently with their surrounding sequences. Figure 1 shows a true operation time series, which contains both abnormal points and abnormal sequences. Operation staff in real operation scene tag the anomalies, and in Fig. 1, these anomalies are marked in red.

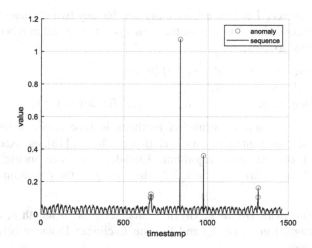

Fig. 1. The real operation data containing the abnormal data (Color figure online)

Figure 1 shows that the abnormal points and abnormal sequences in time series usually have large differences with the values or morphologies of their surrounding points. Therefore, when determining whether a point belongs to an abnormal point, it is necessary to consider the relevant points around it. For the determination of anomalies, the normal sequence model needs to be compared as a sample. Therefore, the definition of time subsequence and sliding window is introduced in this paper as follows.

Definition 2. *Subsequence.* Given a time series with length n, i.e. $X = \{x_t, t = 1, 2, \cdots, n\}$, a subsequence $S_{i,l}$ in time series is defined as a set of continuous points with length $l \leq n$, which is expanded forward from x_i, i.e. $S_{i,j} = \{x_{i-l+1}, x_{i-l+2}, \cdots, x_{i-1}, x_i\}$, where $l \leq i \leq n$.

Definition 3. *Sliding window.* Given a time series X with length n, and a subsequence $S_{i,l}$ with length l, a sliding window $W_{i,m}$ in X is defined as a set of continuous points with length $m(l \leq m \leq n)$, which is expanded forward from x_i and includes $S_{i,l}$, that is $W_{i,m} = \{x_{i-m+1}, x_{i-m+2}, \cdots, x_{i-l}, x_{i-l+1}, x_{i-l+2}, \cdots x_{i-1}, x_i\}$, where $m \leq i \leq n$.

The first problem we need to solve is to detect the abnormal points in a period accurately. For the subsequence that needs to be judged whether abnormal or not, it is necessary to determine whether the subsequence is similar to the rest normal subsequences. In order to avoid Comparison, we introduce the definition of non-self-match.

Definition 4. *Non-self-match*. Given a time series X of length n, a subsequence $S_{i,l}$ and a sliding window $W_{i,m}$, a non-self-match of $S_{i,l}$ is defined as the subsequence $S_{j,l}$ of length l in $W_{i,m}$ which is expanded forward from x_i, that is $S_{j,l} = \{x_{j-l+1}, x_{j-l+2}, \cdots, x_{j-1}, x_j\}(i - m + l \leq j \leq i - l)$.

The definition of non-self-match makes sure that the two subsequences in the given sliding window have no intersection points. When measuring the similarity between two subsequences in a sliding window, we should use a distance-based metric. In mathematics, the distance is defined as follows.

Definition 5. *Distance*. Let S be a non-empty set, for any two elements x and y in S, Distance is a function $d(x, y)$ that maps these two points to a real number and satisfies the following three axioms:

  i. Non-negative: $d(x, y) \geq 0$, $d(x, y) = 0$ iff $x = y$;
 ii. Symmetry: $d(x, y) = d(y, x)$;
iii. Triangle Inequality: $d(x, y) \leq d(x, z) + d(y, z)$ for any $x, y, z \in S$.

The shape-based distance calculation methods in time series include Euclidean distance, cosine distance, and Pearson correlation coefficient [18], etc. According to the characteristic of our proposed algorithm, Euclidean distance metric is the most appropriate, and we confirm it in Sect. 2.2. Here we give the definition of Euclidean Distance.

Definition 6. *Euclidean Distance*. Given a time series X of length n, and two subsequences of length l in X, i.e. $S_{i,l}$ and $S_{j,l}$, the Euclidean Distance between them is defined as follows:

$$EuclideanDist(S_{i,l}, S_{j,l}) = \sqrt{\sum_{q=0}^{l-1} (x_{i-q} - x_{j-q})^2} \tag{1}$$

where $l \leq i, j \leq n$.

Next, we will give the definition of anomaly in time series. First we introduce the most similar non-self-match. Note that the anomaly here is not just for the abnormal points. It is a measure of the abnormal degree of every point in time series.

Definition 7. *The most similar non-self-match*. Given a subsequence $S_{i,l}$ of length l and a sliding window $W_{i,m}$ of length m, the most similar non-self-match $S'_{i,l}$ of $S_{i,l}$ is defined as the non-self-match with the smallest Euclidean distance of $S_{i,l}$ in $W_{i,m}$, that is:

$$S'_{i,l} = S_{j,l}$$
$$s.t. EuclideanDist(S_{i,l}, S_{j,l}) = \min\{EuclideanDist(S_{i,l}, S_{p,l})\} \tag{2}$$

where $S_{p,l}$ is the non-self-match of $S_{i,l}$ in $W_{i,m}$.

Definition 8. Anomaly. Given a time series $X = \{x_t, t = 1, 2, \cdots, n\}$ with length n, and a subsequence $S_{i,l}$ which is expanded forward from x_i, the Anomaly of x_i is defined as the distance between $S_{i,l}$ and $S'_{i,l}$ in the sliding window $W_{i,m}$, that is: $Anomaly(x_i) = EuclideanDist(S_{i,l}, S'_{i,l})$, where $l \leq i \leq n$.

When the length of sliding window and subsequence are given, we can calculate the anomaly of each point in the time series, and the anomaly of the abnormal points in time series is larger than that of the normal points. When an abnormal situation occurs, the anomaly increases significantly. The definition of the abnormal point needs to be introduced.

Definition 9. Abnormal Point. Given a time series $X = \{x_t, t = 1, 2, \cdots, n\}$ with length n, the length of subsequence l, the length of sliding window m, and the threshold K, x_i is an abnormal point iff $Anomaly(x_i) > K$.

2.2 Related Work on Anomaly Detection

Anomaly detection in time series can be applied in many fields and several algorithms have been proposed for various scenes including medicine [16], finance and the Internet. Some anomaly detection algorithms in time series use traditional analysis methods, including ARIMA [9], exponential smoothing [20], and time series decomposition [1, 19]. Other research results use statistical methods for anomaly detection, such as PCA [10], linear regression [6, 15], extreme value theory [17], median theory [5], etc. The rapid development of machine learning algorithms in recent years results in the usage of many machine learning algorithms such as neural network [8], SVDD [4], DBSCAN [15] and so on.

In industry, Internet companies develop time series analysis platforms based on their own business needs. Yahoo's time series analysis system EGADS [3] includes three modules: time series forecasting, time series anomaly detection and alerting module system, which integrates multiple time series analysis and anomaly detection algorithms. In 2014, Twitter proposed an anomaly detection algorithm based on time series decomposition and generalized Extreme Studentized Deviate test [1]. Twitter also put forward a complementary breakout detection algorithm in time series, and provided the R libraries [24, 26] for these two algorithms. Netflix developed the anomaly detection system Surus to ensure the validity of the company's data, and open sourced the algorithm RAD [21], which mainly uses RPCA [23] to detect abnormal points. Linkedin's open source tool, luminol [22], is a lightweight library for time series analysis that supports anomaly detection and correlation analysis.

Both in academia and industry, the measurements of anomaly detection algorithms should include the following aspects:

(1) Accuracy. Anomaly detection is essentially a two-category problem. For any point, a false classification may lead to some irreparable consequences. Therefore, the accuracy of the algorithm is the most important. When measuring the accuracy

of anomaly detection algorithms, the accuracy, recall, and the harmonic mean of the accuracy and recall, F1-Score are usually used.

(2) Offline or online. This measurement should be considered in two aspects. First, in general, in order to maintain the accuracy of the anomaly detection algorithm, it is necessary to update the model and parameters continuously. Second, from the aspect of intelligent operation, the time series data obtained from the monitoring system is streaming, so a proper algorithm should detect the abnormal situation as the points flow in.

(3) Super parameters. Most regression and classification algorithms need to set several super parameters, such as the K value in K-nearest-neighbor algorithm. The values of super parameters tend to have a decisive influence on the effect of the algorithm. The anomaly detection algorithm is no exception. If the number of super parameters is less, and the effect of the algorithm is less affected by the super parameter size, this algorithm is undoubtedly a more stable model.

(4) Time complexity. The detection of anomalies needs to be both accurate and fast, so the time complexity of the algorithm also needs to be considered [13].

(5) The main purpose of the anomaly detection algorithm is to be able to detect outliers in a time series accurately and quickly. Many existing algorithms model the normal points and find the anomaly by comparing the difference between the currently analyzed data and the normal data. If the difference is large enough, the current analyzed point is considered abnormal. Based on this idea, many data mining algorithms are applied to detect time series anomalies, such as linear regression [6, 15], support vector machine [4], neural network [8] and so on. These algorithms usually divide the obtained time series data into a training set and a test set, train the model in the training set and perform detection on the test set. In practical applications, time series data is streaming and changing constantly. Therefore, if the model obtained by training is not be updated in real time, it will be difficult to apply the model to new data. In addition, the variability of normal data and abnormal data makes it difficult to use a single model to detect anomalies accurately during the whole detection period. In summary, an online anomaly detection algorithm can not only run in streaming data, but also update the model itself continuously, which will be more suitable for the actual situation.

3   An Online Anomaly Detection Algorithm

This section introduces the distance-based online anomaly detection algorithm proposed in this paper. Firstly, the main idea of the algorithm is expounded, and then the proposed algorithm is given by formal definition.

3.1   Main Idea

By observing and analyzing the real time series anomaly data in operation, we find that abnormal points usually show a sudden increase or a sudden decrease compared with the surrounding points. The abnormal sequences usually show a different trend from its surrounding points (especially the previous points), as shown in Fig. 2. Figure 2 is a real operation database, which contains both abnormal sequences and abnormal points.

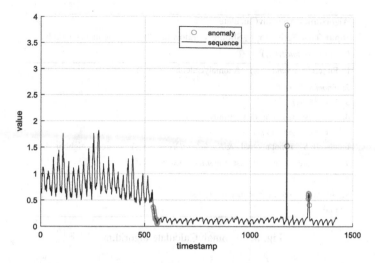

Fig. 2. A real operation data that contains both abnormal points and subsequences

According to the characteristics of abnormal data, we propose an online distance-based anomaly detection algorithm. The main idea is that for every point in the given time series, we calculate the anomaly of the subsequence expanded from that point in the sliding window. In general, the anomaly of abnormal data is significantly larger than that of normal data. Our algorithm uses two specific statistical distributions to fit the anomaly of each point in the time series. The anomaly of normal points often fluctuates around the distribution center, while the anomaly of abnormal points is so large that it is far from the center. Therefore, when the anomaly deviates from the center of the distribution too much, the point is regarded as an abnormal point.

3.2   The Anomaly in Sliding Window

Algorithm 1 *AnomalyCalculate* gives a calculation method for calculating the anomaly of each point in the time series by using a sliding window mechanism. The pseudo code is as follows.

Here we give the specific steps of *AnomalyCalculate*. Given a time series $X = \{x_t, t = 1, 2, \cdots, n\}$ with length n, the length of sliding window m, the length of sub-sequence l, then for every point in the interval $[m, n]$, that is $\{x_i, i = m, m+1, \cdots, n\}$, we have the subsequence $S_{i,l}$, which is expanded from x_i and of length l, and the sliding window $W_{i,m}$, which is expanded from x_i and of length m, where $m \leq i \leq n$. We will find the non-self-match which has the least Euclidean distance with $S_{i,l}$ in $W_{i,m}$, i.e. the most similar non-self-match $S'_{i,l}$. The Euclidean distance between $S_{i,l}$ and $S'_{i,l}$, i.e. $EuclideanDist(S_{i,l}, S'_{i,l})$, is the anomaly of x_i, denoted as $Anomaly(x_i)$, just as the description in definition 8. In order not to compare the current data with the previous abnormal data, algorithm 1 restricts that the most similar non-self-match is normal data (Fig. 3).

After calculating the anomaly of each point in a given time series by Algorithm 1, it is found that when the abnormal point or the abnormal sequence appears, the anomaly

---

Algorithm 1 AnomalyCalculate

Input: Time Series (x_t), Sliding Window length m, Subsequence length l

Output: $Anomaly(x_t)$

1: **Function** $Anomaly(x_t) = $ AnomalyCalculate(x_t, m, l)

2: $Anomaly(x_t) = \vec{0}$

3: For $i=m$ to n

4:    nearest_neighbor_dist=infinity

5:    For $j=i-m+l$ to $i-l$

6:       IF $S_{j,l}$ is not anomaly & $EuclideanDist(S_{i,l}, S_{j,l}) < $ nearest_neighbor_dist

7:       nearest_neighbor_dist=$EuclideanDist(S_{i,l}, S_{j,l})$

8:    End

9: $Anomaly(x_t) \leftarrow$ nearest_neighbor_dist

10:End

Fig. 3. AnomalyCalculate algorithm

will increase significantly. Figure 4 shows that the anomaly is non-negative, and after a period of m (the length of sliding window), the anomaly fluctuate randomly and increase significantly when the abnormal situation occurs.

For comparison, Fig. 4 also shows the anomaly calculated using the cosine distance and the Pearson correlation coefficient. Note that a proper distance metrics should maximum the anomaly of abnormal data and minimum the anomaly of normal data to separate these two categories. From Fig. 4 we can see Euclidean distance is the most appropriate method.

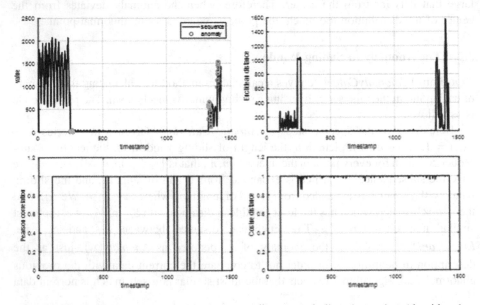

Fig. 4. The operation datasets and its corresponding anomaly line chart using Algorithm 1

3.3   Threshold Selection Mechanism

From the analysis in Sect. 3.2, AnomalyCalculate can maximum the anomaly of abnormal data. However, the operation data obtained in actual scene is streaming data and different time series have different orders of magnitude, so it is not enough to calculate the anomaly. The key is that we should select a threshold, and then if the anomaly of the current point exceeds the threshold, the point should be considered as abnormal. In this paper, we use distribution-fitting method to determine the threshold.

Assume that the anomaly of the points in a time series follows a certain distribution, then the anomaly of abnormal points are so large that they fall outside the $1 - \alpha(0 < \alpha < 1)$ quantile. Therefore, when the anomaly of the current point falls in that part, we consider it as abnormal. After observing the anomaly distribution of massive time series, we choose normal distribution and lognormal distribution to fit the anomaly.

In this paper, we use the recursive calculation method of mean and variance [14] to estimate the mean and variance of the distribution, as calculated below:

$$\mu_n = \tfrac{1}{n}x_n + \tfrac{n-1}{n}\mu_{n-1}$$
$$S_n^2 = \tfrac{n-1}{n}S_{n-1}^2 + \tfrac{n-1}{n^2}(x_n - \mu_{n-1})^2 \tag{3}$$

For the addition of new elements, the forgetting factor λ is introduced into the recursive formula for calculating the mean and variance. Then the mean and variance with forgetting factor are calculated as follows:

$$\mu_n = \sum_{i=1}^{n}\frac{\lambda^{n-i}x_n}{\sum_{i=1}^{n}\lambda^{n-i}} \quad S_n^2 = \sum_{i=1}^{n}\frac{\lambda^{n-i}(x_i - \mu_n)^2}{\sum_{i=1}^{n}\lambda^{n-i}} \tag{4}$$

The recursive calculation methods of the mean and variance are as follows:

$$\mu_n = \tfrac{1-\lambda}{1-\lambda^n}x_n + \tfrac{\lambda(1-\lambda^{n-1})}{1-\lambda^n}\mu_{n-1}$$
$$S_n^2 = \tfrac{\lambda(1-\lambda^{n-1})}{1-\lambda^n}S_{n-1}^2 + \tfrac{\lambda(1-\lambda^{n-1})(1-\lambda)}{(1-\lambda^n)^2}(x_n - \mu_{n-1})^2 \tag{5}$$

3.4   Anomaly Detect

AnomalyCalculate in Sect. 3.2 calculates the anomaly of the points in a given time series. By using the two fitting distributions given in Sect. 3.3 and the recursive calculation method of mean and variance, we can estimate and update the parameters of the two fitting distributions as we calculate the anomaly of each point. Because the mean and variance calculated in initial stages fluctuate greatly, which may lead to the instability of the fitting distribution and then affect the detection effect, the proposed algorithm AnomalyDetect introduces a transition period, in which the mean and variance are not updated. The initial values of mean and variance are calculated by the anomaly of points in the transition period, and the mean and variance after the transition period are updated by formula (3) or formula (5).

Algorithm 2 (AnomalyDetect) gives the specific steps of fitting the anomaly distribution and estimating the parameters while calculating the anomaly of each point in the given time series, delimiting the threshold and determining whether the current point is abnormal, as shown in Fig. 5.

Based on AnomalyCalculate, AnomalyDetect adds several steps including anomaly distribution fitting, parameter estimation, threshold delimiting, and anomaly detection. Figure 6 shows the specific implementation process of AnomalyDetect. As shown in Fig. 6, for the subsequence expanded forward from the current point, AnomalyDetect looks for the most similar non-self-match in the sliding window, which is also expanded forward from the current point. AnomalyDetect calculates the Euclidean distance of the two subsequences as the anomaly of the current point, and calculates the degree of deviation from the distribution center. When the deviation is excessive, the current point is considered an abnormal point. Similarly, in order to prevent comparing current subsequence with the abnormal points, we delimit the most similar non-self-match are all normal data.

Algorithm 2 AnomalyDetect

Input: Time Series (x_t) , Sliding Window length m, Subsequence length l,
transition t, anomaly threshhold $\alpha \in (0,1)$

Output: Anomaly flags $\vec{f}$

1: **Function** $Anomaly(x_t) = \text{AnomalyDetect}(x_t, m, l)$
2: $Anomaly(x_t) \leftarrow \vec{0}$
3: Anomaly flags $\vec{f} \leftarrow \vec{0}$
4: transition_dist $\leftarrow$ null array
5:
6: For $i=m$ to n
7:      nearest_neighbor_dist=infinity
8:      For $j=i-m+l$ to $i-l$
9:          IF $S_{j,l}$ is not anomaly & $EuclideanDist(S_{i,l}, S_{j,l}) < $ nearest_neighbor_dist
10:         nearest_neighbor_dist=$EuclideanDist(S_{i,l}, S_{j,l})$
11:     End
12: End
13: $Anomaly(x_i) \leftarrow$ nearest_neighbor_dist
14: IF $i < m+t$
15:     transition_dist+[nearest_neighbor_dist]
16: End
17: IF $i = m+t$
18:     $\mu \leftarrow \text{mean}(transition\_dist)$
19:     $\sigma^2 \leftarrow \text{var}(transition\_dist)$
20: End
21: IF $i \geq m+t$
22:     Calculate the α-quantile z_α of $N(\mu, \sigma^2)$ or $LN(\mu, \sigma^2)$
23:     IF nearest_neighbor_dist $> z_\alpha$
24:         Anomaly flags $\vec{f}_i \leftarrow 1$
25:     Else
26:         Update μ and σ^2
27:     End
28: End

Fig. 5. AnomalyDetect algorithm

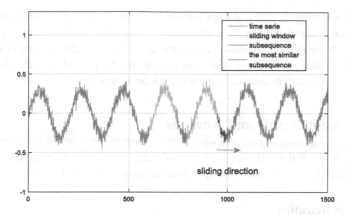

Fig. 6. The specific implementation of AnomalyDetect algorithm

3.5 Complexity Reduction

From the perspective of time complexity, AnomalyDetect calculates Euclidean distance for m times to get the most similar non-self-match. In some scenarios where data points are dense and high efficiency is required, we propose a mechanism to reduce the time complexity for our algorithm.

We use k-means and time-space trade-off mechanism. In the initial sliding window, k-means is used to cluster normal subsequences to get k classes and k class centers. The algorithm maintains two data structures in the detection process: an array is used to mark the classes of each subsequence in the sliding window, and a dictionary is used to store the class centers, as shown in Fig. 7.

value0	value1	value2	label
52.6063	53.2957	186.8987	4
53.2957	186.8987	249.9720	4
186.8987	249.9720	279.8083	9
249.9720	279.8083	264.1173	9
279.8083	264.1173	352.9358	9
...	...	...	...
-1253.8910	-1287.2320	-1229.9050	3
-1287.2320	-1229.9050	-1291.1907	3
-1229.9050	-1291.1907	-1267.7189	3
-1291.1907	-1267.7189	-1281.5156	3
-1267.7189	-1281.5156	-1347.3994	3

0	333.4046	327.2986	316.6243
1	-1212.5169	-1231.5428	-1255.9541
...	...	...	...
9	80.9580	53.0702	45.2936

Fig. 7. Two data structures used to reduce time complexity

While the sliding window moves forward, we compare the current subsequence with class centers and determine it abnormal or not. If it is determined normal, the subsequence in the sliding window will be updated: the first subsequence in the sliding window is discarded, the current subsequence is added at the end, and the class centers of the class to which the two subsequences belong is updated.

4   Experiment Result and Analysis

In this section, several experiments of anomaly detection algorithm are carried out on the actual operation time series datasets, and the results are analyzed.

4.1   Data Preparation

This article uses the actual operation datasets [2] provided by Yahoo!, which contains four subfolders: A1, A2, A3, and A4. The A1 dataset contains 67 real operation time series, and the A2, A3, and A4 datasets each contain 100 pieces of synthetic time series. The synthetic time series is composed of periodicity, trend and noise, and the complexity of the synthetic time series is gradually increased. Figure 8 is the representative timing charts of the four datasets, where the abnormal points are marked in red.

The research on the synthetic data in Yahoo! S5 data shows that the A2, A3, and A4 datasets randomly change the normal points value to generate abnormal data points. The abnormal points are divided into two categories: anomaly and changepoint. The normal data in the A2 dataset is composed of simple trend, single periodic data and

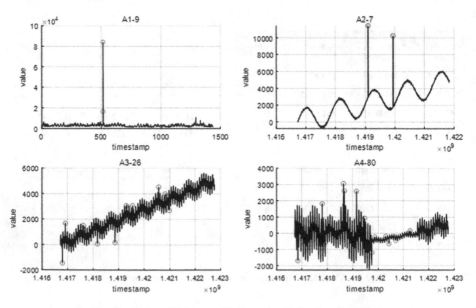

Fig. 8. Yahoo Webscope S5 Datasets (Color figure online)

noise. The abnormal point type is only anomaly. The normal data in the A3 data set consists of a single trend, three periodic data with different cycles and amplitudes, and noise. The abnormal point type is only anomaly. The A4 data set is formed of a trend and three periodic data with different cycles and varying amplitudes, and noise. The abnormal point type includes both anomaly and changepoint. Figure 9 shows the synthetic time series in the A3 and A4 datasets and the trend and period data, labeled with different colors.

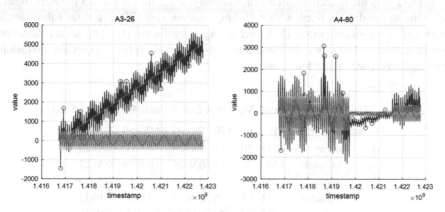

Fig. 9. The synthesis sequence and decomposition sequence of A3 and A4 datasets

4.2 Data Preparation

Anomaly detection problem in time series can be regarded as a two-category problem. Each point in the time series is marked as normal or abnormal, and can also be predicted as normal or abnormal. If the normal is marked as 0, the abnormal flag is 1, then the real situation and the prediction situation can be counted as a contingency table, that is, the confusion matrix, as shown in Table 1.

Table 1. Confusion matrix

Actual	Predicted	
	Positive(1)	Negative(0)
Positive (1)	True Positive (TP)	False Negative (FN)
Negative (0)	False Positive (FP)	True Negative (TN)

Each point in the time series can be labeled as TP, FN, FP, and TN.

F1-Score is another indicator to measure the accuracy of the two-category model. It is the harmonic mean of the precision and recall and considers both of these two evaluation methods.

4.3   Data Preparation

In this paper, we use AnomalyDetect to perform experiments on the Yahoo! S5 datasets. The detection of abnormal data will be performed after a sliding window plus a transition period. While detecting the abnormal points, with the fluctuation of the mean and variance, the anomaly distribution will have a few changes. At the end of the detection process, we can get the anomaly of each point in the given time series, and the anomaly distribution estimated by the final iteration.

Table 2 lists the detection effects of AnomalyDetect in Yahoo! S5 datasets, where each time series data is fixed with a sliding window size (200), a time subsequence length (3), a transition period (50), and a forgetting factor (1). The actual detection process is after a sliding window and a transition period. Table 4 gives the precision, recall and F1-Score of the four datasets.

Table 2. The detection effect of Algorithm 2 on Yahoo! Webscope S5 dataset

Dataset	Algorithm	TP	FP	FN	Precision	Recall	F1 Score
A1	norm	1543	10	111	0.9329	0.9936	0.9623
	lognorm	1543	10	111	0.9329	0.9936	0.9623
A2	norm	461	0	5	0.9893	1	0.9946
	lognorm	461	1	5	0.9893	0.9978	0.9935
A3	norm	766	30	37	0.9539	0.9623	0.9581
	lognorm	766	29	37	0.9539	0.9635	0.9587
A4	norm	572	66	315	0.6449	0.8966	0.7502
	lognorm	577	68	281	0.6725	0.8946	0.7678

As can be seen from Table 2, the detection accuracy of AnomalyDetect is very high, reaching more than 0.95 on the A1–A3 dataset, especially in the real operation dataset A1, the F1-Score also reached 0.96. And in A4 dataset, it reaches more than 0.75. This is the case with the basic ideas of AnomalyDetect. AnomalyDetect is mainly based on the comparison of morphological similarity of different subsequences in time series, not just the correlation of adjacent points. Moreover, AnomalyDetect can realize the universal detection of both abnormal points and abnormal sequences by adjusting the length of subsequences.

Similarly, AnomalyDetect has its shortcomings. Its detection effect on the A4 dataset is not perfect, which is related to the complex and varied form of the A4 dataset.

In this article, we use two open source detection algorithms for comparison. Table 3 lists the detection accuracy of the Twitter anomaly detection algorithm S-H-ESD [24] and Netflix's anomaly detection algorithm RPCA [21] on the Yahoo! Webscope S5 datasets.

The S-H-ESD algorithm is an offline algorithm based on time series decomposition and generalized ESD test. RPCA is also an offline algorithm, mainly based on the Robust PCA algorithm. Both algorithms need to obtain the whole time series data, and

Table 3. The Results of S-H-ESD and RPCA on Yahoo Webscope S5 datasets

Dataset	Algorithm	TP	FP	FN	Precision	Recall	F1-score
A1	S-H-ESD	571	1147	664	0.4623	0.3324	0.3867
	RPCA	636	1033	1655	0.2776	0.3811	0.3212
A2	S-H-ESD	140	172	43	0.765	0.4487	0.5657
	RPCA	447	19	49	0.9012	0.9592	0.9293
A3	S-H-ESD	86	583	0	1	0.1286	0.2278
	RPCA	509	434	77	0.8686	0.5398	0.6658
A4	S-H-ESD	112	454	1156	0.0883	0.1979	0.1221
	RPCA	432	405	411	0.5125	0.5161	0.5143

then the abnormal points are detected. Drawing the F1-score of the four algorithms on the Yahoo S5 dataset into a bar graph can compare the detection effects of the four algorithms more clearly, as shown in Fig. 10.

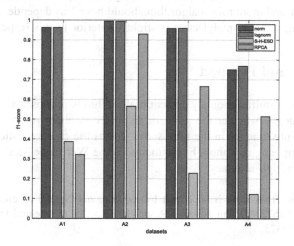

Fig. 10. The F1-score of different algorithms on Yahoo Webscope S5 datasets

As can be seen from Fig. 11, AnomayDetect is significantly better than another two algorithms in term of accuracy. From the perspective of the datasets, the four algorithms perform best in the A2 dataset because of the obvious periodicity of the A2 dataset. If the trend is more obvious, the noise impact is smaller, and the abnormal points are more different from the normal points, then the detection is easier. In addition, as can be seen from Fig. 11, AnomalyDetect has a significant advantage in the A1 dataset. A1 is an real operation dataset. Unlike the synthetic dataset, the timing pattern of A1 is more complex and reflects a real operation situation. And the innovative distance-based algorithm AnomalyDetect is more suitable for real situation data.

In summary, compared with other anomaly detection algorithms, the algorithm shows obvious advantages in the following aspects:

(1) Accuracy. It can be seen from Tables 2 and 3 that the F1-score of the algorithm on the four data sets is relatively high.
(2) Versatility. Usually a single anomaly detection algorithm is not applicable to all time series data. For example, the algorithm for detecting abnormal points does not detect abnormal sequences well. However, based on the similarity between different subsequences, AnomalyDetect can detect both abnormal points and abnormal sequences. What's more, the detection effect of AnomalyDetect on real time series is not inferior to that of synthetic time series.
(3) Online. The analysis in Sect. 2.2 indicates that the online characteristic of a time series anomaly detection algorithm is an inevitable requirement for ensuring the real-time and accuracy. Therefore, AnomalyDetect's online update mechanism makes it significantly better than other algorithms.

Similarly, AnomalyDetect also has its inferior performance. The algorithm involves about four super parameters and is sensitive to the super parameter size. Because the algorithm needs to delimit the threshold, and the model parameters need to be updated continuously, the size of the super parameter plays an important role. As analyzed in Sect. 2.2, a better and more robust algorithm should have less dependence on the super parameters setting, but AnomalyDetect is slightly inferior in this respect.

5 Summary and Prospect

In this paper, a new online anomaly detection algorithm is proposed for the real scene. The algorithm judges whether the point or sequence is abnormal by calculating the anomaly of the subsequence in the time series. It has the characteristics of linear and real-time updating, etc., in Yahoo. Experiments on the Webscope S5 dataset show that the algorithm has high accuracy.

Acknowledgments. This work is supported by the National Natural Science Foundation of China (Grant No. 61672384), Fundamental Research Funds for the Central Universities under Grants No. 0800219373.

References

1. Vallis, O., Hochenbaum, J., Kejariwal, A.: A novel technique for long-term anomaly detection in the cloud. In: HotCloud (2014)
2. Yahoo: S5 - A Labeled Anomaly Detection Dataset, version 1.0 (2015). http://webscope.sandbox.yahoo.com/catalog.php?datatype=s&did=70
3. Laptev, N., Amizadeh, S., Flint, I.: Generic and scalable framework for automated time-series anomaly detection. In: KDD, pp. 1939–1947 (2015)
4. Huang, C., Min, G., Wu, Y., Ying, Y., Pei, K., Xiang, Z.: Time series anomaly detection for trustworthy services in cloud computing systems
5. Sagoolmuang, A., Sinapiromsaran, K.: Median-difference window subseries score for contextual anomaly on time series. In: IC-ICTE (2017)

6. Thill, M., Konen, W., Bäck, T.: Online anomaly detection on the webscope S5 dataset: a comparative study. In: EAIS (2017)
7. Chen, Y., Hu, B., Keogh, E., Batista, G.E.: DTW-D: time series semi-supervised learning from a single example
8. Suh, S., Chae, D.H., Kang, H.-G., Choi, S.: Echo-state conditional variational autoencoder for anomaly detection. In: International Joint Conference on Neural Networks (IJCNN) (2016)
9. Yu, Q., Jibin, L., Jiang, L.: An improved ARIMA-based traffic anomaly detection algorithm for wireless sensor networks. Int. J. Distrib. Sens. Netw. **12**(1), 9653230 (2016)
10. Hyndman, R.J., Wang, E., Laptev, N.: Large-scale unusual time series detection
11. Wei, L., Kumar, N., Lolla, V., Keogh, E., Lonardi, S., Ann Ratanamahatana, C.: Assumption-free anomaly detection in time series. In: 17th International Conference on Scientific and Statistical (2005)
12. Berndt, D.J., Clifford, J.: Using dynamic time warping to find patterns in time series. AAAI Technical Report WS-94-03
13. Chandola, V., Cheboli, D., Kumar, V.: Detecting anomalies in a time series database. Department, University of Minnesota, Technical report 12 (2009)
14. Welford, B.P.: Note on a method for calculating corrected sums of squares and products. Technometrics **4**(3), 419–420 (1962)
15. Watson, S.M., Tight, M., Clark, S., Redfern, E.: Detection of outliers in time series. Institute of Transport Studies, University of Leeds
16. Keogh, Eamonn, Lin, Jessica, Lee, Sang-Hee, Van Herle, Helga: Finding the most unusual time series subsequence: algorithms and applications. Knowl. Inf. Syst. **11**(1), 1–27 (2007)
17. Siffer, A., Fouque, P.A., Termier, A., Largouët, C.: Anomaly detection in streams with extreme value theory. In: Proceedings of the 23rd ACM SIGKDD International Conference (2017)
18. Lin, J., Keogh, E., Lonardi, S. Chiu, B.: A symbolic representation of time series, with implications for streaming algorithms. In: Proceedings of the 8th ACM SIGMOD Workshop on Research Issues in Data Mining and Knowledge Discovery (2003)
19. Chen, Y., Mahajan, R., Sridharan, B., Zhang, Z.-L.: A provider-side view of web search response time. In: Proceedings of the ACM SIGCOMM 2013 Conference on SIGCOMM, vol. 43 (2013)
20. Yan, H.,: Argus: end-to-end service anomaly detection and localization from an ISP's point of view. In: IEEE INFOCOM (2012)
21. Netflix: Surus. https://github.com/Netflix/Surus
22. Linkedin: luminol. https://github.com/linkedin/luminol
23. Candès, E.J., Li, X., Ma, Y., Wright, J.: Robust principal component analysis (2011)
24. Twitter: Anomaly Detection. https://github.com/twitter/AnomalyDetection
25. Laptev, N., Amizadeh, S.: Yahoo anomaly detection dataset S5 (2015). http://webscope.sandbox.yahoo.com/catalog.php?datatype=s\&did=70
26. Twitter: Breakout Detection. https://github.com/twitter/BreakoutDetection
27. Zhang, S., et al.: Rapid and robust impact assessment of software changes in large internet-based services. In: CoNEXT 2015, 01–04 December 2015, Heidelberg, Germany (2015)

Transitive Pseudonyms Mediated EHRs Sharing for Very Important Patients

Huafei Zhu[✉] and Ng Wee Keong

School of Computer Science and Engineering, Nanyang Technological University,
Singapore, Singapore
huafeizhu@gmail.com, awkng@ntu.edu.sg

Abstract. Electronic health record (EHR) greatly enhances the convenience of cross-domain sharing and has been proven effectively to improve the quality of healthcare. On the other hand, the sharing of sensitive medical data is facing critical security and privacy issues, which become an obstacle that prevents EHR being widely adopted. In this paper, we address several challenges in very important patients' (VIPs) data privacy, including how to protect a VIP's identity by using pseudonym, how to enable a doctor to update an encrypted EHR with the VIP's absence, how to help a doctor link up and decrypt historical EHRs of a patient for secondary use under a secure environment, and so on. Then we propose a framework for secure EHR data management. In our framework, we use a transitive pseudonym generation technique to allow a patient to vary his/her identity in each hospital visit. We separate metadata from detailed EHR data in storage, so that the security of EHR data is guaranteed by the security of both the central server and local servers in all involved hospitals. Furthermore, in our framework, a hospital can encrypt and upload a patient's EHR when he/she is absent; a patient can help to download and decrypt his/her previous EHRs from the central server; and a doctor can decrypt a patient's historical EHRs for secondary use under the help and audit by several proxies.

Keywords: Electronic health record · Pseudonym ·
Semantic security · Transitive pseudonym

1 Introduction

Medical tourism is in great demanding [1–7], and since the medical tourists are often very important persons, healthcare service providers may be more likely to care for VIPs such as celebrities, super star athletes, and political leaders and many efforts have been proposed to handle the VIP medical records which are not shared across the public sectors currently in many countries and areas. The designation of VIPs in healthcare usually refers to the patients with great concern for their privacy and confidentiality due to the very high public profiles. To facilitate inter-professional collaboration and to enable disease management

© Springer Nature Switzerland AG 2019
J. Miller et al. (Eds.): ICWS 2019, LNCS 11512, pp. 80–94, 2019.
https://doi.org/10.1007/978-3-030-23499-7_6

and optimal technology support, one may handle VIPs' medical records within a public healthcare sector so that the outsourced EHRs can be accessed anytime, anywhere and anyhow for legitimate users. As important as it is to protect VIPs from bodily harm during the visit, it is equally important to protect them from attacks on the confidentiality via unauthorized access to the electronic medical records and to prevent the identifications of VIPs on various systems being traced [8–13].

1.1   The Motivation Problem

Considering a scenario where a VIP Alice visits a clinic for a medical treatment. She does not want to show the real identity to the clinic, as she is afraid of the exposure of her private medical condition caused by system attacks or reveal from the administrative staff or doctor in the clinic. She does not want to use the same pseudonym for every visit either, because the frequency she visits the clinic, the statistics in medical reports, and the linkage among different treatments and tests (e.g., blood test, X-ray, etc.) may help someone, who has certain background knowledge of Alice, guess her identity from those data. She would like to use a different pseudonym every time she visits the clinic. When Alice registers at the clinic with a new pseudonym, the administrative staff must verify that this pseudonym corresponds to a legal resident. Later when Alice sees a doctor Bob, Bob will pull all Alice's previous EHRs, under her help, from the central server to assist diagnosing, though those EHRs are indexed by different IDs (e.g., Alice's different pseudonyms). Two days later, when a new blood test report is out, Bob needs to update Alice's EHR in the central server, with Alice's absence. One month later, Bob finds Alice's case is special and worth of further research. Then Bob downloads and decrypts all Alice's EHRs generated before her last consultation with him, under the help of some authorities. To summarize the above scenario, when the VIP Alice registers in a medical center, she should not use the real identity, nor the same pseudonym as that was used in previous visits to this medical center. In other words, the local database in a medical center should be private enough to avoid data linkage in case it is compromised or some insider (e.g., administrative person) intentionally or unintentionally reveal the patient data. Furthermore, it can minimize the threat if the EHRs of a person are indexed by different IDs in the central server that are not linkable by adversaries. On the other hand, when a doctor tries to pull historical EHRs of a patient from the central server, he/she must be able to identify which records belonging to this patient and decrypt them for reading. This process sometimes needs to be achieved with the patient's absence, i.e., the patient cannot help to identify and decrypt his/her EHRs.

To achieve this goal, we need to solve the challenges:

- A way to generate pseudonym so that the real identity of a patient cannot be linked with the pseudonym;
- A way to generate multiple non-repeated pseudonyms from a patient's identity, and to verify these pseudonyms belong to the same identity;

- A way to prove to the administrative person during registration that the pseudonym to be registered corresponds to a legal resident;
- A way to search and decrypt all encrypted EHRs of a certain patient, which are indexed by different IDs, in a central server for an authorized action like EHR update or secondary use, when the patient is absent.

1.2   The Related Work

VIPs's EHR data stored in a server should be carefully encoded and protected. The existing cryptographic techniques guarantees the security of encrypted EHR data. However, the process of decryption should consider the absence of patients. In the motivation problem scenario, many medical test results and diagnoses are made when a patient leaves a medical center, so his/her EHR should be updated by the doctor. For the secondary use of EHRs (mainly for research purposes, as agreed in HIPAA) requires a doctor to decrypt certain EHR data. Such research issues have not been well addressed. To protect personal information of VIPs, the de-identification should be introduced. The state-of-the-art pseudonyms can be categorized into two types: irreversible and reversible pseudonyms. Irreversible pseudonyms are pseudonyms that cannot be reversed back to the original data owners' identities. Reversible pseudonyms are pseudonyms that can be reversed back to the back to the original data owners' identities. If one wants to get irreversible pseudonyms, then one-way functions such as cryptographically secure hash functions that modelled as random functions are applied. [14,15] and [16] use hash function to generate pseudonyms and assign a unique pseudonym to each patient while the identity information from every data packet is masked and chopped off in [17]. The l-diversity solution [18] and k-anonymity solution in [19] are fallen into the category of irreversible pseudonyms. If one wants to get reversible pseudonyms, then trap-door permutations such as cryptographically secure symmetric key encryptions are applied. In [20], a trusted third party based solution for generating reversible pseudonyms is presented and analyzed. And in [21], an interesting hardware and software concept is presented which allows the reversible and irreversible encryption of sensitive sample data without the need of electronic connectivity. Although, both irreversible and reversible pseudonyms provide protections of patients' data so that any information held by healthcare providers cannot be linked to an individual, in practice, there are times when for legitimate reasons multiple de-identified records of the same patient may need to be linked, for example, when we need to study the history of a patient medical condition. To guarantee an individual transaction associated with a different pseudonym, we also require that the generated pseudonyms can be efficient re-randomized.

1.3   This Work

In this paper, we propose a novel framework that is secure for VIP EHR data protection and convenient for EHR data sharing among authorized parties. In our framework, there is a Information Center in each hospital that stores the metadata of the EHR generated by the doctors in this hospital, and takes the role to communicate with the central server and the Information Centers in other hospitals for EHR data searching, encryption, decryption and sharing. A doctor's role is as simple as submitting diagnosis to and request for historical medical reports from the Information Center, without caring about EHR searching, encryption, decryption and sharing. A patient can use a different pseudonym in each hospital visit, and controls the public/secret key for the encryption and decryption of his/her EHR.

Organization: the rest of this paper is organized as follows. Section 2 presents technical details on pseudonym generation and verification. Section 3 describes how encryption and decryption are done by the user-controlled public/secrect key. The repository designs for the metadata in each hospital's Information Center and the encrypted EHR data in the central server, as well as how cross-domain queries are performed are discussed in Sect. 4. Finally, we conclude this paper in Sect. 5.

2 Syntax and Security Definition of Pseudonym Generators

Definition 1. *A pseudonym generator $\mathcal{N} \colon D \times A \to R$ is a probability polynomial time (PPT) algorithm such that on input $id_U \in D$ and $aux \in A$, $\mathcal{N}$ outputs a pseudonym $nid_U \in R$, i.e., $nid_U = \mathcal{N}(id_U, aux)$, where D is a domain of user identities, A is an domain of auxiliary strings and R is a domain of pseudonyms.*

$\mathcal{N}$ is irreversible if for every probabilistic polynomial time adversary $\mathcal{A}$, there exists a negligible function $neg(1^{\kappa})$ such that $Pr[id_U \leftarrow \mathcal{A}(nid_U, \perp) | nid_U = \mathcal{N}(id_U, aux)] \leq neg(1^{\kappa})$, where κ is a security parameter and $\perp$ stands for an empty auxiliary string.

$\mathcal{N}$ is reversible if on input a valid nid_U there exists an efficient identity extractor $\mathcal{X}$ such that id_U can be extracted with the overwhelming probability, i.e., $Pr[id_U \leftarrow \mathcal{X}(nid_U, aux)] \geq 1 - neg(1^{\kappa})$, where κ is a security parameter.

To define the security of the pseudonym generator, we consider the following experiment running between $\mathcal{N}$ and an adversary $\mathcal{A}$:

- $\mathcal{N}$ provides $\mathcal{A}$ black-box accesses to the sampling algorithm and the evaluation algorithm for polynomial many pairs $(id_{U_1}, nid_{U_1}), \ldots, (id_{U_l}, nid_{U_l})$, where $id_{U_i} \in D$ is adaptively selected and the adversary $\mathcal{A}$ obtains the corresponding pseudonyms $\{nid_{U_i}\}_{i=1}^{l}$;
- $\mathcal{A}$ outputs two identities id_{x_b} and $id_{x_{\bar{b}}}$. $\mathcal{N}$ randomly selects a bit $b \in \{0, 1\}$ and gives nid_{x_b} to $\mathcal{A}$. Adversary wins the game if it outputs a bit b' such that $b' = b$.

Definition 2 *(Semantic security of pseudonym generators): Let $Adv(\mathcal{A}) = |Pr(b' = b)| - 1/2$. A trapdoor pseudonym generator is semantically secure against chosen-identity attack if $Adv(\mathcal{A})$ is at most a negligible amount.*

We provide an efficient construction of pseudonym generator in the common reference string model, where no trusted third party assumption is made. Our pseudonym generator is based on the ElGamal encryption scheme. Let p be a large prime number, i.e., $p = 2q+1$, p, q are larger prime numbers. Let $G = <g>$ be a cyclic group of order q and H: $\{0,1\}^* \rightarrow Z_p^*$ be a cryptographic hash function. The idea behind our construction is that we allow a pseudonym generator and its insurance company or any other external auditor to collaboratively generate a verifiable common reference string h such that the discrete logarithm $\log_g(h)$ is unknown to all participants and then we will define a pseudonym of user U as a ciphertext $(u = g^r, v = \mathsf{H}(id_U)^2 \times h^r)$ of user's id together with a proof that id_U is encrypted by a Diffie-Hellman quadruple (g, h, g^r, h^r) in zero-knowledge (*notice that id_U should be encoded in the form of $(\mathsf{H}(id_U))^2$ mod p rather $\mathsf{H}(id_U)$ mod p since the value $\mathsf{H}(id_U)$ mod p may not be an element in G*).

Definition 3. *Two ensembles $X = \{X_n\}_{n \in N}$ and $Y = \{Y_n\}_{n \in N}$ is called statistically close if the statistical difference is negligible, where the statistical difference (also known as variation distance) of X and Y is defined as $\Delta(n) = 1/2 \sum_\alpha |\Pr(X_n = \alpha) - \Pr(Y_n = \alpha)|$.*

2.1 Root Pseudonym Generators

Based on the generated common reference string $h \in G$, a user (say, Alice) first provides her National Registration Identity Card (NRIC) to the certificate authority (CA) for verifying that she is a genuine holder of this NRIC (*we identify user U's NRIC with id_U throughout the paper*). If the check is succeed (the validity of a user's NRIC can be verified via a physical contact or a secure channel that has been established between user and the pseudonym generation center), Alice generates a cipher-text $c = (u, v)$, where $u = g^r$ mod p and $v = h^r \times (\mathsf{H}(\mathrm{NRIC}))^2$ mod p of NRIC using ElGamal encryption scheme, and then proves in zero-knowledge that she knows the plain-text $(\mathsf{H}(\mathrm{NRIC}))^2$ of the corresponding cipher-text c. If the proof is valid, then CA issues a certified pseudonym (g, h, g^r, h^r) to Alice. The procedure for generating a pseudonym nid_U of a user U (say, Alice) is described as follows:

- Alice first demonstrates her ownership of the presented NRIC that will be used for applying for her initial pseudonym; If the check is valid, Alice then randomly computes a Diffie-Hellman quadruple (g, h, u, v), where $u = g^r$ mod p and $v = h^r \times (\mathsf{H}(\mathrm{NRIC}))^2$ mod p.
  Let $w \leftarrow \frac{v}{(\mathsf{H}(\mathrm{NRIC}))^2}$ and let π be the following zero-knowledge proof of knowledge that the generated (g, h, u, w) is a Diffie-Hellman quadruple
  - Alice randomly selects $u' = g^{r'}$, $w' = h^{r'}$ and sends (u', w') to the pseudonym generator center $\mathcal{N}$;
  - $\mathcal{N}$ randomly selects a challenge string $e \in Z_q$ uniformly at random and sends it back to the prover Alice;
  - Upon receiving e, Alice computes the response $r'' = r' + er$ mod q, and sends r'' to $\mathcal{N}$.

Let π be a transcript of the above interactive proof $< (u', w'), e, r'' >$
- Upon receiving (u, v) and π, the pseudonym issue checks the valid of π using the auxiliary information NRIC by the following check: $g^{r''} \stackrel{?}{=} u'u^e \bmod p$ and $h^{r''} \stackrel{?}{=} w'w^e \bmod p$; else it outputs 0 and terminates the protocol; If the proof is valid, then a certificate $cert_U$ on the pseudonym $nid_U \leftarrow (u, v)$ will be issued.

We call $(nid_U, cert_U)$ be a root pseudonym of user U. We stress that the zero-knowledge proof should be performed and verified in a secure and authenticated channel since any leakage of zero-knowledge proof results in the user can be traced back efficiently. It is clear that the proof π is zero-knowledge and the proposed pseudonym generator is semantically secure assuming the decisional Diffie-Hellman problem defined over prime filed Z_p^* is hard. As a result, the proposed pseudonym is zero-knowledge and it is semantically secure assuming the decisional Diffie-Hellman problem defined over prime filed Z_p^* is hard.

2.2   Transitive Pseudonyms

In this section two methods for attesting pseudonyms are introduced and formalized: directly and indirectly attested pseudonyms. Informally, a directly attested pseudonym is a new pseudonym generated at session α which is attested by the previous pseudonym generated at session $\alpha-1$. An indirectly attested pseudonym is a new pseudonym generated at session α which is attested by a previously generated pseudonym generated at session β $(\beta < \alpha - 1)$.

Direct Attestation. As usual in the real world, a user should register in the front desk before he/she is treated by a healthcare provider. during this initial registration, a user should demonstrate the healthcare provider that he/she is a valid user registered in a pseudonym distribution authority so that in case that a dispute occurs, the id of this registered user can be revealed (under what condition, an id of the registered user should revealed by law is out of the scope of this paper).

In our setting, a user will simply show that she/he is a genuine holder of $<nid_U, cert_U>$. The user then refreshes the initial pseudonym for the current registration. Let $(g, h, g^{r'}, h^{r'}(H(NRIC))^2 \bmod p)$ be a pair of refreshed pseudonym. The user proves in zero-knowledge the fact that $(g, h, g^r, h^r(H(NRIC))^2 \bmod p)$ and $(g, h, g^{r'}, h^{r'}(H(NRIC))^2 \bmod p)$ are ciphertexts of the same scratched user id to the healthcare registration desk. Let $\bar{u} = \frac{u'}{u}$ and $\bar{v} = \frac{v'}{v}$. Notice that the prover (Alice) knows r and r' and hence she knows the difference $\bar{r} = r - r'$ such that $\bar{u} = g^{\bar{r}}$ and $\bar{v} = h^{\bar{r}}$. Since $(g, h, g^r, h^r(H(NRIC))^2 \bmod p)$ is a certified pseudonym, it follows that we need to prove the following two things: (1) A proof of knowledge r such that $u = g^r$ in $<nid_U, cert_U>$ and (2) a proof of knowledge such that $(g, h, \bar{u}, \bar{v})$ is a Diffie-Hellman quadruple. The details of performs are processed below

<u>Protocol 1:</u> A proof of knowledge r such that $u = g^r$ in $<nid_U, \text{cert}_U>$

- Alice chooses a random string $s \in [1, q-1]$ and computes $\widehat{u} = g^s$, then sends $\widehat{u}$ to the healthcare provider H;
- H chooses a random string $f \in [1, q-1]$ uniformly at random and sends f to Alice;
- Alice computes $t = s + rf \bmod q$ then sends t to H
- H checks the equation: $g^t = \widehat{u}u^f \bmod p$. If the condition is satisfied then accept otherwise reject.

<u>Protocol 2:</u> A proof of knowledge such that $(g, h, \overline{u}, \overline{v})$ is a Diffie-Hellman quadruple

- Alice randomly selects $\overline{u}' = g^{\overline{r}'}$, $\overline{v}' = h^{\overline{r}'}$ and sends $(\overline{u}', \overline{v}')$ to the pseudonym generator center $\mathcal{N}$;
- $\mathcal{N}$ randomly selects a challenge string $e \in Z_q$ uniformly at random and sends it back to the prover Alice;
- Upon receiving e, Alice computes the response $\overline{r}'' = \overline{r}' + e\overline{r} \bmod q$, and sends $\overline{r}''$ to $\mathcal{N}$.
- H checks the equation: $g^{\overline{r}''} = \overline{u}'\,\overline{u}^e \bmod p$ and $h^{\overline{r}''} = \overline{v}'\overline{v}^e \bmod p$. If the condition is satisfied then accept otherwise reject.

Let π be the concatenation of transcripts of Protocol 1 and Protocol 2. We show that the successful proof π guarantees (g, h, u', v') and (g, h, u, v) are encryptions of the same NRIC.

Theorem 1. *The newly generated pseudonym (g, h, u', v') and the previously generated pseudonym (g, h, u, v) are encryptions of the same NRIC.*

Proof. One can verify that both Protocol 1 and Protocol 2 are complete, sound and zero-knowledge. By Protocol 1, we know that Alice is the genuine holder $<nid_U, \text{cert}_U>$ since Alice proves her knowledge r such that $u = g^r$, where (g, h) are common reference strings such that the knowledge of $\log_g h$ is unknown to all participants.

By Protocol 2, we know that $(g, h, \overline{u}, \overline{v})$ is a Diffie-Hellman quadruple. This means that there exists a value $\delta \in Z_q$ such that $\overline{u} = g^\delta$ and $\overline{v} = h^\delta$. Recall that $\overline{u} = \frac{u'}{u}$ and $\overline{v} = \frac{v'}{v}$, it follows that $u' = ug^\delta = g^{r+\delta}$ and $v' = vh^\delta = h^{r+\delta}(\text{H(NRIC)})^2$ (which is guaranteed by $<nid_U, \text{cert}_U>$). As a result, (u', v') is a random refreshment of (u, v) such that both ciphertetxts are encryptions of the same plaintext NRIC.

Let π be a zero-knowledge proof of the statement that $(g, h, g^r,$ $h^r(\text{H(NRIC)})^2 \bmod p)$ and $(g, h, g^{r'}, h^{r'}(\text{H(NRIC)})^2 \bmod p)$ are ciphertexts of the same scratched user id. Form Lemma 2, we know that the newly generated pseudonym $(g, h, g^r, h^r(\text{H(NRIC)})^2 \bmod p)$ binds the user's NRIC. Therefore, if the proof is accepted, the healthcare provider will issue a certificate $\text{cert}_U^{(H)}$ to this newly generated pseudonym denoted by $\text{nid}_U^{(H)}$. The internal database d_H

of the healthcare provider H stores the following table privately. Notice that we store π in the internal repository since it is a proof that $\text{nid}_U^{(H)}$ is valid and it is a witness for issuing a certificate $\text{cert}_U^{(H)}$ and future auditing

$$\boxed{(\text{nid}_U, \text{cert}_U)\,\big|\,(\text{nid}_U^{(H)}, \text{cert}_U^{(H)})\,\big|\,\pi}$$

Indirect Attestation. The following are illustrative examples for the introduction of the indirect attestation:

For a treatment in the hospital registered with $\text{nid}_U^{(H_i)}$, there could be many related diagnoses such as blood test, X-ray check etc. If these diagnoses are outsourced using the same $\text{nid}_U^{(H_i)}$, then these results can be linked trivially. To solve the problem, instead of re-generation a new pseudonym for patient Alice, we would like to re-randomize $\text{nid}_U^{(H_i)}$ to get a new $\text{nid}_U^{(H_{i,j})}$ for registered at the department $H_{i,j}$ in the hospital H_i and then proves to $H_{i,j}$ her knowledge that both $\text{nid}_U^{(H_i)}$ and $\text{nid}_U^{(H_{i,j})}$ are ciphertexts that bind the same NRIC.

- For a patient Alice who registered initially at hospital H_i, is now to register at hospital H_j. In this case, the user may chooses $(\text{nid}_U, \text{cert}_U)$ or $(\text{nid}_U^{(H_i)}, \text{cert}_U^{(H_i)})$ as a witness to attest a newly generated pseudonym $(\text{nid}_U^{(H_j)}, \text{cert}_U^{(H_j)})$ at H_j. If $(\text{nid}_U, \text{cert}_U)$ is used to attest $(\text{nid}_U^{(H_j)}, \text{cert}_U^{(H_j)})$, there exists an obvious linkage between $(\text{nid}_U^{(H_i)}, \text{cert}_U^{(H_i)})$ and $(\text{nid}_U^{(H_j)}, \text{cert}_U^{(H_j)})$ since both are attested by $(\text{nid}_U, \text{cert}_U)$. To resist the linkability attack, we would like to use $\text{nid}_U^{(H_i)}$ to attest a newly generated pseudonym $\text{nid}_U^{(H_i)}$. Such a procedure is called indirect attestation.

Based on the above discussions, we can now formalize the structure of indirect (recommended) attestations. Suppose that $(\text{nid}_U, \text{cert}_U)$ is used to attest $(\text{nid}_U^{(H_1)}, \text{cert}_U^{(H_1)})$, and $(\text{nid}_U^{(H_1)}, \text{cert}_U^{(H_1)})$ is used to attest $(\text{nid}_U^{(H_2)}, \text{cert}_U^{(H_2)})$ and so on. We can now construct an attestation path: $(\text{nid}_U, \text{cert}_U) \rightarrow (\text{nid}_U^{(H_1)}, \text{cert}_U^{(H_1)}) \rightarrow (\text{nid}_U^{(H_2)}, \text{cert}_U^{(H_2)}) \rightarrow \cdots \rightarrow (\text{nid}_U^{(H_k)}, \text{cert}_U^{(H_k)})$. Since each zero-knowledge proof binds the original NRIC, it follows that there is an indirect linkage between the root $(\text{nid}_U, \text{cert}_U)$ the destination node $(\text{nid}_U^{(H_k)}, \text{cert}_U^{(H_k)})$. This means that the concept of indirect attestation can be formalized in the notion of transitive graphs.

Definition 4. *A graph $G = (V, E)$ has a finite set V of vertices and a finite set $E \subseteq V \times V$ of edges. The transitive closure $G^* = (V^*, E^*)$ of a graph $G = (V, E)$ is defined to have $V^* = V$ and to have an edge (u, v) in E^* if and only if there is a path from u to v in G.*

In terms of the notion of transitive graph, a direct attestation is an edge between two nodes in a graph G while indirect attestation is an edge defined in its corresponding transitive closure graph G^*. As a result, the notion of indirect attestation can be viewed as a natural extension of the notion of the direct attestation (if the number of intermediate nodes in a path is zero). We will further demonstrate that the introduced indirectly attested pseudonym is a useful tool for the cross-domain query of outsourced EHRs.

3   User Controlled Encryptions

In this section, a user controlled encryption scheme is proposed and analyzed. The idea behind our construction is that when a user U initially registers to a healthcare service provider H, the generated plain electronic health record is first processed in a private sector within H. This is because the main function of a doctor is to examine a patient's health and to find causes and solutions for the illness. As a consequence, a health record stored in the private database (managed by the healthcare provider) should only be accessible by the doctors and healthcare staffs who are involved in the treatment. An access to the user's EHR by a doctor or a healthcare staff is logged and audited. All healthcare professionals are also bound by law and professional ethics to keep user medical information strictly confidential during the period when the generated EHR are stored and processed in the private sector. To outsource the healthcare records, the plain EHR will be first encrypted by the user specified public key encryption scheme that is generated on the fly. The resulting ciphertexts are transferred to the public sectors. Below is a detailed construction of our protocol.

3.1   One-the-fly Public Key Generation

After the initial registration in H, a user Alice invokes a cryptographically strong pseudo-random generator G which takes the current state as an input and outputs $(s', k) \leftarrow G(s)$, where $s \in \{0, 1\}^m$ in the current state and $s' \in \{0, 1\}^m$ is the next state and $k \in \{0, 1\}^m$ is the current output. We assume that Alice enciphers k as $K = g^k \bmod p$. K is then securely transferred via secure channel established between user and the healthcare provider (say, SSL via the web interface). The secret key sk used for enciphering the generated EHRs is encrypted by K.

3.2   Threshold Decryption

As mentioned earlier, in some cases a doctor needs to decrypt an EHR without the presence of the patient, e.g., the doctor needs to update the EHR or the doctor needs to use the EHR for further research (secondary use of EHR). In such cases, we need a practical decryption mechanism to obtain a plain EHR without a patient's assistance. In this paper, we will use the notion of threshold encryption.

In real world, enterprises often delegate the security verification of incoming people (to its premises) to companies which have specialized skill set in doing such job. Based on stated policies of an organization, these security companies verify various credentials of incoming people, before they are allowed to enter the premises of the organization. We apply this approach in the context of threshold encryptions. Let $T_1, \ldots, T_m$ be m decryption proxies (servers) not necessary within the hospital (e.g., an insurance company, or a certificate issuing center can be designated decryption proxies). A user will process an l-out-of-m threshold public key encryption scheme for supporting, e.g., the secondary use of the encrypted EHRs:

- H randomly selects a polynomial $f(x) = f_0 + f_1 x + \cdots + f_{l-1} x^{l-1}$, where $f_0 = k$;
- Each processing center T_i is given a pair shares $(t_i, f(t_i))$ $(i = 1, \ldots, m)$, where t_i is an id of T_i;

We are able to provide an efficient solution to the problem stated in the motivation problem: Two days later, doctor Bob needs to update Alice's EHR that was encrypted and outsourced by the Information Center. One month later, Bob finds Alice's case is special and worth of further research. Then Bob downloads and decrypts all Alice's EHRs generated before her last consultation with him, under the help of some authorities. To serve such requests, i.e., the hospital H makes a decryption query of the ciphertext $(u, v) = (g^r, sk \times K^r)$, the Information Center will randomly select l decryption servers among the specified m proxies and send the corresponding u to the selected servers. Once the Information Center gets the m values $u^{f(t_i)}$ $(i = 1, \ldots, m)$, it can retrieve the plain EHR by the Lagrange interpolation formula.

If a public-key encryption secure against adaptively chosen ciphertext attack is used for encrypting a symmetric key sk that will be used to encipher the generated EHRs (say, the Cramer-Shoup's encryption scheme [22]), one needs to generate more randomness from k. An obvious solution is to invoke a new instance of the underlying pseudo-random generator G^* which takes as input k and runs recursively to output $(k_1, k_2, k_3, k_4, k_5, k_6) \in [1, q-1]^6$ such that $X = g^{k_1} h^{k_2} \bmod p$, $Y = g^{k_3} h^{k_4} \bmod p$ and $Z = g^{k_5} h^{k_6} \bmod p$. To encrypt a message $m = H(\text{NRIC})^2$, the Cramer-Shoup's encryption algorithm chooses $r \in [1, q-1]$ uniformly at random, then computes $u_1 = g^r \bmod p$, $u_2 = h^r \bmod p$, $v = mZ^r \bmod p$, $e = H(u_1, u_2, e)$ and $w = X^r Y^{re} \bmod p$. (u_1, u_2, v, w) is called an encryption of the message m. The Canetti and Goldwasser's threshold public key cryptosystem secure against adaptive chosen ciphertext attack constructed from the Cramer and Shoup's encryption can be applied here. We refer to the reader [23] for more details.

4 Storage and Query

In our framework, the metadata of EHRs, i.e., the owner of each EHR and how each EHR links other EHR under the same owner are stored locally in the Information Center in each participating hospital. The encrypted EHR data are outsourced to the central server for sharing. This section describe how the EHR metadata and data storages are designed.

4.1   In-Hospital Repository

Although the encrypted EHR data are outsourced to the central server, the local database in the Information Center of each hospital should store some metadata about the EHRs generated in the hospital and their patient owners. The purpose of in-hospital data storage is to record the certified pseudonyms of the patients who accepted treatment in the hospital, and also to offer guidance to link each EHR to the previous EHRs of the same patient since this link is important for the secondary use of EHRs but should not be exposed in the central server.

Recall that an internal transcript generated during a patient's registration comprises of the following items: the previously generated and certified pseudonym ($\mathrm{nid}_U^{(H_{i-1})}$, $\mathrm{cert}_U^{(H_{i-1})}$), a newly generated and certified pseudonym ($\mathrm{nid}_U^{(H_i)}$, $\mathrm{cert}_U^{(H_i)}$), a proof π as well as a public-key K generated on the fly for EHR encryption. Thus the in-hospital database of a hospital H_i is designed as:

$$R_{H_i}(Pre\text{-}nym, Pre\text{-}cert, New\text{-}nym, New\text{-}cert, Proof, PK)$$

Table 1 shows an example local database table for a hospital H_i.

Table 1. An example local database table for the hospital H_i

Pre-nym	Pre-cert	New-nym	New-cert	Proof	PK
nid_{U_1}	cert_{U_1}	$\mathrm{nid}_{U_1}^{(H_i)}$	$\mathrm{nid}_{U_1}^{(H_i)}$	$\pi_{U_1}^{(H_i)}$	K_{U_1}
$\mathrm{nid}_{U_2}^{(H_j)}$	$\mathrm{cert}_{U_2}^{(H_j)}$	$\mathrm{nid}_{U_2}^{(H_i)}$	$\mathrm{nid}_{U_2}^{(H_i)}$	$\pi_{U_2}^{(H_i)}$	K_{U_2}
...	...	...	...	...	...
$\mathrm{nid}_{U_n}^{(H_k)}$	$\mathrm{cert}_{U_n}^{(H_k)}$	$\mathrm{nid}_{U_n}^{(H_i)}$	$\mathrm{nid}_{U_n}^{(H_i)}$	$\pi_{U_n}^{(H_i)}$	K_{U_n}

We can see that each tuple contains the pseudonym of a patient that is certified by the CA or a previous visited hospital, and the new pseudonym certified by H_i. We need to emphasize that the proof π is also necessary to be stored. This is because each hospital will be aperiodically audited. The auditing will be done by checking the proof to show that the hospital is not cheating on each certified pseudonym. A tuple can be identified by either *New-nym* or *PK*. The different identifiers are used for searching and linking EHRs of a same patient under the circumstance that the patient is absent or present. The details will be covered in Sect. 6. Note that different pseudonyms will be used even if the same patient visits H_i multiple times.

The hospital will also temporarily store the EHR of a patient, before encrypting and uploading it to the central server. This period is rather short. Once the encrypted EHR is outsourced, the hospital should not maintain a copy. In the case that the database in a hospital is attacked, there will be no EHR exposed. Also, from the metadata, the adversary can only infer a one-level linkage of pseudonym, i.e., $\mathrm{nid}_{U_2}^{(H_j)}$ and $\mathrm{nid}_{U_2}^{(H_i)}$ are the same patient, but cannot reverse either his/her identity or medical condition.

4.2   Outsourced EHR Repository

The central server storage is designed as:

$$R \ (Nym, \ PK, \ EK, \ eEHR)$$

We assume that the secret key sk that will be used to encrypt the outsourced EHRs is created by the ElGamal encryption scheme. This is reasonable assumption since sk is one-time used for each K (similar with the notion of one-time encryption). When a personal health record d is created by a doctor in the hospital H, this data d will be encrypted by K using the ElGamal encryption scheme $c_K \ (:= (u_K, v_K)) = (g^r, sk \times K^r)$. The corresponding storage of the encrypted EHR is:

$$\boxed{nid_U^{(H)} \ | \ K \ | \ c_K \ | \ AES(sk, \ d)}$$

4.3   Patient-Aided Query

Now we consider the case that a patient Alice consults a doctor in a hospital, and needs to help the doctor find out all his/her previous EHRs in the central server, including the ones generated by other hospitals and the ones generated in this hospital before. In this case, Alice will invoke the pseudo-random number generator which takes a seed s as input and outputs (s', k). Recursively, she obtains $(k_1, \ldots, k_i)$ and hence obtains $K_1, \ldots, K_i$ accordingly as the public keys generated in previously visited hospitals. Then Alice searches the database in the central server using the generated index $K_1, \ldots, K_i$ to download all encrypted EHRs, and perform decryption.

4.4   Patient-Absent Query

As illustrated, sometimes a doctor needs to find out and decrypt a patient's EHRs when the patient is not around. If the doctor would like to update an EHR he/she produced before, he should submit the request to the Information Center, and the Information Center will help to download the EHR and decrypt it based on the threshold decryption. After updating the EHR, the Information Center will encrypt it and replace the one in the central server. Now we consider the secondary use of EHR. Assume a doctor would like to obtain all historical EHRs (that may be generated by different hospitals) of a patient for research purpose, he/she needs to do it collaboratively with the central server and the Information Centers of all involved hospitals. The procedure is shown in Algorithm.

Algorithm 1 Inter-hospital EHR searching

Input: the current eEHR d of the patient with pseudonym p in the hospital H, the
 database $DB_{H'}$ of an involved hospital H', the database DB_s of the central server
Output: a set S of all plain-text EHRs of the patient that were generated before d
 1: let H decrypt d by threshold decryption and put the plain-text EHR into S
 2: search DB_H for the previous pseudonym that was used to generate p by the patient,
    denoted by p'
 3: **while** the authority that certified p' is not the CA **do**
 4:    let H' denote the hospital that certified p'
 5:    send request to H'
 6:    H' finds and decrypts the eEHR by p' from DB_s, and save the plain-text into S
 7:    H' search $DB_{H'}$ for the previous pseudonym used to generate p'
 8:    update p' as the newly found pseudonym
 9: **end while**
10: return S as all the plain-text EHRs by the patient

Suppose a doctor D_i at hospital H_i and wants to query all the previous medical reports of a user U_2. Then the Information Center in H_i will search the local database, as shown in Table 1, and find that U_2 visited the hospital H_j before visiting H_i (from the second tuple in Table 1). Then the Information Center will send a request to the Information Center in H_j. The Information Center in H_j will go through a threshold decryption and send the EHR generated by H_j to H_i. Furthermore, H_j will recursively request another hospital for the previous EHR, until all EHRs of the patient are found.

5   Computation Complexity

All computations are measured with the multiplications mod$p$. Since a computation g^x mod$p$ on average is roughly $1.5\log_2[(p-1)/2]$ assuming that x is randomly distributed in $(p-1)/2$ using the standard square-and-multiplication method, where $p-1 = 2q$ and q is a large prime number. It follows that the computation complexity of Protocol 1 is $4.5\log_2(q)$ modular multiplications and Protocol 2 is $9\log_2(q)$ modular multiplications. Hence the transitive attestation is very efficient.

6   Conclusion

In this paper, a novel approach has been proposed and analyzed for securely handling the VIP EHRs to the public sector. Our method leverages the notion of trapdoor pseudonym generators. The transitive property of the proposed pseudonym generators benefits the healthcare professionals performing cross-domain queries efficiently. Our user controlled encryption protecting the outsourced healthcare records from attacks on the confidentiality and preventing the identifications of VIPs on various systems being traced.

References

1. Sadlier, C., Bergin, C., Merry, C.: Healthcare globalization and medical tourism. Clin. Infect. Dis. **58**(11), 1642–1643 (2014)
2. Ivanov, S., Webster, C., Mladenovic, A.: The microchipped tourist: implications for European tourism. Social Science Electronic Publishing (2014)
3. Beladi, H., Chao, C.C., Ee, M.S., Hollas, D.: Medical tourism and health worker migration in developing countries. Econ. Model. **46**, 391–396 (2015)
4. Fombelle, P.W., Sirianni, N.J., Goldstein, N.J., Cialdini, R.B.: Let them all eat cake: providing VIP services without the cost of exclusion for non-VIP customers. J. Bus. Res. **68**(9), 1987–1996 (2015)
5. Dang, H.S., Huang, Y.F., Wang, C.N.: Estimation of the market size of medical tourism industry using grey models - case study in South Korea. In: Estimation of the Market Size of Medical Tourism Industry Using Grey Models - Case Study in South Korea, pp. 46–50 (2016)
6. Arunotai, P.: An investigation of tourism information on destination management organization websites as the pull factor: a case study of health and wellness tourism information. In: 2017 11th International Conference on Software, Knowledge, Information Management and Applications (SKIMA), pp. 1–8 (2017)
7. Zhao., H.: An investigation of tourism information on destination management organization websites as the pull factor: a case study of health and wellness tourism information. In: ICISS 2018 Proceedings of the 2018 International Conference on Information Science and System, pp. 102–106 (2018)
8. Yang, C.C., Leroy, G., Ananiadou, S.: Smart health and wellbeing. ACM Trans. Manag. Inf. Syst. **4**(4), 15:1–15:8 (2013). https://doi.org/10.1145/2555810.2555811
9. Yang, C.C.: Patient centered healthcare informatics. IEEE Intell. Inf. Bull. **15**(1), 1–5 (2014)
10. Yang, C.C., Veltri, P.: Intelligent healthcare informatics in big data era. Artif. Intell. Med. **65**(2), 75–77 (2015). https://doi.org/10.1016/j.artmed.2015.08.002
11. Spagnuelo, D., Lenzini, G.: Transparent medical data systems. J. Med. Syst. **41**(1), 8:1–8:12 (2017). https://doi.org/10.1007/s10916-016-0653-8
12. Daniels, M., Rose, J., Farkas, C.: Protecting patients' data: an efficient method for health data privacy. In: ARES 2018, Proceedings of the 13th International Conference on Availability, Reliability and Security (2018)
13. Alabdulhafith, M., Alqarni, A., Sampalli, S.: Customized communication between healthcare members during the medication administration stage. In: MobileHCI 2018 Proceedings of the 20th International Conference on Human-Computer Interaction with Mobile Devices and Services (2018)
14. Riedl, B., Neubauer, T., Goluch, G., Boehm, O., Reinauer, G., Krumboeck, A.: A secure architecture for the pseudonymization of medical data. In: ARES, pp. 318–324 (2007)
15. Quantin, C., Jaquet-Chiffelle, D.O., Coatrieux, G., Benzenine, E., Fa, A.: Medical record search engines, using pseudonymised patient identity: an alternative to centralised medical records. Int. J. Med. Inf. **80**(2), 6–11 (2011)
16. Nugroho, H.A., Priyana, Y., Prihatmanto, A.S., Rhee, K.H.: Pseudonym-based privacy protection for steppy application. In: 2016 6th International Annual Engineering Seminar (InAES), pp. 138–143 (2016)
17. Sarkar, S., Chatterjee, S., Misra, S., Kudupudi, R.: Privacy-aware blind cloud framework for advanced healthcare. IEEE Commun. Lett. **21**(11), 2492–2495 (2017). https://doi.org/10.1109/LCOMM.2017.2739141

18. Shah, A., Abbas, H., Iqbal, W., Latif, R.: Enhancing E-healthcare privacy preservation framework through L-diversity. In: 2018 14th International Wireless Communications and Mobile Computing Conference (IWCMC) (2018)
19. Sweeney, L.: K-anonymity: a model for protecting privacy. Int. J. Uncertainty, Fuzziness Knowl.-Based Syst. **10**(5), 557–570 (2002)
20. Hillen, C.: The pseudonym broker privacy pattern in medical data collection. In: 2015 IEEE TrustCom/BigDataSE/ISPA, Helsinki, Finland, 20–22 August 2015, vol. 1, pp. 999–1005 (2015). https://doi.org/10.1109/Trustcom.2015.475
21. Ihmig, F.R., Wick, H., Hichri, K., Zimmermann, H.: RFID for anonymous biological samples and pseudonyms. In: 2011 IEEE International Conference on RFID-Technologies and Applications, RFID-TA 2011, Sitges, Spain, 15–16 September 2011, pp. 376–380 (2011). https://doi.org/10.1109/RFID-TA.2011.6068665
22. Cramer, R., Shoup, V.: A practical public key cryptosystem provably secure against adaptive chosen ciphertext attack. In: Krawczyk, H. (ed.) CRYPTO 1998. LNCS, vol. 1462, pp. 13–25. Springer, Heidelberg (1998). https://doi.org/10.1007/BFb0055717
23. Canetti, R., Goldwasser, S.: An Efficient *threshold* public key cryptosystem secure against adaptive chosen ciphertext attack (extended abstract). In: Stern, J. (ed.) EUROCRYPT 1999. LNCS, vol. 1592, pp. 90–106. Springer, Heidelberg (1999). https://doi.org/10.1007/3-540-48910-X_7

A Novel Coalitional Game-Theoretic Approach for Energy-Aware Dynamic VM Consolidation in Heterogeneous Cloud Datacenters

Xuan Xiao[1], Yunni Xia[1(✉)], Feng Zeng[4], Wanbo Zheng[2(✉)], Xiaoning Sun[1],
Qinglan Peng[1], Yu Guo[3], and Xin Luo[5]

[1] Software Theory and Technology Chongqing Key Lab, Chongqing University,
Chongqing 400044, China
xiayunni@hotmail.com
[2] Data Science Research Center, Faculty of Science,
Kunming University of Science and Technology, Kunming 650500, China
zwanbo2001@163.com
[3] School of Public Administration, Sichuan University, Chengdu 610064, China
[4] Discovery Technology (shenzhen) limited, Shenzhen, China
[5] Chongqing Key Laboratory of Big Data and Intelligent Computing,
Chongqing Institute of Green and Intelligent Technology,
Chinese Academy of Sciences, Chongqing 400714, China

Abstract. Server consolidation technique plays an important role in energy management and load-balancing of cloud computing systems. Dynamic virtual machine (VM) consolidation is a promising consolidation approach in this direction, which aims at using least active physical machines (PMs) through appropriately migrating VMs to reduce resource consumption. The resulting optimization problem is well-acknowledged to be NP-hard optimization problems. In this paper, we propose a novel merge-and-split-based coalitional game-theoretic approach for VM consolidation in heterogeneous clouds. The proposed approach first partitions PMs into different groups based on their load levels, then employs a coalitional-game-based VM consolidation algorithm (CGMS) in choosing members from such groups to form effective coalitions, performs VM migrations among the coalition members to maximize the payoff of every coalition, and close PMs with low energy-efficiency. Experimental results based on multiple cases clearly demonstrate that our proposed approach outperforms traditional ones in terms of energy-saving and level of load fairness.

Keywords: Energy-aware · Dynamic VM consolidation ·
Load fairness · Merge-split method · Coalitional game ·
Heterogeneous clouds

1 Introduction

Nowadays, cloud computing is becoming an increasingly popular computational paradigm featured by the ability to provide elastic services over the internet

© Springer Nature Switzerland AG 2019
J. Miller et al. (Eds.): ICWS 2019, LNCS 11512, pp. 95–109, 2019.
https://doi.org/10.1007/978-3-030-23499-7_7

for a huge number of global users. With the rapid growth of cloud services, cloud infrastructures and their supporting datacenters are becoming increasingly complex, energy-requiring, and expensive with varying resource configurations and heterogeneous architectural setups. According to [1], electricity demand for world-wide datacenters is expected to increase by over 66% over the period of 2011–2035. Hence, resource and energy management become major concerns of both cloud providers and users. However, today's datacenters are still limited in ways of effectiveness of energy efficiency and energy management strategies. Among various energy management and energy saving technologies, dynamic VM consolidation is one of the most effective ones. Consolidation refers to the live migration operations of VMs between hosts with slight performance loss [2]. The aim of dynamic VM consolidation is to reduce the energy consumption of consolidation activities through live migration of VMs instead of static or planned ones. It is capable of turning idle active PMs into sleeping mode for energy saving. This technique considerably improves resource utilization and energy efficiency. In this work, we propose a novel energy-aware and merge-and-split-based coalitional game-theoretic approach for dynamic VM consolidation for heterogeneous cloud with varying resource configurations. The proposed approach involves multiple steps: (1) dividing PMs into three groups based on their workloads, (2) performing a coalitional game to improve the utilization, (3) letting PMs compete with each other and forming coalitions by using merge and split operations. To validate our proposed approach, we conduct extensive simulative studies based on multiple cases and show that our approach clearly outperforms traditional ones in terms of energy-saving and load fairness.

2   Literature Review

2.1   VM Consolidation Algorithms for Energy Management

Recently, considerable research efforts have been paid to the VM consolidation and related energy performance optimization problems. Related methods fall into two major categories, namely the dynamic server provisioning methods and dynamic VM consolidation ones [9]. The latter refers to the technique of reallocating VMs using live migration according to their real-time resource demand and switching idle hosts to the sleep mode. Various consolidation methods are heuristic-based or meta-heuristic-based. E.g., Buyya et al. [3] proposed a consolidation mechanism using two fixed threshold values calculated based on processors' utilization rates. He et al. [4] proposed an local-regression-based algorithm featured by a combination of local regression algorithm with the minimum-migration-time VM selection policy. Huang et al. [5] proposed a M-Convex VM consolidation method based on the semi-quasi M-convex optimization framework, which is capable of adaptively adapting its solutions according to the optimization objectives. Murtazaev et al. [6] developed the Sercon framework and considered an all-or-none migration strategy, where all the VMs in one active PM are tentatively migrated to other active PMs. If the migration is successful, a new placement scheme with a reduced number of active PMs is performed.

The above operation is iterated until no improvement can be made. Farahnakian et al. [7] used an online optimization metaheuristic algorithm called Ant-Colony-System to find near-optimal solutions for dynamic consolidations and showed that their proposed approach achieved good energy savings while meeting quality-of-service(QoS) constraints. They defined a multi-objective function which considers both the number of dormant PMs and the number of migrations. Wu et al. [8] proposed an improved-group-genetic-algorithm-based VM consolidation method to optimize trade-off between migration costs and energy consumption in heterogeneous clouds. Zhang et al. [9] presented a heterogeneity-aware resource monitoring and management system that is capable of performing dynamic capacity provision in heterogeneous datacenters. Duan et al. [10] proposed an improved ant-colony algorithm for energy-efficiency optimization by leveraging a prediction model based on fractal mathematics and a scheduler based on an improved ant colony algorithm.

2.2 Game-Theoretic Scheduling in Cloud

Recently, it is shown that game theory models and related methodologies can be effective in dealing with multi-constraint-multi-task scheduling and planning problems. Game-theoretic algorithms are featured by low time-complexity in comparison with heuristics, and thus can be highly suitable for scheduling and managing time-critical cloud systems. Extensive efforts were paid in this direction. E.g., Guo et al. [12] used a cooperative game model to guide VM consolidation with load and energy constraints, which is tested in a homogeneous cloud environment. Paul [13] proposed an uncooperative game-theoretic algorithm for dynamic VM consolidation problem in cloud computing. Xue et al. [14] used a coalitional game model to schedule the tasks in cloud. They proposed the merge-and-split-based mechanism to reduce the cost of tasks execution and increase the profit of cloud resource providers. Guazzone et al. [15] devise an algorithm, based on cooperative game theory that allows a set of cloud providers to cooperatively set up their federations in such a way that their individual profit is increased with respect to the case in which they work in isolation. A careful investigation into above contributions suggests that they are still limited in several ways: (1) most existing works considered energy-reduction and migration-cost-saving as objectives. However, the tradeoff between load fairness and energy-saving in heterogeneous clouds was less studied [20]; (2) various works aimed at closing as many PMs as possible in optimizing energy efficiency. However, it can be misleading and problematic to do so due to the fact that PMs in heterogeneous clouds are with varying energy-consumption characteristics and turning off fewer energy-requiring PMs may be more attractable than turing off more energy-saving ones. and (3) various existing works address cloud heterogeneity by considering heterogeneous PMs and VMs while ignoring the heterogeneity of workloads. However, it should be noted that in reality workloads can be heterogeneous as well [16,17]. Our proposed method therefore aims at appropriately addressing the above issues and overcoming related limitations.

3   System Model

As widely acknowledged [3,4], the power consumption of a PM, $P(u)$, is mainly decided by its resource utilization u according to (1). In (1), P_{max} denotes the energy-consumed by a fully-loaded PM, and α denotes the proportion of idle time of a PM.

$$P(u) = \alpha P_{max} + u(1 - \alpha)P_{max} \tag{1}$$

According to [3], α is usually around 0.7. Note that the utilization of a CPU can be time-varying, we thus use $u(t)$ instead of u in (2). The total energy consumed, denoted by ξ, can be estimated through an integration form as (2), where t_0 denotes the starting time, and T the period during which a PM is running.

$$\xi = \int_{t_0}^{t_0+T} P(u(t))\, dt \tag{2}$$

It is assumed a datacenter has m types of heterogeneous machines, t_s is the time that the VM consolidation starts, and t_e is the time that VM consolidation ends. f_k is the energy consumed by a PM of type k per unit time. Let b_k denotes the energy consumed by all the machines of type k per unit time before consolidation. We have:

$$b_k = n_k * \int_{t_s-T}^{t_s} f_k \tag{3}$$

where n_k denotes the number of machines of the kth type. Let a_k denotes the energy consumed by all the machines of type k per unit time after consolidation and it can be similarly calculated as:

$$a_k = n_k * \int_{t_e}^{t_e+T} f_k \tag{4}$$

Next, we should consider the energy consumed by VM migrations in a consolidation process. h represents the energy consumed by migration. In this paper, we adopt the function of migration-cost proposed by [12]. It is caculated by (5).

$$h = \int_{t_s}^{t_e} \Delta P_s(t)\, dt + \int_{t_s}^{t_e} \Delta P_d(t)\, dt + q \tag{5}$$

where $\int_{t_s}^{t_e} \Delta P_s(t)$ and $\int_{t_s}^{t_e} \Delta P_d(t)$ are the increased energy consumption of the source and destination PM respectively. q is the increased energy consumption as a result of turning on a PM, which is a constant value. If we do not need to turn on a new PM as the destination PM, when a VM is migrated, then $q = 0$. Based on the above assumptions and configurations, the problem we are interested in can thus be formulated in (6).

$$Max \ \ S = \int_{t_s}^{t_e} \sum_{k=1}^{m} (b_k - a_k) - h$$

$$s.t. \sum_{j=1}^{m} d_{ij} = 1, j = 1, 2, 3 \ldots, u_j > 0 \tag{6}$$

where d_{ij} is a boolean variable to indicate whether the ith VM is placed on the jth PM. If the ith VM is placed on the jth PM, then let $d_{ij} = 1$; otherwise, $d_{ij} = 0$. u_j is the utlization of PM_j, and PM_j shouldn't be an empty PM. S denotes the energy saved by the VM consolidation approach. The above formulation aims at maximizing the energy saved by the VM consolidation approach, i.e., energy saved by consolidation with the constraints that every VM can only be placed on one PM and there is no idle PMs.

4 The Coalitional Game-Theoretic Approach

According to [21,22], a coalitional game Γ consists of two essential elements as shown in (7): (1) a set of players $N = \{1, 2 \ldots\}$, in this paper, PMs are modelled as players; (2) a characteristic value v that specifies the value created by different subsets of the players. i.e., the payoff of a coalition C. Here maximizing the payoff $v(C)$ means maximizing the energy-efficiency of a coalition.

$$\Gamma = (N, v) \tag{7}$$

Players of the game choose to join or not to join a coalition by deciding whether more energy-saving could be achieved. To facilitate the handling of the coalitional game over coalitions of PMs, we first partition PMs into three groups, i.e., E, H, and L, which contains PMs with extrahigh load, high load and low load respectively, according to two load thresholds, i.e., t_1 and t_2:

$$t_1 = Q_1, \ t_2 = Q_3 \tag{8}$$

where t_1 equals Q_1, which denotes the first quartile of the workloads placed on all PMs. t_2 equals Q_3, which denotes the third quartile of the workloads placed on all PMs. In our proposed algorithm, the merge-and-split-based coalitional games are performed to maximize v of any coalition, i.e., payoff, as shown in (9). We define the utilization of a coalition as v which equals the average utilization of PMs in the coalition C except the PMs with extrahigh load.

$$Max \ v$$

$$v = \frac{1}{n} \sum_{j=1}^{n} u_j \tag{9}$$

$$s.t. \ 0 < u_j \le x_j, \ \mathrm{PM}_j \notin E, \ \mathrm{PM}_j \in C$$

where u_j denotes the real-time utilization of PM_j. x_j is the maximum utilization permitted of PM_j. n is the number of PMs in the coalition except the PMs with extrahigh load. In a coalitional game, the merge operation refers to grouping multiple PMs into a single coalition. The split operation works in the opposite direction, where workload from an extra-highly-loaded PM is distributed through multiple PMs. Only on condition that the payoff v, i.e. the energy-efficiency of a coalition is higher than the average one of all coalition members when they are running individually, the PMs are merged to form a coalition. (10)-(a)/(b)/(c)/(d) denote the precondition for the merge of an extra-highly-loaded PM and a lowly-loaded PM, the split of an extra-highly-loaded PM, the merge of lowly-load PMs, and the merge of PMs with high load, respectively.

$$
\begin{aligned}
&(a) \ \forall PM_j \in E, PM_i \in L, C = \{PM_i, PM_j\} \\
&v(C) > mean(u_j, u_i) \\
&(b) \ \forall PM_j \in E, u_j < v(C), \\
&C = \{PM_i, PM_k\}, PM_i, PM_k \in L/H \\
&(c) \ \forall PM_j, PM_i \in L, C = \{PM_i, PM_j\} \\
&v(C) > mean(u_j, u_i) \\
&(d) \ \forall PM_j, PM_i \in H, C = \{PM_i, PM_j\} \\
&v(C) > mean(u_j, u_i)
\end{aligned}
\tag{10}
$$

where u_i denotes the utilization of PM_i. Note that the operations enabled by the (a)(b)(c)(d) preconditions happen with the alphabetic order of these preconditions to ensure that PMs with extrahigh/low load are handled before those with high load. The steps of the above operations are implemented through Algorithm 1. Figure 1(a) illustrates a typical example of three kinds of merge operations. As can be seen, VM_{1-5} are on an extra-highly-loaded PM while VM_{25} is on a PM with low load, according to the algorithm, the two PMs are thus merged in a coalition and then form two highly-loaded PMs. VM_{29-30} are

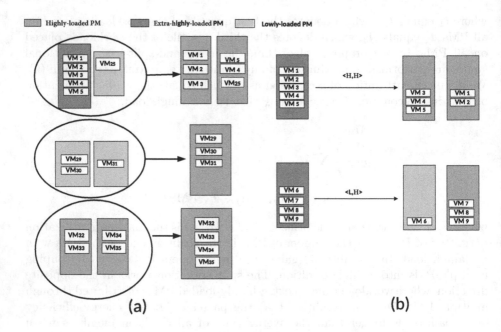

Fig. 1. Merge-and-split-based method of coalition formation

Algorithm 1. CGMS(E, H, L) algorithm

Input: E,H,L
Output: Updated E,H,L

1 Step 1:
2 **for** *each PM_j in E* **do**
3   **for** *each PM_i in L* **do**
4   **if** *PM_i, PM_j can be merged according to (10)-a* **then**
5   migrate the source VM from PM_j to PM_i ;
6   **end**
7   **end**
8 **end**
9 Step 2:
10 **for** *each PM_j in E* **do**
11   **if** *PM_j can be split according to (10)-b* **then**
12   migrate the source VM from PM_j to a new PM;
13   **end**
14 **end**
15 Step 3:
16 **for** *each PM_j, PM_i in L* **do**
17   **if** *PM_i, PM_j can be merged according to (10)-c* **then**
18   migrate the source VM from PM_j to PM_i;
19   **if** *PM_j is empty* **then**
20   close PM_j
21   **end**
22   **end**
23 **end**
24 Step 4:
25 **for** *each PM_j, PM_i in H* **do**
26   **if** *PM_j, PM_i can be merged according to (10)-d* **then**
27   migrate the source VM from PM_j to PM_i;
28   **if** *PM_j is empty* **then**
29   close PM_j
30   **end**
31   **end**
32 **end**

---

on a lowly-loaded PM while VM_{31} is on another PM with low load, the two lowly-loaded PMs are thus merged in a coalition and then form a PM with high load. VM_{32-33} are on a PM with high load while VM_{34-35} are on another PM with high load, the two highly-loaded PMs are thus merged in a coalition and then form a PM with high load. In Fig. 1(b), only extra-highly-loaded PMs undergo split operations. As can be seen, VM_{1-6} are on an extra-highly-loaded PM. This PM is thus splitted to two PMs with high load, which contain $VM_{3,4,5}$ and $VM_{1,2}$ respectively. After the game, numbers of extra-highly-loaded and lowly-loaded PMs are reduced while that of the PMs with high load is increased, thereby consolidating tasks into a reasonable number of PMs while avoiding both waste of resources caused by idle PMs and potential performance degradations of extra-highly-loaded PMs. The aim of the coalitional game is thus to finally form a PM group G that contains PMs which are working in a high-efficiency state for saving energy.

$$G = \{PM_j \mid PM_j \in H \wedge u_j <= x_j\} \tag{11}$$

The coalition can be gradually formed by using Algorithm 1. Note that in lines 5, 12, 18, 27 in the pseudo codes stipulate that the resulting load of the destination PM is still subject to the load constraint, i.e., a PM should not be extra-highly-loaded. We consider d as the measure of load fairness.

$$d = (n_E + n_L)/n_H \tag{12}$$

where n_E, n_L, n_H are the number of PMs in E, L, and H, respectively. According to (12), a lower d indicates better load fairness. In this work, we consider load fairness [16,17,20] as an important metric and the optimization algorithm aims at fairly distributing workloads among PMs to aviod hotspots.

5   An Illustrative Example of CGMS

Example Analysis. We consider the example shown in Fig. 3 as an illustrative example of the effect of the merge-and-split process: a datacenter contains multiple PMs, whose indexes are shown in the X-label. The workload of each PM is based on CoMon workload traces [18] collected from 10 days during march and April 2011, which is collected from roughly 400–450 active PlanetLab nodes every 5 min within 10 days. Every PM contains 4 VMs with varying workloads as shown in Fig. 2. According to the workload data and (8), t_1 and t_2 are set as 20 and 60, respectively. As shown in Fig. 3, $L/H/E$ groups are marked blue/green/red. During the process, lowly-loaded and extra-highly-loaded PMs are turned into PMs with high load. The new PMs in H are marked by purple in Fig. 3(c)(d). The new PMs in L are marked by black in Fig. 3(c). As can be seen in Fig. 4(a), H is enlarged while E and L shrink. Thus, the overall energy efficiency is optimized

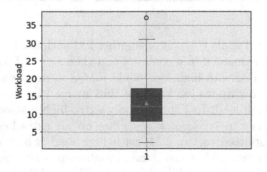

Fig. 2. VM workload used in example

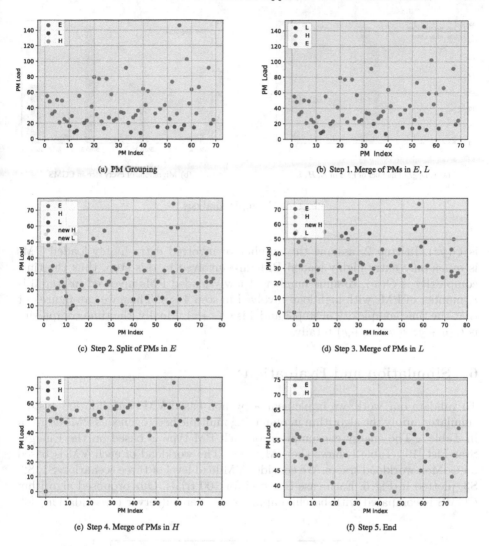

Fig. 3. An example of CGMS (Color figure online)

while the workload constraint for PMs is kept. Finally, number of migrations of every step is shown in Fig. 4(b). It is obvious that if a datacenter contains a lot of lowly-loaded PMs, a great number of VM migrations is required.

Time Complexity Analysis. The overall computational complexity of our approach can be analyzed by examing the group, merge, and split operations. In our algorithm, assuming that the number of PMs is g, the group operation's time complexity is $O(g)$. In step 1 assume the number of extra-highly-loaded PMs is y, number of lowly-loaded PMs is z, thus in step 1 the time complexity

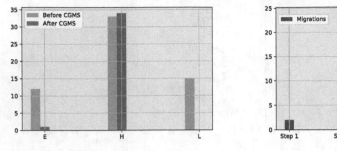

(a) Change of number of PMs in E, H, L (b) Migrations of every step in CGMS

Fig. 4. Example analysis

is $O(yz)$. In step 2, assume the number of involved extra-highly-loaded PMs is w, as only extra-highly-loaded PMs are involved in this step, thus the time complexity is $O(w)$. Assume number of lowly-loaded PMs involved in step 3 is r, number of PMs with high load involved in step 4 is s. Thus, we can figure out that the time complexity of step 3 and 4 is $O(s+r)$. Finally, the time complexity is $O(g + yz + w + s + r)$ totally.

6   Simulation and Evaluation

To validate our work, we implement a python-based VM consolidation system simulator, apply the algorithm in managing multiple heterogeneous PMs as given in Table 1. The energy consumption of each PM type is based on the Energy-Star-List [19]. Table 2 shows the VM types. The workload of each VM is based on CoMon workload traces. We consider VM load level of three scenarios: S1, S2, S3, plotted in Fig. 5. Each case is tested for 100 trials. Our proposed algorithm CGMS is compared with baseline approaches: Sercon(server consolidation) [6],

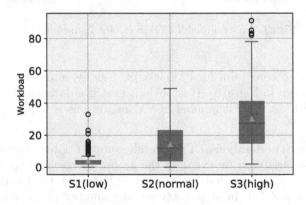

Fig. 5. Workload used in experiments

IGGA (improved group genetic algorithm) [8], and CGHO [12] (cooperative game in homogeneous cloud). Sercon is kind of improved greedy method to decrease the energy-cost and migration-cost, which inherits some properties of First-Fit and Best-Fit. Sercon used a migration threshold to control the migration efficiency. IGGA is kind of metaheuristic method using an improved genetic algorithm for VM consolidation. CGHO is another cooperative-game-theoretic algorithm tested in a homogeneous environment.

Table 1. VM configurition

VM instance	Memory	CPU
Micro	613 M	500 MIPS
Small	1.7 GB	1000 MIPS
Large	3.75 GB	2500 MIPS
Extra large	4 GB	2500 MIPS

Table 2. PM configurition

PM instance	DELL R515	HP DL380G8	HP DL585G7
Memory	16 GB	32 GB	64 GB
Idle power	213 W	109 W	258 W
Peak power	420 W	276 W	396 W

Energy-Saving and Load Fairness. We first evaluate the energy-saving, i.e., S modelled in (6), and load fairness, i.e., d in (12), between CGMS and baseline algorithms. As shown in Fig. 6(a) (c) (e), when the number of PMs ranges from 60 to 500, our method achieves higher energy-saving (32.30% higher than Sercon in three scenarios on average; 20.03% higher than CGHO on average; and 14.28% higher than IGGA on average). The energy-saving increases with the number of PMs and outperforms baseline ones as well. As shown in Fig. 6(b)(d)(f), CGMS achieves better load fairness (85.71% lower than Sercon in three scenarios on average; 42.02% lower than CGHO on average; and 70.32% lower than IGGA on average) in all scenarios with varying PM numbers.

Computational Cost. Fig. 7 depicts the required runtime of each approach. With increase of N, the runtime of CGMS and CGHO increase slowly. Sercon is the fastest one, due to the characteristic of greedy heuristic algorithm. IGGA is a meta-heuristic algorithm. Its runtime rises smoothly with the number of PMs going up. As a result, CGMS keeps a relatively low cost, which is acceptable for most datacenters in different scales.

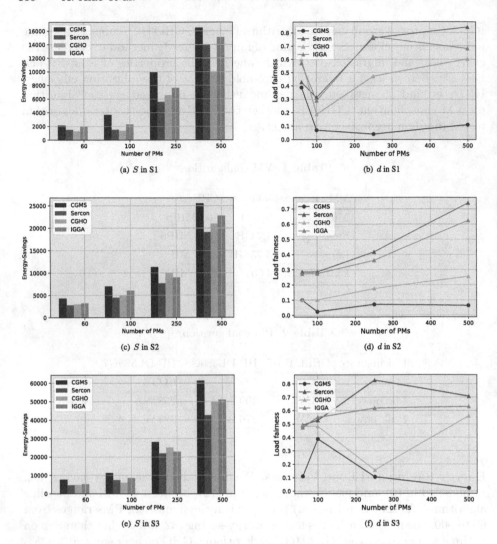

Fig. 6. Algorithm comparison in S1, S2, S3

The Number of Migrations. As shown in Table 3, we clearly see that Sercon achieves the least number of migrations in most cases, because it employs a greedy strategy in deciding when and which to migrate. However, it achieves the worst energy-saving. In contrast, CGMS achieves the second-least migrations (13.90% lower than CGHO on average; and 8.82% lower than IGGA on average) while clearly outperforms Sercon in term of energy-saving.

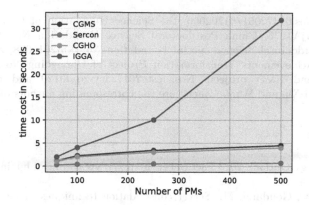

Fig. 7. Computation time of each approach

Table 3. Migrations in S1, S2, S3

Scenarios	Number of PMs	CGMS	IGGA	Sercon	CGHO
S1	60	34.6	37.5	30.1	40.2
	100	167.2	193.5	100.1	192.4
	250	322.2	405.2	226.3	365.0
	500	630.0	721.0	461.4	621.5
S2	60	16.8	15.3	15.6	24.9
	100	45.4	52.1	39.1	57.4
	250	169.0	185.6	137.8	190.4
	500	154.9	194.0	190.2	255.1
S3	60	18.3	16.1	12.0	30.4
	100	37.0	36.1	29.8	50.2
	250	151.8	170.5	155.3	181.8
	500	246.0	275.3	262.2	256.8

7   Conclusion and Future Work

In this work, we present a coalitional game approach for optimizing the energy
efficiency of VM consolidation in heterogeneous cloud datacenters. The experiments results demonstrate that our approach clearly outperforms traditional
approaches in terms of energy-saving and load-balancing. The following issues
should be addressed as future work: (1) reducing migrations, number of migrations is expected to be optimized for a better level. (2) fault tolerance, it is
promising to develop the fault tolerant mechanism based on our approach.

Acknowledgment. This work is supported in part by the International Joint Project
funded jointly by the Royal Society of the UK and the National Natural Science Foundation of China under grant 61611130209, National Science Foundations of China

under grants Nos.61472051/61702060, the Science Foundation of Chongqing under No. cstc2017jcyjA1276, China Postdoctoral Science Foundation No. 2015m570770, Chongqing Postdoctoral Science special Foundation No. Xm2015078, and Universities' Sci-tech Achievements Transformation Project of Chongqing No. KJZH17104, Chongqing grand R&D projects Nos. cstc2017zdcy-zdyf0120 and cstc2017rgzn-zdyf0118. Yunni Xia and Wanbo Zheng are the corresponding authors of this work.

References

1. World Energy Outlook 2013 Fact Sheet. http://www.tp-ontrol.hu/index.php/TP_Toolbox
2. Varasteh, A., Goudarzi, M.: Server consolidation techniques in virtualized datacenters: a survey. IEEE Syst. J. **11**(2), 772–783 (2017)
3. Beloglazov, A., Buyya, R.: Adaptive threshold-based approach for energy-efficient consolidation of virtual machines in cloud datacenters. In: Proceedings of the 8th International Workshop on middleware for Grids, Clouds and e-Science ACM, pp. 1–6 (2010)
4. Beloglazov, A., Buyya, R.: Optimal online deterministic algorithms and adaptive heuristics for energy and performance efficient dynamic consolidation of virtual machines in cloud datacenters. Concurr. Comput. Pract. Exp. **24**, 1397–1420 (2012)
5. Huang, Z., Tsang, D.H.K.: M-Convex VM consolidation: towards a better VM workload consolidation. IEEE Transact. Cloud Comput. **4**, 415–428 (2016)
6. Murtazaev, A., Oh, S.: Sercon: server consolidation algorithm using live migration of virtual machines for green computing. IETE Techn. Rev. **28**(3), 212–231 (2011)
7. Farahnakian, F., et al.: Using ant colony system to consolidate VMs for green cloud computing. IEEE Transact. Serv. Comput. **8**, 187–198 (2015)
8. Wu, Q., Ishikawa, F., Zhu, Q., Xia, Y.: Energy and migration cost-aware dynamic virtual machine consolidation in heterogeneous cloud datacenters. IEEE Transact. Serv. Comput. **1**(1), 99 (2016)
9. Zhang, Q., Zhani, M.F., Boutaba, R., Hellerstein, J.L.: Dynamic heterogeneity-aware resource provisioning in the cloud. IEEE Transact. Cloud Comput. **2**, 14–28 (2015)
10. Duan, H., et al.: Energy-aware scheduling of virtual machines in heterogeneous cloud computing systems. Future Gener. Comput. Syst. **74**, 142–150 (2017)
11. Bharathi, P.D., Prakash, P., Kiran, M.V.K.: Energy efficient strategy for task allocation and VM consolidation in cloud environment. In: 2017 Innovations in Power and Advanced Computing Technologies, i-PACT 2017, pp. 1–6, January 2017
12. Guo, L., et al.: A game based consolidation method of virtual machines in cloud datacenters with energy and load constraints. IEEE Access. **6**, 4664–4676 (2018)
13. Paul, A.K., Sahoo, B.: Dynamic virtual machine placement in cloud computing. Indian J. Sci. Technol. 9(29) (2015)
14. Xue, F., Wu, Z.: Cloud tasks coalitional game scheduling based on merge and split mechanism. Comput. Eng. Des. (2018)
15. Guazzone, M., Anglano, C., Sereno, M.: A game-theoretic approach to coalition formation in green cloud federations. In: IEEE/ACM International Symposium on Cluster, Cloud and Grid Computing IEEE, pp. 618–625 (2014)
16. Guo, M., Guan, Q., Ke, W.: Optimal scheduling of VMs in queueing cloud computing systems with a heterogeneous workload. IEEE Access. **6**, 15178–15191 (2018)

17. Ruiu, P., et al.: Workload management for power efficiency in heterogeneous datacenters. In: Proceedings - 2016 10th International Conference on Complex, Intelligent, and Software Intensive Systems, CISIS 2016, pp. 23–30 (2016)
18. Park, K., Pai, V.S.: CoMon: a mostly-scalable monitoring system for PlanetLab. ACM SIGOPS Oper. Syst. Rev. **40**(1), 65–74 (2006)
19. Energy Star Computer Server Qualified Product List. https://www.energystar. gov/ia/products/prod_lists/enterprise_servers_p_prod_list.xls
20. Xu, M., Tian, W., Buyya, R.: A survey on load balancing algorithms for virtual machines placement in cloud computing. Concur. Comput. Pract. Exp. **29**(1), e4123 (2016)
21. Myerson, R.B.: Game Theory, Analysis of Conflict. Harvard University Press, Cambridge (1991)
22. Saad, W., Han, Z., Debbah, M., Hjorungnes, A., Basar, T.: Coalitional game theory for communication networks: a tutorial. IEEE Sig. Process. Mag. **26**(5), 77–97 (2009)

An Efficient Traceable and Anonymous Authentication Scheme for Permissioned Blockchain

Qianqian Su[1,2], Rui Zhang[1,2(✉)], Rui Xue[1,2], and You Sun[1,2]

[1] State Key Laboratory of Information Security,
Institute of Information Engineering, Chinese Academy of Sciences,
Beijing 100093, China
{suqianqian,zhangrui,xuerui,sunyou}@iie.ac.cn
[2] School of Cyber Security, University of Chinese Academy of Sciences,
Beijing 100049, China

Abstract. Blockchain has become a hot topic in recent years. Many applications apply permissioned blockchain to achieve secure data sharing across organizations such as healthcare blockchain. In the permissioned blockchain, on the one hand, the blockchain system is required to support efficient and dynamic authentication for adding and deleting users in a distributed environment. On the other hand, in some particular applications such as healthcare domain, users prefer to keep anonymity in the process of authentication. Although many solutions for anonymous authentication have been proposed, they often require the participation of a central trusted party in the process of authentication and are not efficient enough. In this paper, we focus on designing an efficient traceable and anonymous authentication scheme, which supports efficient authentication while without revealing user's identity information and does not requires the participation of a central trusted party. While, in case of dispute, the identity of users can be revealed. Moreover, the proposed scheme is able to support dynamic adding and deleting users. Finally, we analyze the security and privacy properties of the proposed scheme and evaluate its performance in terms of computational cost. The experimental results show that the proposed scheme is more efficient than exist schemes and can be easily deployed in the permissioned blockchain.

Keywords: Authentication · Anonymous · Traceable · Permissioned blockchain

1 Introduction

Recently, blockchain [13] as a breaking new technology attracts more and more attention to academia and industry due to its decentralization and tamper-proof characteristics. Permissioned blockchain is one type of blockchain. Unlike the

J. Miller et al. (Eds.): ICWS 2019, LNCS 11512, pp. 110–125, 2019.
https://doi.org/10.1007/978-3-030-23499-7_8

permissionless blockchain [11], permissioned blockchain such as R3 [7], Hyper-Ledger fabric [2], Ripple [3], FISCO [1] requires trusted nodes to authorize permissions to users to read information stored on the blockchain. One important application of permissioned blockchain is that it can achieve data sharing among authorized users.

Consider the following scenario: users (nodes) from different organizations, such as healthcare centers, pharmacies, insurance companies, researchers, and patients, maintain a permissioned blockchain together to share electric healthcare records (EHRs). One key challenge in this scenario is efficiently authenticating users from different organizations in a distributed network. Apparently, the traditional authentication schemes, which requires a central trusted party to authenticate users, cannot be directly applied in this scenario. Moreover, users usually prefer to keep their identity anonymity in the process of authentication. For example, a patient is willing to share his EHRs with other healthcare providers and researchers, but he does not want to blockchain provider and other users to know his real identity. While, in the event of a medical incident or dispute, users' identity can be revealed.

Our goal is to design an efficient traceable and anonymous authentication scheme that can be applied to the permissioned blockchain. To achieve this goal, the following problems should be taken into consideration. (1) The authentication scheme used in permissioned blockchain should be implemented in a distributed manner. Unlike the centralized manner in which a central authentication entity is needed in the authentication phase, the identity of users should be verified without the help of the central authority. (2) In order to protect the privacy of users, the anonymous property should be supported in the authentication scheme. (3) The system should support dynamic adding and revocation of users after system has been initialized.

The main contributions of this paper can be summarized as follows. We present a novel authentication scheme for permissioned blockchain which can efficiently achieve anonymous authentication without the participant of a central trusted party. The real identity of users can be revealed when disputed occurs. The proposed scheme also can support dynamic joining and revocation of users after the system has been initialized. The experimental results show that the proposed scheme is more efficient than exist schemes and can be easily deployed in the permissioned blockchain.

2   Related Work

Numerous anonymous authentication protocols have been proposed. In general, researches on anonymous authentication schemes are classifies into two types: three-party (password, smart card and biometric) schemes [5,6,16,18] and two-party (password and smart card) schemes [8,10,14,15,17].

Zhu et al. [18] proposed a three-party authentication scheme but the proposed scheme failed to provide user anonymity and backward secrecy, and it is susceptible to forgery attack. Gope et al. [5] proposed an efficient scheme which fulfilled strong user anonymity but it requires large storage to store pseudo-identities. Moreover, it is not secure against desynchronization attack and DoS attack because users require to update their pseudo-identities. Wu et al. [16] proposed a scheme which fulfilled strong user anonymity and strong key establishment property but it is not secure against desynchronization attack due to the pseudo-identity of users need to update. Meanwhile, some two-party schemes were also proposed, but their computational costs were very high. Ni et al. proposed an anonymous mutual authentication protocol by utilizing the BBS+ signature in [10], but their scheme cannot protect the privacy of user. Yang et al. introduced the concept of two-party anonymous authentication scheme, and proposed a pseudo-identity-based authentication scheme in [17]. Unfortunately, the proposed scheme is vulnerable to private key reveal attack and has heavy computation overhead at users side. Jo et al. proposed an efficient pseudo-identity two-party authentication scheme in [15]. Their scheme employs signcryption to minimize the number of pseudo-identities stored on users side.

These existing anonymous authentication schemes are difficult to be applied to the distributed permissioned blockchains scenario for the following reasons. First of all, in the three-party authentication schemes, the third trusted parity participates in the authentication process. If this connection is interfered and broken by an adversary, corresponding users cannot get successful access of their services. Secondly, users requires a huge storage capacity to store all corresponding public keys of group managers in advance, since those schemes employ cryptography methods to help users authenticate the group manager. Without knowing these public keys of group managers, the user cannot verify the signatures generated by a group manager during authentication. In addition, group managers require multiple interactions with each other, since they need to download and update its whole revocation list or other parameters from the other group managers periodically.

3   Preliminaries

In this section, we review some preliminary cryptography knowledge, including bilinear map, Discrete Logarithm (DL) problem, q-SDH problem, Bonen-Boyens SDH equivalence, Forking Lamma and anonymous authentication.

3.1   Bilinear Pairings

Let G_1, G_2 and G_T be three multiplicative cyclic groups of the order q, where q is a large prime number. Let g_1, g_2 be the generator of G_1 and G_2, respectively. We say a map $e : G_1 \times G_2 \to G_T$ is a bilinear pairing if it satisfies:

(1) Bilinearity: For any $P \in G_1, Q \in G_2$ and $a, b \in Z_q^*$, $e(P_1^a, Q_1^b) = e(P_1, Q_1)^{ab}$.
(2) Non-degeneracy: Whenever g_1 is a generator of G_1 and g_2 is a generator of G_2, $e(g_1, g_2) \neq 1$.
(3) Computability: There is an efficient algorithm to compute $e(P, Q)$ for any $P \in G_1, Q \in G_2$.

A bilinear parameter generator $\mathcal{G}en$ is a probabilistic algorithm that takes a security parameter k as input and outputs $(q, G_1, G_2, G_T, e, g_1, g_2)$ as bilinear parameters.

3.2 Discrete Logarithm (DL) Problem

For $x \in Z_q^*$, given $g, g^x \in G_1$ as input, output x. The DL assumption in G_1 holds if it is computationally infeasible to solve the DL problem in G_1.

3.3 q-SDH Problem

Takes $(q+2)$ tuple $(g_1, g_2, g_2^\gamma, ..., g_2^{\gamma^q})$ as the input, output a SDH pair and that equals $(g_1^{1/(x+\gamma)}, x)$ where $x \in Z_p^*$. If $|Pr[A(g_1, g_2, g_2^\gamma, ..., g_2^{\gamma^q}) = (g_1^{1/\gamma+x}, x)] \geq \epsilon$, the algorithm A has an advantage ε in solving $q-SDH$ in (G_1, G_2). This problem is considered hard to solve in polynomial time and ϵ should be negligible.

3.4 Bonen-Boyens SDH Equivalence

Given a $q-SDH$ instance $(g_1, g_2, g_2^\gamma, ..., g_2^{\gamma^q})$, and then applying the Boneh and Boyen's Lemma found in [4] we could obtain $g_1 \in G_1$, $g_2 \in G_2$, $w = g_2^\gamma$ and $(q-1)$ SDH pairs (A_i, x_i) (such that $e(A_i, wg_2^{x_i}) = e(g_1, g_2)$) for each i. Any SDH pair besides these $(q-1)$ ones can be transformed into a solution to the original q-SDH instance.

3.5 The Forking Lamma

Given only public data as input, if an adversary $\mathcal{A}$ with polynomial computation ability can find a valid signature $(M, \delta_0, c, \delta_1)$ with non-negligible probability, then there exists a replay with a different oracle, which can output new valid signatures $(M, \delta_0, c', \delta_1')$ with non-negligible probability where $c \neq c'$.

3.6 Anonymous Authentication

The anonymous authentication scheme [9] consists of the following algorithms:

- **Setup** (1^k). Takes security parameter k as input, outputs the system parameters *params*, the master private key $msk = \{u, v\}$, the master public key $mpk = \{U_1, U_2, V_1\}$, and a hash function H.
- **KeyGen** $(params, msk, i)$. Takes parameters *params*, master private key msk and the identity of user i as inputs, outputs an anonymous key $AK_i = (s_i, S_i)$ for user i.
- **PseudoGen** $(params, AK)$. Takes parameters *params* and anonymous key AK as inputs, outputs temporary private keys $(x_1, x_2, ..., x_l)$ and corresponding public keys $(Y_1, Y_2, ..., Y_l)$.

- **Sign** $(params, S, x, Y, m)$. Takes parameters $params$, an anonymous key AK, a temporary private key pairs (x, Y) and message m as inputs, generates an anonymous certification $Cert$ and a signature σ as outputs.
- **Verify** $(params, m, \sigma, Cert)$. Takes parameters $params$, the message m, certification $Cert$ and signature σ as inputs, output 1 if $Cert$ and σ is valid, or output $\perp$ otherwise.
- **Open** $(params, msk, Cert)$. Takes parameters $params$, master private key msk and certification $Cert$ as inputs, output the identity of user i.

4 Definitions

4.1 System Model

The model of the proposed scheme involves a trusted third party (TTP) and N organizations. Each organization contains a control center (CCenter), an authentication dealing module (ADM) and M users. For clarity and without loss of generality, we simplify the system model with only one TTP and two organizations, and each organization contains a user, as shown in Fig. 1.

- *Organization (Org)*: Organization is the participant of the system and maintainer of the permissioned blockchain. These organizations can be hospitals, Banks or companies. Every organization contains a control center (CCenter), an authentication dealing module (ADM) and M users.
- *Trusted Third Party (TTP)*: TTP is assumed powered with sufficient resources, and fully trusted by all organizations. The main tasks of TTP are (1) managing the registration of the organization, joining and revoking, (2) generating and distributing private key pairs (sk, pk) for CCenters. It's worth mentioning that TTP will remain offline after initialization until there is an organization joining or revoking.
- *Control Center (CCenter)*: CCenter is the manager of an organization. CCenter is responsible for (1) generating public parameters and master private keys, and (2) managing the registration of users, joining and revoking.
- *Authentication Dealing Module (ADM)*: ADM is responsible for handling the authentication process, including verify the identity and generate the request response.

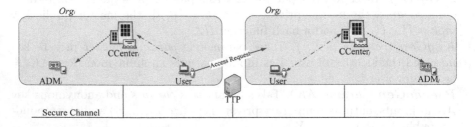

Fig. 1. System model

- *Users*: Users access to organizations to obtain some services or data. In this paper, we consider the scenario where a user requests services or data from other organizations within the system.

4.2   Formal Definition of the Proposed Scheme

In this section, we formally define the algorithms that form the proposed scheme.

Definition 1: A traceable and anonymous authentication scheme consists of the following algorithms:

- **SSetup**(λ, ID_{Org}) is an algorithm run by TTP. Taking a security parameter λ and the identity of the Org as the input, this algorithm outputs private key pairs (pk, sk) for $CCenter$ belongs to ID_{Org}.
- **CSetup**(λ, pk, sk) is an algorithm run by $CCenter$. Taking a security parameter λ and key pairs (sk, pk) generated by TTP as the input, each $CCenter$ outputs the system parameters gpk, the master private key $gmsk$, and the partial key Δ.
- **KeyGen**$(gpk, gmsk, U)$ is an algorithm run by $CCenter$. Taking the system parameters gpk, the master private key $gmsk$ and the users identity U as the input. This algorithm outputs an authorized anonymous key ASK for U.
- **ProofGen**(gpk, M, ASK, Δ) is an algorithm run by the user U. Taking the system parameters gpk, a message M, the authorized anonymous key ASK of the user U and the partial key Δ as the input, this algorithm outputs a certification $Cert$ on the message M.
- **ProofVer**$(gpk, M, Cert, \Delta)$ is an algorithm run by ADM. Taking the system parameters gpk, the certification $Cert$, the signature σ, the partial key Δ, and the message M as the input, this algorithm outputs $true$ for a valid proof $Cert$ and $false$ otherwise.
- **Reveal**$(gpk, gmsk, Cert)$ is an algorithm run by $CCenter$. Taking the system parameters gpk, the master private key $gmsk$ and the certification $Cert$ as the input, this algorithm outputs an identity for a valid certification or $false$ otherwise.
- **KeyUpdate**$(gpk, gmsk)$ is an algorithm run by $CCenter$. Taking the system parameters gpk and the master private key $gmsk$ as the input, this algorithm outputs the partial key Δ.

We say that a traceable and anonymous authentication scheme is correct, meaning that for any message M, any non-revoked user U registered to $CCenter$ belonging to a non-revoked organization ID_{Org}, if $(pk, sk) \leftarrow$ **SSetup**(λ, ID_{Org}), $(gpk, gmsk, \Delta) \leftarrow$ **CSetup**(λ, pk, sk), $ASK \leftarrow$ **KeyGen**$(gpk, gmsk, U)$, $Cert \leftarrow$ **ProofGen**(gpk, M, ASK, Δ), then **ProofVer**$(gpk, M, Cert, \Delta) \rightarrow true$.

4.3   Security Definitions

In this section, we formally define the security prosperities that must be required to the proposed scheme.

Definition 2 (Anonymity): A traceable and anonymous authentication scheme is anonymity if the advantage of the success probability of any polynomial-time adversary $\mathcal{A}$ in the following experiment is negligible.

- **Setup:** The adversary $\mathcal{A}$ chooses an organization labeled as ID_{Org}, and the TTP runs $(pk, sk) \leftarrow$ **SSetup**(λ, ID_{Org}), The $CCenter$ runs $(gpk, gmsk, \Delta) \leftarrow$ **CSetup**(λ, pk, sk). Give the public parameters $(pk, gpk, ID_{Org}, \Delta)$ to the adversary $\mathcal{A}$.
- **KeyGen Query:**
  (1) The adversary $\mathcal{A}$ chooses a user U_i and issues it to the challenger C.
  (2) The challenger C maintain a query list (initialize as empty) to save the queried user's identity and its ASK. After receiving U_i from the adversary $\mathcal{A}$, if U_i is in the query list, the challenger C obtain its ASK_i. Otherwise, the challenger C runs $ASK_i \leftarrow$ **KeyGen**$(gpk, gmsk, U_i)$, and adds (U_i, ASK_i) to the query list.
  (3) After that, the challenger C sends ASK_i to the adversary $\mathcal{A}$.
- **ProofGen Query:**
  (1) The adversary $\mathcal{A}$ chooses a user U_i and a message M, and issues it to the challenger C.
  (2) If U_i is in the query list, the challenger C runs $Cert \leftarrow$ **ProofGen**(gpk, M, ASK_i, Δ), and sends $Cert$ to the adversary $\mathcal{A}$. If U_i is not in the query list, the challenger C runs $ASK_i \leftarrow$ **KeyGen**$(gpk, gmsk, U_i)$, and adds (U_i, ASK_i) to the query list. After that, the challenger C runs $Cert \leftarrow$ **ProofGen**(gpk, M, ASK_i, Δ), and sends $Cert$ to the adversary $\mathcal{A}$.
- **Challenge:**
  (1) The adversary $\mathcal{A}$ sends a message m^*, and two identities U_0 and U_1 to the challenger C.
  (2) The challenger C randomly chooses a bit $b \in \{0, 1\}$, runs $ASK_b \leftarrow$ **KeyGen**$(gpk, gmsk, U_b)$ and $Cert_b \leftarrow$ **ProofGen**$(gpk, m^*, ASK_b, \Delta)$.
  (3) The challenger C sends $Cert_b$ to the adversary $\mathcal{A}$.
- **Guess:** After receiving $Cert_b$, the adversary $\mathcal{A}$ outputs a guess b'.

We say the adversary $\mathcal{A}$ succeeds, if $b' = b$. Otherwise, the adversary $\mathcal{A}$ fails.

Definition 3 (Traceability): We say that a traceable and anonymous authentication scheme is traceable, meaning that for any message M, any non-revoked user U registered to $CCenter$ belonging to a non-revoked organization, if $(pk, sk) \leftarrow$ **SSetup**(λ, ID_{Org}), $(gpk, gmsk, \Delta) \leftarrow$ **CSetup**(λ, pk, sk), $ASK \leftarrow$ **KeyGen**$(gpk, gmsk, U)$, $Cert \leftarrow$ **ProofGen**(gpk, M, ASK, Δ), then **Reveal**$(gpk, gmsk, Cert) \rightarrow U$.

Definition 4 (Unlinkability): A traceable and anonymous authentication scheme is unlinkability if the advantage of the success probability of any polynomial-time adversary $\mathcal{A}$ in the following experiment is negligible.

- **Setup:** The setup is the same as in Definition 2.
- **KeyGen Query:** The keygen query is the same as in Definition 2.
- **ProofGen Query:** The proofgen query is the same as in Definition 2.
- **Challenge:**
  (1) The adversary $\mathcal{A}$ sends a message m^*, and two identities U_0 and U_1 to the challenger C.
  (2) The challenger C randomly chooses a bit $b \in \{0, 1\}$, runs $ASK_b \leftarrow$ **Key-Gen**$(gpk, gmsk, U_b)$ and $Cert_b \leftarrow$ **ProofGen**$(gpk, m^*, ASK_b, \Delta)$. And the challenger C randomly chooses a bit $b' \in \{0, 1\}$, runs $ASK_{b'} \leftarrow$ **Key-Gen**$(gpk, gmsk, U_{b'})$ and $Cert_{b'} \leftarrow$ **ProofGen**$(gpk, m^*, ASK_{b'}, \Delta)$.
  (3) The challenger C sends $Cert_b$ and $Cert_{b'}$ to the adversary $\mathcal{A}$.
- **Guess:** After receiving $Cert_b$ and $Cert_{b'}$, the adversary $\mathcal{A}$ outputs a guess *yes* or *no*.

We say the adversary $\mathcal{A}$ succeeds, if $b' = b$ and the adversary A output *yes*, or $b' \neq b$ and the adversary A outputs *no*.

Definition 5 (Unforgeability): A traceable and anonymous authentication scheme is unforgeability if the success probability of any polynomial-time adversary $\mathcal{A}$ in the following experiment is negligible.

- **Setup:** The setup is the same as in Definition 2.
- **KeyGen Query:** The keygen query is the same as in Definition 2.
- **ProofGen Query:** The proofgen query is the same as in Definition 2.
- **Forge:** The adversary $\mathcal{A}$ generates a forged certification $Cert^*$ based on a never queried m^* and U^*, and sends the forged certification $Cert^*$ to the challenger C.
- **Output:** The challenger C runs the **Reveal**$(gpk, gmsk, Cert)$ algorithm. If **Reveal**$(gpk, gmsk, Cert)$ returns U_i which has been queried, the challenger C outputs *false*. Otherwise, the challenger C runs the **ProofVer**$(gpk, M, Cert^*, \Delta)$ algorithm and outputs the result *true/false*.

We say the adversary $\mathcal{A}$ succeeds, if the challenger outputs *true* for the forged certification $Cert^*$.

5   The Proposed Scheme

5.1   Overview

In our proposed scheme, TTP generates private key pairs (pk, sk) for CCenters, and CCenter generates its system parameters gpk, master private key $gmsk$ and partial key Δ; meanwhile, it issues an authorized anonymous key ASK_i and a partial key Δ to user U_i. When U_i belonging to Org_i wants to access to Org_j, U_i generates the request message M and computes a certification $Cert$. After that, U_i sends $(M, Cert)$ to $Org_r (r = 1, 2, ..., N, r \neq i)$. On received $(M, Cert)$, the $ADM_r (r = 1, 2, ..., N, r \neq i)$ belonging to Org_r will check the valid of $Cert$. If the verification is passed and $r \neq j$, the ADM_r saves M in its local memory; if the verification is passed and $r = j$, the ADM_r not only saves M, but also generates response. Otherwise, the ADM_r reject the message. By leveraging anonymous authentication, the identity of U_i can be anonymously verified, and CCenter can use gpk and $gmsk$ to reveal the identity of U_i when a dispute occurs.

When Org_{new} wants to join in the system after system initialization, TTP invokes the **SSetup** algorithm to generate private key pairs (pk, sk) for it. Similarly, when U_{new} wants to join in Org, the $CCenter$ belonging to Org invokes the **KeyGen** algorithm for U_{new}. When Org_{exit} is revoked, TTP adds its label ID_{Org} the revoked list (RL) and publish its key pairs to unrevoked organizations. When U_{exit} is revoked, $CCenter$ invokes the **KeyUpdate** algorithm to obtain a new partial key Δ and publish it to non-revoked users. It should be noted that although TTP is introduced in our system, it cannot interrupt the authentication process for TTP will be offline after the system initialization unless there are organizations want to join in or leave out the system.

5.2   Details of the Proposed Scheme

In this section, we construct our proposed scheme, and show the details of the proposed scheme as follows.

SSetup(λ, ID_{Org}): TTP generates and distributes the private key pairs (sk, pk) for $CCenter$ belonging to Org. The private key pairs (sk, pk) is used to exchanges information between $CCenters$.

CSetup(λ, pk, sk): $CCenter$ generates the bilinear parameters $(q, G_1, G_2, G_T, e, g_1, g_2)$ by running $\mathcal{G}en$, chooses two random numbers $a, b \in Z_q^*$, a public collision-resistant hash function $H : \{0,1\}^* \rightarrow Z_q^*$, a signature scheme Π, a random value t_0, and computes $A_1 = g_1^a$, $A_2 = g_2^a$, $B = g_1^b$, $\Delta = g_1^{1/(H(t_0)+a)}$. After that, $gpk = (q, G_1, G_2, G_T, e, g_1, g_2, A_1, A_2, B, H, \Pi)$, $gmsk = (a, b)$.

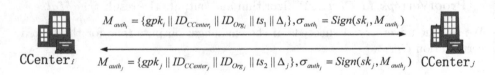

$$M_{auth_i} = \{gpk_i \| ID_{CCenter_i} \| ID_{Org_i} \| ts_1 \| \Delta_i\}, \sigma_{auth_i} = Sign(sk_i, M_{auth_i})$$

CCenter$_i$ $M_{auth_j} = \{gpk_j \| ID_{CCenter_j} \| ID_{Org_j} \| ts_2 \| \Delta_j\}, \sigma_{auth_j} = Sign(sk_j, M_{auth_j})$ **CCenter**$_j$

Fig. 2. Information exchange between CCenters

It is noted that $CCenter$ needs to exchange essential informations with each other, as shown in Fig. 2. $CCenter_i$ generates M_{auth_i} and signs it by $Sign(sk_i, M_{auth_i})$, where gpk_i is its system parameters, $ID_{CCenter_i}$ is its identity, ID_{Org_i} is its organization's label, ts is timestamps. Then, $CCenter_i$ sends M_{auth_i} and its signature to $CCenter_j (j \neq i)$. If ts is valid, and the signature is verified by $Verify(sk_i, M_{auth_i})$, M_{auth_i} will be stored in ADM_j by $CCenter_j$.

KeyGen$(gpk, gmsk, U)$: $CCenter$ selects a random number $s_i \in Z_q^*$ such that $s_i + a \neq 0 \ mod \ q$, and computes $S_i = g_1^{1/(s_i+a)}$. Let $ASK_i = (s_i, S_i)$,

$CCenter$ stores the tuple (U_i, S_i^a) in the user index table. After that, $CCenter$ sends (ASK_i, Δ_i) to the user U_i.

ProofGen(gpk, M, ASK, Δ): U_i first generates the access request M, where $M = \{ID_{Org_i}||ID_{Org_j}||operation||t_1\}$, ID_{Org_i} is the label of organization that U_i belongs to, ID_{Org_j} is the label of organization that U_i is going to communicate with, and t_1 is a timestamp. Then, U_i selects four random numbers $r, r_1, r_2, r_3 \in Z_q^*$, and computes:

$$T_1 = A_1^r, T_2 = S_i \cdot B^r, \delta = r \cdot s_i \bmod q, R_1 = A_1^{r_1}, R_2 = T_1^{r_2}/A_1^{r_3};$$
$$R_3 = e(T_2, g_2^{r_2})/e(B, A_2^{r_1} \cdot g_2^{r_3}), c = H(M, A_1, B, T_1, T_2, R_1, R_2, R_3, \Delta);$$
$$s_1 = (r_1 + c \cdot r) \bmod q, s_2 = (r_2 + c \cdot s_i) \bmod q, s_3 = (r_3 + c \cdot \delta) \bmod q.$$

After that, U_i sets $Cert = \{T_1||T_2||c||s_1||s_2||s_3\}$.

ProofVer$(gpk, M, \Delta, Cert)$: ADM_r first checks the valid of t_1. If t_1 is invalid, it rejects the message and outputs $false$. Otherwise, it computes:

$$R_1' = A_1^{s_1}/T_1^c, R_2' = T_1^{s_2}/A_1^{s_3}, R_3' = e(T_2, g_2^{s_2} \cdot A_2^c)/(e(B, A_2^{s_1} \cdot g_2^{s_3}) \cdot e(g_1, g_2^c)).$$

ADM_r checks $c = H(M', A_1, B, T_1', T_2', R_1', R_2', R_3', \Delta')$, where Δ' is $CCenter_i$ shared to $CCenter_r$ during the $CSetup$ phase. If the above equation holds, it outputs $true$ indicating that the proof is valid. Otherwise, it outputs $false$.

After the verification is passed, ADM_r checks ID_{Org_j}, if $r \neq j$, Org_r is not the organization that U_i wants to communicate to. Then ADM_r stores $M||Cert$; If $r = j$, ADM_r not only stores it, but also dealing with the request.

Reveal$(gpk, gmsk, Cert)$: The $CCenter$ computes $S_i^a = T_2^a/T_1^b$, and looks up the user index table corresponding to S_i^a. If (U_i, S_i^a) is in the user index table, it outputs U_i. Otherwise, it outputs $false$.

KeyUpdate$(gpk, gmsk)$: The $CCenter$ chooses a random value t_0' to compute a new partial key Δ, and publish it to non-revoked users and other $CCenters$. And then the non-revoked users and other $CCenters$ update their Δ.

Dynamic Join and Revocation: When an organization wants to join in the system after system initialization, TTP invokes the **SSetup** algorithm to generate private key pairs (pk, sk) for it. Similarly, when a user wants to join in an organization, the $CCenter$ belonging to the organization invokes the **KeyGen** algorithm for the user. And the $CCenter$ sends (ASK, Δ) to the user, where ASK is generated by invoking the **KeyGen** algorithm, and Δ is generated by **CSetup** algorithm during the system initialization.

As shown in Fig. 3, when an organization is revoked, TTP adds its label ID_{Org} to the revoked list (RL) and publish its key pairs to unrevoked organizations. When a user is revoked, the $CCenter$ invokes the **KeyUpdate** algorithm to obtain a new partial key Δ and publish the new Δ to non-revoked users. We illustrate this process in Fig. 4.

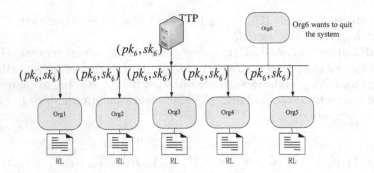

Fig. 3. Organization exit

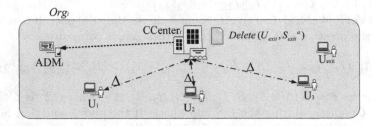

Fig. 4. User exit

6   Security and Performance Analyses

In this section, we first prove that the proposed scheme is correct and achieves the security requirements described in Sect. 4, and then evaluate the performance of the proposed scheme.

6.1   Security Analysis

Theorem 1 (Correctness). *If and only if the certificate Cert are valid, the request message can pass the authentication and be accepted.*

Proof. It is because the following equations hold:

$$R_1' = A_1^{s_1}/T_1^c = A_1^{r_1+c\cdot r}/A_1^{c\cdot r} = A^{r_1} = R_1 \tag{1}$$

$$R_2' = T_1^{s_2}/A_1^{s_3} = T_1^{r_2+c\cdot s_i}/A_1^{r_3+c\cdot \delta} = T_1^{r_2}/A_1^{r_3} = R_2 \tag{2}$$

$$
\begin{aligned}
R_3' &= \frac{e(T_2, g_2^{s_2} \cdot A_2^c)}{e(B, A_2^{s_1} \cdot g_2^{s_3}) \cdot e(g_1, g_2^c)} \\
&= \frac{e(T_2, g_2^{r_2})}{e(B, A_2^{r_1} \cdot g_2^{r_3})} \cdot \frac{e(S_i \cdot B^r, g_2^{c\cdot s_i} \cdot A_2^c)}{e(B, A_2^{c\cdot r} \cdot g_2^{c\cdot \delta}) \cdot e(g_1, g_2^c)} \\
&= \frac{e(T_2, g_2^{r_2})}{e(B, A_2^{r_1} \cdot g_2^{r_3})} = R_3
\end{aligned}
\tag{3}
$$

Theorem 2 (Traceability). *Each certification Cert generated by a registered user U_i belonging to Org, the identity of U_i can be traced by CCenter belonging to Org.*

Proof. If the $Cert$ is generates by a registered user U_i belonging to Org, then the $CCenter$ belonging to Org can get U_i's identity. It is because of $T_2^a/T_1^b = (S_i^a g_1^{r \cdot a \cdot b})/g_1^{r \cdot b \cdot a} = S_i^a$ holds. By looking up the user index table corresponding to S_i^a, $CCenter$ can obtain the identity of U_i.

Theorem 3 (Anonymity). *The proposed scheme is anonymity if DL assumption holds in (G_1, G_2).*

Proof. The adversary $\mathcal{A}$ gives $U_{i(0)}$, $U_{i(1)}$ and the message m to the challenger C, and the challenger C chooses a random toss $b \in \{0, 1\}$, and generates $Cert_b$. Give $Cert_b$ to the adversary $\mathcal{A}$, where $Cert_b = \{T_{1(b)} \| T_{2(b)} \| c_{(b)} \| s_{1(b)} \| s_{2(b)} \| s_{3(b)}\}$, $b \in \{0, 1\}$. If the advantage that the adversary $\mathcal{A}$ with polynomial computation ability to guess the correct b is negligible, the proposed scheme is said to be anonymity.

Suppose that adversary $\mathcal{A}$ can break the anonymity of the proposed scheme, and then it means the adversary $\mathcal{A}$ has a non-negligible advantage to guess the correct b in the above statement. More specifically, given $U_{i(0)}$ and $U_{i(1)}$ and the message m, the adversary $\mathcal{A}$ has a non-negligible advantage to distinguish the tuple $Cert_0$ from $Cert_1$. From the proposed scheme, we have $Cert_0 = \{T_{1(0)} \| T_{2(0)} \| c_{(0)} \| s_{1(0)} \| s_{2(0)} \| s_{3(0)}\}$, $Cert_1 = \{T_{1(1)} \| T_{2(1)} \| c_{(1)} \| s_{1(1)} \| s_{2(1)} \| s_{3(1)}\}$, where $T_{1(i)} = A_1^{r(i)}$, $T_{2(i)} = S_i B^{r(i)}$, $c = H(m, A_1, B, T_{1(i)}, T_{2(i)}, R_{1(i)}, R_{2(i)}, R_{3(i)}, \Delta)$, and $r_{(i)}, s_{1(i)}, s_{2(i)}, s_{3(i)}$ are randomized values for $i = \{0, 1\}$.

If the adversary $\mathcal{A}$ has the ability to distinguish $Cert_0$ from $Cert_1$, it means $\mathcal{A}$ break DL problem, and it contradicts with DL assumption. Thus, it is impossible for $\mathcal{A}$ to distinguish $Cert_0$ from $Cert_1$ with a non-negligible probability, and the proposed scheme is anonymous.

Theorem 4 (Unforgeability). *The proposed scheme is unforgeability if SDH is hard in (G_1, G_2).*

Proof. Given a forged certification $Cert^*$ based on a message m^*, where $Cert^* = \{T_1 \| T_2 \| c_b \| s_1 \| s_2 \| s_3\}$. The probability that **ProofVer**$(gpk, m^*, Cert^*, \Delta)$ outputs *true* is negligible.

Suppose the adversary $\mathcal{A}$ can forge a certification $Cert^* = \{T_1 \| T_2 \| c_b \| s_1 \| s_2 \| s_3\}$ on message m^*. Let $M = m^*$, $\delta_0 = \{T_1, T_2\}$, $\delta_1 = \{s_1, s_2, s_3\}$ and $c = c_{(b)}$. The valid $Cert$ on m^* can be viewed as a tuple $<M, \delta_0, c, \delta_1>$. According to Forking Lemma, we can extract a tuple $<\delta_0, c', \delta_1'>$ from $<\delta_0, c, \delta_1>$, where $c' \neq c$. Thus we can create a new SDH tuple denoted as (s_i', S_i') without the knowledge of a.

Using the two tuple $< \delta_0, c', \delta_1' >$ from $< \delta_0, c, \delta_1 >$, we could extract a new SDH tuple, Let $\Delta c = c - c'$, $\Delta s_1 = s_1 - s_1'$, $\Delta s_2 = s_2 - s_2'$ and $\Delta s_3 = s_3 - s_3'$. Divide the two instance of the equations used previously in proving correctness of the proposed scheme. One instance with c' and the other is with c to get the following:

- Dividing $T_1^c/T_1^{c'} = A_1^{s_1}/A_1^{s_1'}$ we get $A_1^{r'} = T_1$, where $r' = \Delta s_1/\Delta c$.
- Dividing $T_1^{s_2}/T_1^{s_2'} = A_1^{s_3}/A_1^{s_3'}$ we get $\Delta s_3 = r'\Delta s_2$.
- Diving $(e(g_1, g_2)/e(T_2, A_2))^{\Delta c}$ will lead to

$$e(T_2, g_2)^{\Delta s_2} e(B, A_2)^{-r'\Delta c} e(B, g_2)^{-r'\Delta s_2} = (e(g_1, g_2)/e(T_2, A_2))^{\Delta c}$$

Letting $s_i' = \Delta s_2/\Delta c$, we get

$$e(g_1, g_2)/e(T_2, A_2) = e(T_2, g_2)^{s_i'} e(B, g_2)^{-r'} e(B, g_2)^{-r's_i'}$$

This could be rearranged as $e(g_1, g_2) = e(T_2 B^{-r'}, A_2 g_2^{s_i'})$. Let $S_i' = T_2 B^{-r'}$, we get $e(S_i', A_2 g_2^{s_i'}) = e(g_1, g_2)$. Hence, we obtain a new SDH pair (s_i', S_i') breaking Boneh and Boyens theorem. Thus, it is impossible for the adversary $\mathcal{A}$ to generates a forged certification $Cert^*$ and the certification can pass the verification. Thus, the proposed scheme is unforgeability.

Theorem 5 (Unlinkability). *The proposed scheme is unlinkability if DL assumption holds in (G_1, G_2).*

Proof. Unlinkability is covered through full anonymity. If the scheme was linkable, the adversary of the anonymity game can query a proof of U_i and later in the challenge phase include U_i among the users he wants to be challenged upon. The adversary does not to guess the generator of the proof he obtains in the challenge phase, because he can just link it thus breaking full anonymity.

In other words, similarly to the proof in Theorem 3, given U_0 and U_1 and the message m, the challenger response $Cert_b$ and $Cert_{b'}$ to the adversary $\mathcal{A}$, where $b \in \{0, 1\}$ and $b' \in \{0, 1\}$. If the scheme was linkable, the adversary $\mathcal{A}$ has non-negligible advantage to guess whether $b = b'$. It means that the adversary $\mathcal{A}$ has the ability to distinguish $Cert_0$ from $Cert_1$ by solving DL problem, and it contradicts with DL assumption. Thus, it is impossible for $\mathcal{A}$ to guess whether $b = b'$ with a non-negligible probability, and the proposed scheme is unlinkability.

6.2   Performance Analysis

We first analyze the overhead of the proposed scheme for proof generation, proof verifies, identity reveal and dynamic join and revocation. And then, we make the experimental evaluation of the proposed scheme.These experiments are carried out on a Linux machine with an Intel Pentium processor of 2.70 GHz and 8 GB memory.

To generate the proof, the user needs to conduct 1 hash operation, 3 additions, 2 divisions, 6 multiplications, 7 exponentiations in G_1, 3 exponentiations in G_2, 2 bilinear pairings and 1 division in G_T. To verify the proof, ADM needs to conducts 1 hash operation, 2 divisions, 3 multiplications, 5 exponentiations in G_1, 5 exponentiations in G_2, 4 bilinear pairings and 1 division in G_T. When a new organization wants to join in the system, TTP needs to distribute key pairs for it. When an organization wants to leave out the system, TTP needs to add its key pairs to revoked list (RL) and distribute RL to unrevoked organizations. When a new user wants to join an organization, the $CCenter$ needs to conduct 1 exponentiation in G_1. When a user wants to leave out its organization, the $CCenter$ needs to conduct 1 eFan2016AFan2016Axponentiation in G_1.

Next, we show the experimental evaluation of the proposed scheme. Firstly, We present the time cost of key generation in Fig. 5. The X-axis presents the number of users. The Y-axis represents the corresponding time overhead. Figure 6 shows that the time cost in proof generation, verifying and identity revealing. The X-axis presents the number of certificate should be generate (verified/revealing). The Y-axis represents the corresponding time overhead. Figure 7 presents the time cost of user join and revocation. The X-axis represents the number of added (revoked) users, and the Y-axis represents the time cost. As described in dynamic join and revocation phase, when a new user joins, there is no impact on the old users for it is only needed that $CCenter$ computes ASK and sends (ASK, Δ) to the new user. Therefore, the time cost only happens in $CCenter$ side. When the user exit, it is needed that $CCenter$ generates a new Δ and sends it to unrevoked users.

In Fig. 8, we compare the time cost of certification generation with the scheme in [12]. It is should note that the scheme in [12] is designed to enable data sharing for the same group in the cloud. Shen's scheme [12] uses group signature to achieve anonymity and traceability. Therefore, we illustrate the efficiency of our scheme by comparing our scheme with [12]. The X-axis presents the number of generated certificate. The Y-axis represents the corresponding time overhead. From Fig. 8, we can see that the time cost of our scheme is more smaller than that of [12]. Figure 9 shows the time cost of verifying in [12] and our proposed scheme. The X-axis presents the number of verified authentication. The Y-axis represents the time cost. From Figs. 8 and 9, it is easily observed that the proposed scheme has advantages in terms of efficiency authentication.

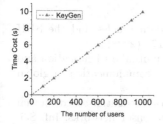

Fig. 5. The time cost of key generation

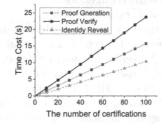

Fig. 6. The time cost of proof generation, verification and identity reveal

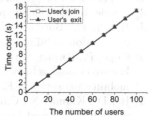

Fig. 7. The time cost of users join and revocation

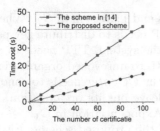
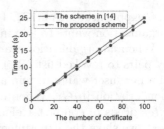

Fig. 8. The comparison of the time cost of generation

Fig. 9. The comparison of the time cost of verify

7   Conclusion

In this paper, we design a traceable and anonymous authentication scheme with high security and efficiency for permissioned blockchain. In the proposed scheme, an organization can efficiently verify the identity of users in a distributed and anonymous manner. Besides, the proposed scheme can support the traceability of user. In terms of dynamic change in organizations or users, we design an efficient and secure method that supports dynamic joining and revocation for organizations and users. The results of the security and performance analyses demonstrate that the proposed scheme can achieve the required security requirements and achieve efficient authentication.

Acknowledgment. The authors acknowledge the support from National Key R&D Program of China under Grant No.2017YFB1400700 and National Natural Science Foundation of China under Grant No.: 61472414, 61772514, 61602061.

References

1. Fisco. https://en.wikipedia.org/wiki/FISCO
2. Hyperledger. https://www.hyperledger.org
3. Ripple. https://en.wikipedia.org/wiki/Ripple
4. Boneh, D., Boyen, X.: Short signatures without random oracles and the SDH assumption in bilinear groups. J. Cryptol. **21**(2), 149–177 (2008)
5. Gope, P., Hwang, T.: Lightweight and energy-efficient mutual authentication and key agreement scheme with user anonymity for secure communication in global mobility networks. IEEE Syst. J. **10**, 1–10 (2015)
6. He, D., Kumar, N., Chilamkurti, N.: A secure temporal-credential-based mutual authentication and key agreement scheme for wireless sensor networks. Inf. Sci. **321**, 1–6 (2013)
7. Higgins, S.: Inside R3CEV's plot to bring distributed ledgers to wall street. https://www.coindesk.com/r3cev-distributed-ledger-wall-street
8. Lai, C., Li, H., Liang, X., Lu, R., Zhang, K., Shen, X.: CPAL: A conditional privacy-preserving authentication with access linkability for roaming service. Internet Things J. IEEE **1**, 46–57 (2014)

9. Lu, R., Lin, X., Luan, T.H., Liang, X., Shen, X.: Pseudonym changing at social spots: an effective strategy for location privacy in vanets. Veh. Technol. IEEE Transact. **61**, 86–96 (2012)
10. Ni, J., Zhang, K., Lin, X., Yang, H., Shen, X.: AMA: Anonymous mutual authentication with traceability in carpooling systems. pp. 1–6, May 2016
11. Satoshi, N.: A peer-to-peer electronic cash system (2008)
12. Shen, J., Zhou, T., Chen, X., Li, J., Susilo, W.: Anonymous and traceable group data sharing in cloud computing. IEEE Transact. Inf. Forensics Secur. **13**, 1–1 (2017)
13. Swan, M.: Blockchain: Blueprint for a New Economy. O'Reilly Media, Sebastopol (2015)
14. Tsai, J.L., Lo, N.W., Wu, T.C.: Secure handover authentication protocol based on bilinear pairings. Wirel. Pers. Commun. **73**(3), 1037–1047 (2013)
15. Wang, D., Wang, P.: Two birds with one stone: two-factor authentication with security beyond conventional bound. IEEE Transact. Dependable Secure Comput. **15**, 1–22 (2016)
16. Wu, F., et al.: A novel and provably secure authentication and key agreement scheme with user anonymity for global mobility networks: a novel and provably secure authentication and key agreement scheme with user anonymity for global mobility networks. Sec. Commun. Netw. **9**, 3527–3542 (2016)
17. Yang, G., Huang, Q., Wong, D., Deng, X.: Universal authentication protocols for anonymous wireless communications. Trans. Wireless. Comm. **9**, 168–174 (2010)
18. Zhu, J., Ma, J.: A new authentication scheme with anonymity for wireless environments. IEEE Transact. Consum. Electron. **50**, 231–235 (2004)

A Web-Service to Monitor a Wireless Sensor Network

Rayanne M. C. Silveira[1]([✉]), Francisco P. R. S. Alves[1], Allyx Fontaine[2], and Ewaldo E. C. Santana[3]

[1] Departament of Electrical Engineering, Federal University of Maranhão, Maranhão, Brazil
rayanne.silveira@aluno.ecp.ufma.br
[2] Université de Guyane, UMR Espace-Dev, Cayenne, France
[3] Departament of Mathematics, State University of Maranhão, Maranhão, Brazil

Abstract. In recent years, the interest in the Internet of Things has been growing, and WSN is a promising technology that could be applied in many situations. Regardless of the nature of the application, WSNs are often used for data acquisition, to obtain information from an environment of interest, so it is essential to consider how this data will be made available to users. Over the last years, an increasing number of web services have been used to deal with databases and final users, providing familiar interfaces and multi-platform access to those data. To address this problem, our study proposes a web application based on MVC architecture to monitor, organize and manage devices and data in a wireless sensor network. Here, is presented a functional evaluation of the proposed system and a discussion regarding the test results.

1 Introduction

Currently, the use of Wireless Sensor Networks (WSNs) has been a recurrent topic in several studies describing the different types of problems in which this technology can be applied. WSNs are communication networks composed of devices that exchange information through a channel. Usually, there are three types of devices: routers, end devices and a coordinator [1].

This scientific interest affects positively the popularization of this technology, since, coupled with the advances in microelectronics, there has been a growth in the development of commercial technologies that can be used for the construction of WSNs [2]. With the emergence of these technologies, the use of WSNs and, mobile sensing in general, has approached real problems, becoming a viable alternative to solve several problems [3] such as distributed monitoring, automation, and data acquisition, for example.

Regardless of their application, WSNs have their operation based on specific sensors to carry out the readings expected by the designer and to transmit them from wireless technology. These networks can capture a physical state from different points and concentrate this information in a single point for analysis.

J. Miller et al. (Eds.): ICWS 2019, LNCS 11512, pp. 126–146, 2019.
https://doi.org/10.1007/978-3-030-23499-7_9

After data concentration, a microcontroller is generally used to export the data in a way that they can be processed and used to generate useful information.

Tools that simplify the access and reading of the data obtained are essential in applications in which the sensors that make the acquisition are in hard-to-access locations. In precision farming, for example, a field that has invested in the use of technologies to obtain information that optimizes its production process, it is often unfeasible to collect the information only in the place where the reading was carried out, because of logistical reasons or even because of the impossibility of interaction with the place. Several methods have been proposed to help precision farming to gather data, and with the proper analytic tools, the changes during the season can be monitored [4].

Among the various tools that can be used to export the data obtained by WSN, web applications have shown to be promising tools. Furthermore, they allow the tracking of data collection in real time. Composed of a database and a graphical interface, this tool makes access to the desired data simple by providing access via a computer or a smartphone via the internet.

To address the problem of accessing information obtained in WSNs, in this paper, we propose a web-service based on MVC (Model-View-Controller) architecture to monitor, organize and manage devices and data in a wireless sensor network. Here, a functional evaluation of the proposed system will be presented and the test results will also be discussed. This paper has two main goals: (i) develop a web application to monitor and manage the values generated by the network and (ii) describe the interaction between the WSN developed for testing and the proposed system. The main contribution is the MVC Web service that was used to organize all data collected by a WSN, using a friendly and intuitive interface, and make these data available for many researchers and, as a result, increase the number of soil temperature and moisture databases. The next section presents a few works that have a similar proposal. Section 3 describes the proposed system architecture and functionalities. Section 4 shows the implementation of the system. Section 5 describes the experimentation and the results of the validation process before we present our conclusions.

2 Related Work

It is well known that the acquisition of data is a fundamental step for the monitoring of environments of interest. However, only performing the acquisition is not enough; it is also essential to allow the user to have easy access to this information. In the Internet, when it comes to the application of certain things, like Wireless Sensor Networks, there are many challenges such as energy consumption, routing protocols and, one of the biggest challenges: storing and interpretation of the data generated in those applications [5].

Something relevant is to make sure that the application, a WSN or another IOT application, has a low energy consumption. In [6] is presented an algorithm that reduces the energy consumption in heterogeneous cloud computing with a high success rate. When it comes to WSNs this type of proposal is prevalent, [7] and [8], for example, deal with techniques to save energy in WSNs.

In [5] the author presents a proposal similar to our paper, aiming to develop a web platform for data acquisition with tools for processing and analysis of data. The main objective was to develop a web platform, called CLUeFARM, which provides farmers with a way to monitor their farm from a distance through the internet. To assess the application, the author performed tests with response time for each service offered by the platform. Despite the satisfactory results, it is worth mentioning that the sensors and equipment used are complex and expensive. Our system uses a less expensive technology, the Xbee, that also has an easier configuration.

[9] presents a service related to soil management, within a platform that supplies integrated support for greenhouse activities, in addition to the CLUeFARM. Monitoring, assessing, and managing farm operations can provide enormous benefits in terms of productivity. To prioritize these items, the author proposes a service related to soil management, within a platform that supplies integrated support for greenhouse activities. In the work's experiments, a possible conclusion is that even though the proposed web-service is an extension of CLUeFARM, it may operate independently.

Another important topic was discussed in [10], in which the author presents a low-cost technology to build wireless sensor networks. The main gold was achieved, and the proposal presents a low-cost technology in comparison with technologies like the Libelium system. To deal with all the produced data, they also propose a Web Application. However, compared to the application of our paper, his application is quite simple, and just shows the values obtained with the WSN.

In [11], the authors propose a web-service to manage information from a green farm, like our project. The difference is that, in this case, the web application is a service-oriented platform. The main objective is to provide support in the management process and business development, and to increase the quality of products grown in farms. It also offers services for data processing and an algorithm to gather data. To validate their proposal, they made an experiment and an analysis to see the time needed to send notifications to users in case of an event.

In order to develop these services, a lot of frameworks and tools could be used. Knowing that there are diverse ways to build web applications, study [12] proposes a novel approach for Web service interface decomposition using a Formal Concept Analysis (FCA) framework. The authors made the validation of their method on 26 real-world Web services and obtained results that show that their method performs significantly better than other discussed techniques in terms of design quality improvement.

In [5,9,13], another type of framework is used: the MVC framework. Based in three layers of development, the MVC consists of models, views, and controllers. In each mentioned work, the authors used this kind of architecture because it promotes clean code, good practices, and it improves user interaction and interfaces. In the last few years, a lot of frameworks that use this architecture were used, the Laravel is one of the most popular ones.

Considering all presented platforms, our proposed system used a web-service as a tool to monitor, organize and visualize data collected by a WSN. To build this application, we have used the Laravel framework because it is a MVC framework, compatible with many browsers and it provides features that help in the fast development of scalable and modular applications [5]. Communications are based on HTTP protocol with the WSN to store the produced data.

3   Web-Service

Like any application, a web software is based on an architecture that will define how it will work. Our system is no different. In this section, we will describe the main features of our system: the architecture, the functionalities (system requirements and implementation) and the tools used to develop the application back-end and front-end.

3.1   Architecture of the System

The proposed system is a web service based on queries made by clients and answers sent by a server. The communication between client and server is performed using the Hypertext Transfer Protocol (HTTP), verbs (GET, POST, DELETE, and others), and it features a Representational State Transfer application (RESTful). Using this type of architecture decreases the number of queries because in this case all data will be sent using a single request into one JSON object through an HTTP POST request [14].

Usually, when the amount of exchanged information between an application and a web-service is big, data are converted into convenient structured formats such as XML [15] or JavaScript Object Notation (JSON). According to [16], in recent years developers have replaced XML with the JSON format to transfer data. Indeed, JSON is a lightweight data interchange format that is easy for humans to read and write, as well as easy for machines to parse and generate.

Looking for an efficient application with this behavior, our system was developed using a framework in PHP called Laravel. This framework is an open source tool for PHP development. It is largely applied as it has an organized code structure that makes it easier to read and modify the code. It also supplies tools needed for large and robust applications [17]. The Laravel uses a MVC architecture, therefore the development of the system followed this architecture.

The MVC is responsible for dividing the application in three layers of development: models, views and controllers. This design pattern is frequently used to develop web applications because it combines some technologies that are usually divided into a set of layers [18]. The model layer is responsible for organizing the data, communicating with the database and accessing all stored data. The view layer is the one that will build the graphical user interface. The controller layer is the most important and complex part: it is responsible for managing models and views, and processing the information from models to show in views [19].

The system works as described in Fig. 1. It shows the functionality of each layer and how these layers will interact with the final user. Our system will have a database to store all the data collected by the WSN. This exchange of information will be made by the coordinator device that acts like a client. It will send the information gathered to a cloud database through a POST request.

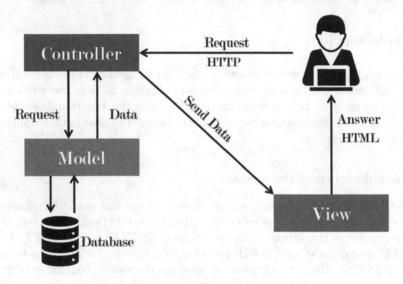

Fig. 1. MVC architecture

Therefore, the application must contain a functionality that gives the system the ability to organize in the database the data received by the microcontroller. The database model follows the entity-relationship (ER) pattern and is outlined in Fig. 2. There are three types of data: data, devices, and users, which are represented in the ER Diagram as entities.

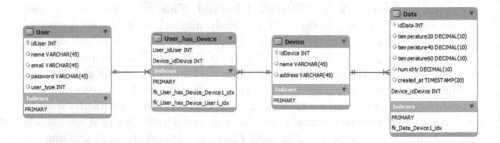

Fig. 2. Entity-Relationship diagram

The ER Diagram (Fig. 2) shows the relation between entities and their attributes. The Device entity has an id field, a device identifier (name) and the MAC address of this device. Each device performs a series of readings, these readings are stored in another table, symbolized by the Data entity. This table contains fields for an id, for the values of the three temperatures, for the value of the humidity, data about the time the sample was sent to the system and, finally, an identifier of the equipment that has sent the value.

The User entity has fields that store information about users that can use the system. They have an id, name, email, password and can also fill a field to define which type of user they are. The last table in the database is the result of a relation between the user and the device. This relation was added in order to improve the functionality of a user and a device. The database is managed by MySQL, a robust and relational open source tool that is widely used in Web applications. This tool is already well-established in the literature, giving speed and reliability to the system [2].

Another important aspect for a Web service is its security. Our system contains a login system with password protocol security to restrict access to certain functionalities. The Laravel also uses the CSRF (Cross Site Request Forgery) tokens to prevent fake requests and has protection against XSS (Cross Site Scripting) and SQL Injection.

The web application will be hosted in a server and will be available on the internet. This requirement is important because this type of application was chosen, specifically, to use the WSN to collect data for future studies, like an international research project.

3.2 Functionalities

For the development of the system, we studied all the functional and non-functional requirements that the system should have. Functional requirements are requirements that express functions that a certain software must be able to perform or provide, while non-functional ones address system constraints and quality attributes [20].

Therefore, the functional requirements in Table 1 and the non-functional requirements in Table 2 were determined.

In Table 1, the first requirement (FR01) is the CRUD (Create, Read, Update and Delete) of users. This is not the most important feature of the system, but it ensures that new users can register to use, FR02, performs the same role, but for another entity, in this case it refers to the devices that make up the network. The third CRUD, FR03, performs the same role to the Entity Data.

Next requirements, FR04 and FR05, deal with the main functionality of the system: displaying the data obtained by WSN. The data display was implemented in two ways: through tables and graphs. Both data are filtered based on the address of the device that has sent the data. In addition to visualization, making data suitable for computational analysis is also important. Therefore, the requirement FR06 indicates the need for a function to export the data generated by the WSN in a format that simplifies their analysis. The format used was CSV (Comma-Separated Values), since it can be used to import data into several computational tools.

Table 1. Functional requirements

id	Name	Description
FR01	CRUD user	Create, read, update and delete users
FR02	CRUD device	Create, read, update and delete devices
FR03	CRUD data	Create, read, update and delete devices
FR04	Show data	Show in a table a data collection from a device in a defined time
FR05	Show charts	Generate charts with selected data
FR06	Export data	Generate and download a CVS with interest data
FR07	Link user and device	Allow the user to just see the data from a chosen device

Table 2. Non-functional requirements

id	Name	Description
NFR01	Uniqueness of users	
NFR02	Uniqueness of links	Between a user and a device
NFR03	Uniqueness of devices	
NFR04	Types of user	There are three types of users
NFR05	Admin privileges	Just an admin could create, update or delete
NFR06	Guest restrictions	The guest user can just read statistical information
NFR07	Common user restrictions	The common user can read statistical information and create charts, CSV files and make link with devices
NFR08	Create data	The data could just be created by WSN

The last requirement is the only one that has medium priority because although it is not an essential functionality of the system, it will contribute positively to its usability. This requirement (FR07) allows users to create a link with a certain device, so it can follow a device to which it is linked in a personalized page, facilitating the visualization of the data, since the network can have more than 100 devices.

In Table 2, some of the non-functional requirements are listed. The first three non-functional requirements are only system constraints, which should prevent conflicts and duplication in the database. NFR04 defines three types of users: admin, common and guest. The NF05 defines the privileges of an admin user. NF06 defines the limitations of a guest user. And, the NF07, defines limitations to the common users. The NFR08 is an important restriction, it defines that only the WSN can send information to the system.

After defining all the requirements, the functionalities were implemented, and the restriction and privileges were defined according to the non-functional requirements. To help the visualization and comprehension of the system, we present in Fig. 3 the Use Case Diagram that illustrates all the functionalities available for each type of user. In this diagram, it is possible to see the interaction between the WSN and the system.

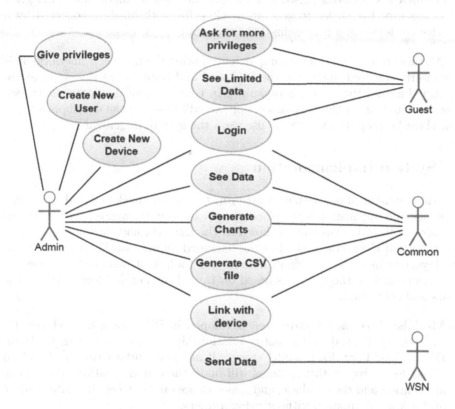

Fig. 3. Use case diagram

In this system, three main functionalities are highlighted and described below: see data, generate charts and generate CSV. All other functionalities play an administrative work that is very important. Besides the three mentioned, it is interesting to point out the importance of the "link with device". This function allows the user to select devices and to visualize more easily the desired data. Since our system will be used by researchers from different countries and the monitoring area for each device could not be related to everyone, this function is useful.

– **See Data:** the main objective of the proposed system is to monitor the data collected by the WSN, so it is fundamental to implement a function to allow the visualization of these data. This information is shown on a web page.

– **Generate Charts:** all data collected by the WSN will be used, processed and analyzed by a group of researchers. So in addition to showing data, it is interesting to show these data as temporal series, in charts, in order to produce more efficient analyses. These charts are generated according to the chosen device and could be personalized to show just information about one defined time interval.

– **Generate CSV:** this personalized application has a functionality that gives to the user the choice to generate a CSV file with all data collected by a selected device in a personalized time interval.

All these functionalities were implemented using the Laravel framework. This framework was used to develop the back-end and front-end of this application. As stated above, the system is organized in tree layers of development: model, view and control. In the next subsection we will describe the development and how these layers interact with the user and the system in general.

4   System Implementation

The development of our system consists in two layers: back-end and front-end. The back-end application is the place where logic is implemented. The front-end is where an intuitive interface is shown to the user; through this interface, they can access all the services listed in the back-end application [5]. To build these two layers we used the framework Laravel as a tool. As it was mentioned before, the architecture of the system is based on three layers of development: models, views and controllers.

– **Models:** three models have been developed in PHP using Laravel, one for each entity defined in the entity-relationship diagram (see Fig. 3): Data, Device, and User. Each model stores all necessary information to build an object for a given entity. A model will make the communication between the application and the database, and make all operations to read, create, update and delete information without using a query.

– **Controllers:** three controllers have been developed, one for each model. It was defined a DataController, a DeviceController and a UserController. The controller rules the application logic [13]. Each controller has functions that deal with the related data. For example, functions to create or delete a user are implemented in the UserController. A function is called according to the URL that the user puts on their browser. The control of that function will be called through a route made by a mechanism from Laravel, a route file that defines the patch and the corresponding function to execute.

– **Views:** it is the front-end of this application: all the web pages that compose the system. It is responsible for getting all information requests and showing them in a HTML file. There are many views in the proposed system, but just a few of them will be shown and discussed in this section.

The system has three perspectives: one for common logged users, one for guest users and one for logged administrator users (admin user). When a guest user access the platform and they are not logged, they only have access to a presentation page with some information about the project SenCSoil-Guyamazon, a Franco-Brazilian Program of cooperation in research, capacity building and innovation in the Amazon. From this page, the user can only access the login page (Fig. 4), where they can log in into the platform using an account or the register page and where they can ask to create a new account.

Fig. 4. Login page

After authentication, there is two kinds of users: the common and the admin. The main difference between those two is that only the admin will be able to access functionalities such as: accept a new user (giving privileges), create a device, create a user, delete devices or users, and update information in devices or users. The main functionalities of the system are available for both users. The first one, to see data, is accessed through the web page shown in Fig. 5a. As mentioned in the requirements subsection, there are two options to see the data, in a chart (see Fig. 5b) or in a table (see Fig. 5c). In the same screen, it is possible to make a link with a device, putting it in your "My Devices" list. The plot of the chart and table rows shows all data from the selected devices, independently of the time when it was created.

All devices for which the user has pressed the "add to my devices" option will be displayed on another page, illustrated in Figure 6. The large number of devices that the network can have, due to the great scalability of the system, make this mechanism essential to facilitate access to data and graphics of a device of interest.

The second main functionality is the chart generation, and the third, the generation of CSV files, they both have the same view pattern, illustrated in Fig. 7. The user must fill two date and time fields, one for the start date of interest and the second for the ending date. This time interval defines which data will be selected, thus seeking only those that were generated in the requested

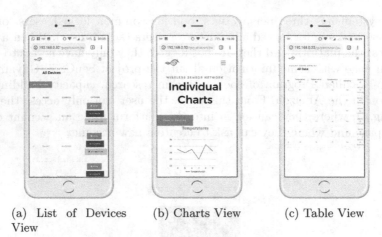

(a) List of Devices View   (b) Charts View   (c) Table View

Fig. 5. Types of data visualization

Fig. 6. My devices view

time interval. The other fields allow the user to select the device from which they want to export data, as well as the data type, since the network stores different types of data, such as temperature and humidity.

In the generate graph screen, after filling all the fields, the user is directed to a page with a chart, similar to Fig. 5b. If the choice is to generate a CSV, the file will be downloaded in the browser. In the administrator's view, in addition to the possibility to register users, the device display screen (see Fig. 5a) will also contain the options to edit or delete the device. The visualization in table format (Fig. 5c), to the admin user also has buttons to edit or delete the data from the system.

Fig. 7. Generate Chart/CSV view

5 Experiments and Results

This stage is divided into two parts. In the first one, we describe the development of the WSN and the algorithm that describes the communication between it and our system. In the second part, we make an evaluation of the usability of our system.

5.1 Wireless Sensor Network

To make some experiments and check the communication between the proposed system and the Wireless Sensor Network, we have used a simple network composed by XBee modules based on the 802.15.4/Zigbee protocol that built a low-power, low maintenance, and self-organizing WSN [21]. To build a WSN, after defining the technology used as a device (in our case the XBee), it is necessary to define the role of these devices in the network.

As mentioned previously, from a functional and operational point of view the nodes of a WSN can be configured as Coordinator, Router or End Device. According to [1], the coordinator is a device that manages all the functions that define the network in order to ensure its integrity and keep it active. In a ZigBee network, there is just one coordinator. The router is a device that can join an existing network, send, receive, and forward information to other network nodes. The end device is a device that can join existing networks, send and receive information, but cannot act as a messenger among other devices.

It is also necessary to define the quantity of devices and how they will be organized, more specifically the topology. The topology defines how the connections will be between all devices. There are three main kinds of topology: tree, mesh and star. In this paper, we have used the star topology because sometimes, mesh topology has a bigger number of lost packages than star topology [22] and this is an important measurement of quality of the service provided by a WSN. The star topology also has a lower delay rate compared to the mesh topology.

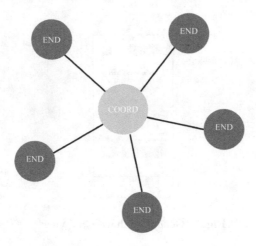

Fig. 8. Star topology

However, according to [8], in the case of precision agriculture, this is not a very important property.

In the star topology, as shown in Fig. 8, the coordinator node is at the center of the star and is connected to a circle of end devices. Any messages in the system must pass through the coordinator node which forwards them as required to devices in the network. The end devices do not communicate directly with each other and only communicate with the coordinator. The advantage of this topology is the simplicity of its implementation and the fact that the data packets between source and destination follow at most two communication links. The disadvantage of this topology is the lack of alternative paths, for the packets, between source and destination, and that all communications must pass through the coordinator.

Once the topology is defined, it is possible to implement the network. As mentioned before, to build the experimental WSN we have used the Xbee module, knowing that it is a practical tool that permits an easy and quick configuration of a network. The model used was XBee Pro S2C, powered by a 9V rechargeable battery. Since the input voltage of the XBee is 5V, an auxiliary circuit with a voltage regulator was used. The assembly made is shown in Fig. 9.

The first type of data to be collected by the proposed WSN will be of interest to researchers working with soil properties analysis. Therefore, the first experiments were carried out with the purpose of collecting different temperatures, from different soil depths and the humidity on its surface. For the acquisition of temperatures, the analog temperature sensor LM35, shown in Fig. 10a, was used and for humidity reading, the capacitive sensor shown in Fig. 10b was used.

In the XBee network, all the end devices send the data placed to the coordinator of the network, which is in a controlled location, with constant power. In addition to the XBees, the NodeMCU development module Esp8266, shown in Fig. 11, was used to perform the communication with the proposed system,

Fig. 9. Module XBee Pro S2C

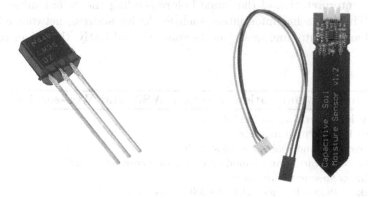

(a) LM35 Temperature sensor   (b) Capacitive humidity sensor

Fig. 10. Sensors used

which through serial communication with the XBee coordinator receives all readings from the network. In the NodeMCU, a routine has been implemented that interprets the data received from the XBee and formats it to send them to the database through an HTTP request. In this case, NodeMCU will play the role of Client and send the message in JSON format.

5.2   Algorithm in WSN

The software embedded (see Algorithm 1) in the NodeMCU was developed using the Arduino platform, in addition to the module's own Wi-Fi communication libraries, the JSON library, which performs the conversion of the message to be sent to the desired format. As mentioned, the connection between the NodeMCU and the Xbee Coordinator is made by serial communication. However, the data sent to the NodeMCU has a specific format, according to the communication

Fig. 11. Module NodeMCU ESP8266 [23]

protocol used by the coordinator. The XBee uses a predetermined frame pattern for each type of message one wants to send. Therefore, it was necessary to perform an interpretation of the frame before sending the actual values to the database. The frame has information such as device address, network address, configuration of digital and analog ports enabled, and lastly, the values read by each port.

Algorithm 1. Comunication Between WSN and Web-service

---

1 **If there is something in Serial Port**:
2   Save Hexadecimal message;
3   Convert To find real values of sample;
4   Take temperature and humidity values and convert to JSON;
5   Make connection with Host;
6   Make a POST Request with the JSON message;
7 **Else:**
8   Wait for a message;

The communication between WSN and the web application was successful. Therefore, to validate the interface, an usability analysis was performed. As the platform went through the evaluation stage, and it is not yet available online, we chose to perform an evaluation using heuristic and the cognitive walkthrough method.

5.3   Usability Evaluation

Heuristic evaluation is a method that identifies usability problems based on usability principles or usability heuristics, making it possible to evaluate the usability of the system [24]. According to [24], this kind of method is more efficient if it is combined with another evaluation method, like cognitive walkthrough. This one is a usability evaluation method in which one or more evaluators analyze a series of tasks, make questions from the user's perspective and check if the systems support the proposed goals.

To evaluate the proposed system, the method proposed by [24] was applied. Firstly, it is necessary to define all heuristics used in the process, showed in Table 3. After this is important to point out the scale that was used: (0) heuristic not applicable; (1) not fulfilled; (2) partially fulfilled; and, (3) fully fulfilled, following what was made in [24,25]. To make this evaluation we have selected three professionals with experience in software development and software engineering.

Table 3. Nielsen 10 heuristic principles [24,25]

id	Name	Description
HP1	Visibility of system status	The system should always keep users informed about what is going on, through appropriate feedback within a reasonable time
HP2	Match between system and the real word	The system should speak the users' language, with words, phrases and concepts familiar to the users. Make the information appear in a natural and logical order
HP3	User control freedom	"Emergency exit" to leave the unwanted state without having to go through an extended dialogue. Support undo and redo
HP4	Consistency and standards	Users should not have to wonder whether different Words, situations, or actions mean the same thing
HP5	Error prevention	Even better than good error messages is a careful design which prevents a problem from occurring in the first place
HP6	Recognition rather than call	Instructions for use of the system should be visible or easily retrievable whenever appropriate
HP7	Flexibility and efficiency of use	Allow users to tailor and speed up frequent actions
HP8	Aesthetic and minimalist design	Dialogues should not contain information which is irrelevant or rarely needed
HP9	Help users recognize, diagnose, and recover from error	Error messages should be expressed in plain language (no codes), precisely indicate the problem, and constructively suggest a solution
HP10	Help and documentation	Any such information should be easy to search, focused on the user's task, list concrete steps to be carried out, and not be too large

For the cognitive walkthrough the author [24] proposes a task analysis and an interview with a questionnaire. For the interview, we use the four questions questionnaire proposed, and we added three questions from the Post-Study System Usability Questionnaire (PSSUQ) [26], an IBM questionnaire to evaluate usability of systems. All selected questions are listed in Table 4. The scale also was applied to the heuristic: (0) not applicable; (1) not fulfilled; (2) partially fulfilled and (3) fully fulfilled. This evaluation was made by three selected developers that work with web applications development.

Table 4. Cognitive walkthrough questionnaire

id	Question
Q01	Is the control for the action visible?
Q02	Will the interface allow the user to produce the effect the action has?
Q03	Will users succeed in performing this action?
Q04	Will users notice that the correct action has been executed successfully?
Q05	Was it simple to use this system?
Q06	Was I able to efficiently complete the tasks and scenarios using this system?
Q07	Was the organization of information on the system screens clear?

5.4   Results

In the heuristic evaluation, it was possible to identify some problems in the interface, however it is important to point out that they are all linked to the absence of feedback in user operations, in which it was verified that it is not possible to identify success or failure in operations of addition or exclusion in the system. All the results are presented in Table 5, in which values from 0 to 3 determine how many valuers pointed to a given response.

Analyzing Table 5, it is possible to prove the previous assertion, since the items HP1, HP5, and HP9 indicated as not fulfilled are related to the absence of messages and the ability to retrieve the user error. The other problems encountered, HP6 and HP10 are related to the lack of help or system documentation that can contribute to the execution of the tasks by the user. In HP10, only one valuer considered this question incomplete, while one valuer considered it partially filled by the existence of a list of features and a use case diagram. Under the same criteria, the last valuer considered this information sufficient and considered it fully fulfilled.

Among the problems found in the majority can be considered of low gravity. However, it is worth mentioning that the absence of success or failure status in operations is considered as an absence of high severity, and that, due to the MVC architecture of the system, can be easily corrected. In a general analysis the evaluation was positive, with 50% of the heuristics at least partially fulfilled.

In the cognitive walkthrough evaluation, in addition to the answers of the questionnaire, comments were also made by the evaluators. First, two of the three evaluators believed that the functionality of editing a data produced by the network is unnecessary since the intention is to receive the values and that in a first analysis there would be no reason to modify them. Another problem

Table 5. Heuristic results

Heuristic	Not applicable	Not fulfilled	Partially fulfilled	Fully fulfilled
HP1	0	3	0	0
HP2	0	0	1	2
HP3	0	0	3	0
HP4	0	0	0	3
HP5	0	3	0	0
HP6	0	2	1	0
HP7	3	0	0	0
HP8	0	0	0	3
HP9	0	3	0	0
HP10	0	1	1	1

pointed out was a non-flexible database and web service, if the user wants to select a new sensor they have to change a lot of fields and adapt the views to deal with this new type of data.

In the analysis of the scenarios and the execution of the tasks, a few problems were found, the most relevant being the absence of confirmation messages of success or failure to create a device or user. In Table 6 are the answers of each valuer for the applied questionnaire. The id corresponds to the question, and 'Ev' represents each valuer.

Table 6. Cognitive walkthrough questionnaire answers

id	Ev 1	Ev 2	Ev 3
Q01	2	2	3
Q02	2	3	3
Q03	2	2	2
Q04	1	1	1
Q05	3	3	3
Q06	2	3	3
Q07	3	3	3

With the results presented in Table 6, it is possible to confirm that the scenario of confirmation of success in the operation was the most irregular in the view of the evaluators, just like in the heuristic evaluation. It is possible to perceive that, in a general analysis, the results of the evaluation were positive. The three questions from PSSUQ received a positive evaluation, even with the adaptation that was made, since this questionnaire consists of affirmations.

6   Conclusion and Future Work

The proposed system was developed to provide access to information collected by a Wireless Sensor Network, given that this is a tool that is becoming increasingly popular for data acquisition. In order to make information available in different countries and with an intuitive and user-friendly interface, a web-service has been proposed.

When it come to its development, a MVC architecture was chosen due to the organization and modularization of the code, facilitating possible changes, such as those pointed out in the evaluation stage. To confirm the communication between the WSN and the application, a network with XBee for the network composition and the NodeMCU device Esp8266 for communication with the web-service was used. The tests performed between the network and the application only sought to prove that the software developed for the embedded system could perform such a function.

The star topology used has limitations, once contact is lost with the coordinator this node is lost. However, the coordinator is in a controlled environment to prevent failures, and the distance between the nodes was not big enough to build a mesh network. In the future, to prevent failures in the coordinator, we can perform tests using a backup node that periodically checks to see if the coordinator has any problems.

The main goal of this work was not high security, a future work will be done in order to use new techniques to reinforce security. However, the analysis of the usability of the system allowed us to conclude that despite the negative aspects pointed out here, the application managed to reach the requirements for which it has been developed. This makes it necessary to execute new steps, firstly correcting the errors identified in the evaluation and, in sequence, putting the application online to analyze factor such as performance and other usability metrics with the final users.

References

1. Faludi, R.: Building Wireless Sensor Networks: with ZigBee, XBee, Arduino, and Processing. O'Reilly Media Inc., Newton (2010)
2. Wheeler, A.: Commercial applications of wireless sensor networks using ZigBee. IEEE Commun. Mag. **45**(4), 70–77 (2007)
3. Gai, K., Qiu, M.: Reinforcement learning-based content-centric services in mobile sensing. IEEE Netw. **32**(4), 34–39 (2018)
4. Huuskonen, J., Oksanen, T.: Soil sampling with drones and augmented reality in precision agriculture. Comput. Electron. Agric. **154**, 25–35 (2018)
5. Colezea, M., Musat, G., Pop, F., Negru, C., Dumitrascu, A., Mocanu, M.: Cluefarm: integrated web-service platform for smart farms. Comput. Electron. Agric. **154**, 134–154 (2018)
6. Gai, K., Qiu, M., Zhao, H.: Energy-aware task assignment for mobile cyber-enabled applications in heterogeneous cloud computing. J. Parallel Distrib. Comput. **111**, 126–135 (2018)

7. Xu, L., O'Hare, G.M., Collier, R.: A balanced energy-efficient multihop clustering scheme for wireless sensor networks. In: 2014 7th IFIP Wireless and Mobile Networking Conference (WMNC), pp. 1–8. IEEE (2014)
8. Rault, T., Bouabdallah, A., Challal, Y.: Energy efficiency in wireless sensor networks: a top-down survey. Comput. Netw. **67**, 104–122 (2014)
9. Serrouch, A., Mocanu, M., Pop, F.: Soil management services in CLUeFARM. In: 2015 14th International Symposium on Parallel and Distributed Computing (ISPDC), pp. 204–209. IEEE (2015)
10. Silva, M.S.d.: Rede de sensores sem fio de baixo custo para monitoramento ambiental. Master's thesis, Faculdade de Engenharia Elétrica e Computaçã - FEEC (2013)
11. Musat, G.A., et al.: Advanced services for efficient management of smart farms. J. Parallel Distrib. Comput. **116**, 3–17 (2018)
12. Daagi, M., Ouniy, A., Kessentini, M., Gammoudi, M.M., Bouktif, S.: Web service interface decomposition using formal concept analysis. In: 2017 IEEE International Conference on Web Services (ICWS), pp. 172–179. IEEE (2017)
13. Gracia, J., Bayo, E.: An effective and user-friendly web application for the collaborative analysis of steel joints. Adv. Eng. Softw. **119**, 60–67 (2018)
14. Reynolds, D., Ball, J., Bauer, A., Griffiths, S., Zhou, J.: CropMonitor: a scalable open-source experiment management system for distributed plant phenotyping and IoT-based crop management. bioRxiv (2018)
15. Serrano, D., Stroulia, E., Lau, D., Ng, T.: Linked rest APIs: a middleware for semantic rest API integration. In: 2017 IEEE International Conference on Web Services (ICWS), pp. 138–145. IEEE (2017)
16. Kao, K.C., Chieng, W.H., Jeng, S.L.: Design and development of an IoT-based web application for an intelligent remote SCADA system. In: IOP Conference Series: Materials Science and Engineering, vol. 323, pp. 012025. IOP Publishing (2018)
17. Wadkar, K., Koshti, P., Parab, D., Tamboli, S.: V-Buddy: a learning management system. In: 2018 Second International Conference on Electronics, Communication and Aerospace Technology (ICECA), pp. 539–541. IEEE (2018)
18. Badurowicz, M.: MVC architectural pattern in mobile web applications. Actual Prob. Econ. **6**, 305–309 (2011)
19. Latief, M., Kandowangko, N., Yusuf, R.: Designing web database application for local medicinal plants of Gorontalo using MVC architecture. In: IOP Conference Series: Materials Science and Engineering, vol. 288, p. 012098. IOP Publishing (2018)
20. Sommerville, I., et al.: Software Engineering. Addison-wesley, Boston (2007)
21. Boonsawat, V., Ekchamanonta, J., Bumrungkhet, K., Kittipiyakul, S.: XBee wireless sensor networks for temperature monitoring. In: the Second Conference on Application Research and Development, ECTI-CARD 2010, Chon Buri, Thailand. Citeseer (2010)
22. Soijoyo, S., Ashari, A.: Analysis of Zigbee data transmission on wireless sensor network topology. Analysis **8**(9), 145–151 (2017)
23. Kodali, R.K., Soratkal, S.: MQTT based home automation system using ESP8266. In: 2016 IEEE Region 10 Humanitarian Technology Conference (R10-HTC), pp. 1–5. IEEE (2016)
24. Pilco, H., et al.: Analysis and improvement of the usability of a tele-rehabilitation platform for hip surgery patients. In: Nunes, I.L. (ed.) AHFE 2018. AISC, vol. 781, pp. 197–209. Springer, Cham (2019). https://doi.org/10.1007/978-3-319-94334-3_21

25. Nielsen, J., Molich, R.: Heuristic evaluation of user interfaces. In: Proceedings of the SIGCHI conference on Human factors in computing systems, pp. 249–256. ACM (1990)
26. Rosa, A.F., Martins, A.I., Costa, V., Queirós, A., Silva, A., Rocha, N.P.: European Portuguese validation of the post-study system usability questionnaire (PSSUQ). In: 2015 10th Iberian Conference on Information Systems and Technologies (CISTI), pp. 1–5. IEEE (2015)

Automated Hot_Text and Huge_Pages: An Easy-to-Adopt Solution Towards High Performing Services

Zhenyun Zhuang(✉), Mark Santaniello, Shumin Zhao, Bikash Sharma, and Rajit Kambo

Facebook, Inc., 1 Hacker Way, Menlo Park, CA 94025, USA
{zhenyun,marksan,szhao,bsharma,rkambo}@fb.com

Abstract. Performance optimizations of large scale services can lead to significant wins on service efficiency and performance. CPU resource is one of the most common performance bottlenecks, hence improving CPU performance has been the focus of many performance optimization efforts. In particular, reducing iTLB (instruction TLB) miss rates can greatly improve CPU performance and speed up service running.

At Facebook, we have achieved CPU reduction by applying a solution that firstly identifies hot-text of the (software) binary and then places the binary on huge pages (i.e., 2 MB+ memory pages). The solution is wrapped into an automated framework, enabling service owners to effortlessly adopt it. Our framework has been applied to many services at Facebook, and this paper shares our experiences and findings.

Keywords: Huge pages · Hot-text · Performance · iTLB miss

1 Introduction

Large Internet companies like Facebook feature large amount of back-end servers which serve billions of users that have various types activities (e.g., messaging, video streaming). These servers run many types of services [1]. Given the large scale of the Facebook computation/storage infrastructure, it is important to ensure our services are running efficiently.

Many types of performance improvement works have been done at various layers (e.g., OS, compiler, application/code level, storage level) targeting different services. At Facebook, we have been treating performance improvement works seriously (e.g., [2,3]) by various types of optimizations. Over the years, we have achieved significant amount of efficiencies and better service performance across the fleet. To gain concrete understanding of the cost-saving scale, consider a service that runs on 100 K servers. Assuming the service is bottlenecked by CPU usage, and a performance improvement effort that saves 1% on server CPU usage will result in about 1 K servers being saved.

Performance improvement of services requires software profiling to identify the top performance bottlenecks, root-causing the fundamental issues, proposing

© Springer Nature Switzerland AG 2019
J. Miller et al. (Eds.): ICWS 2019, LNCS 11512, pp. 147–162, 2019.
https://doi.org/10.1007/978-3-030-23499-7_10

solutions to address the issues, implementing the solutions, and testing to verify the effectiveness of the solutions. We have been continuously profiling thousands of services across our fleet for various types of performance inefficiencies. We found that CPU resource is one of the most common performance bottlenecks, hence improving CPU performance has been the focus in many performance efforts.

One type of service inefficiency is high iTLB (instruction Translation Lookaside Buffer) miss rate, which causes CPU to run ineffectively[1]. The penalty of iTLB misses is significant as the access latency difference between *hit* and *miss* can be 10–100 times of difference. A *hit* only takes 1 clock cycle, while a *miss* takes 10–100 clock cycles. To understand more about such latency penalty, let's assume *hit* and *miss* take 1 and 60 cycles, respectively. Thus a 1% miss rate will result in average access latency being 159 cycles, or 59% higher than not having any misses (i.e., 1 cycle).

For a service that experiencing high iTLB miss rate, reducing iTLB miss rates can greatly improve CPU performance and speed up service running time. Various optimization approaches that impprove the software binaries can be applied to reduce iTLB misses. Overall there are three types of optimizations based on the different stages of compiling the source code (i.e., compile/link/post-link time). Examples include optimizing compiler options to reorder functions so that hot functions are located together, or using FDO (Feedback-Driven Optimization) [4] to reduce the size of code regions. In addition to such compiler optimizations that help reduce iTLB miss rate, we also place the binary code on huge pages to further speed up the running services.

In this work, we combine both types of optimizations (i.e., identifying *hot-text* to co-locate frequently accessed functions and deploying the optimized binary on *huge pages*) to reduce iTLB miss rates. More importantly, we design and implement an automated work flow to make the optimizations transparent and maintenance-free for service owners. As a result, various services can benefit from this solution with minimum efforts, practically rendering this easy-to-adopt solution as a "free lunch optimization" for service owners.

Note that though the *hot-text* optimization mostly applies to services written in statically compiled languages (e.g., C/CPP), *huge page* optimization can apply to all services. Given the fact that many of largest scale backend infrastructures in the world (e.g., Facebook, Google, Microsoft) are written in C/CPP, thanks to C/C++'s high efficiency, our proposed solution can be applied to many services running on these infrastructures. Furthermore, for dynamically compiled languages (e.g., Java), the insights gained in this work can also help improve their compiling performance (e.g., in JVM).

This work shares our design, efficiency gains and some issues found. In particular, we focus on the key questions that could be asked by potential adopters including:

- What is the performance issue this solution addresses? For instance, why is high iTLB miss rate bad?

---

[1] Please refer to Sect. 2 for detailed explanations of iTLB misses.

– What is the design of the solution (i.e., how does it work internally)?
– How much code change is needed?
– How much maintenance overhead is involved?
– What is the downside of this solution?
– How to verify the optimization is applied to my service?

The following writing is organized as follows. Section 2 provides relevant background knowledge. Section 3 walks through the high level design, followed by detailed work flow of the solution in Sect. 4. Section 5 presents performance results of applying this solution. Some related issues are discussed in Sect. 6, and related works are presented in Sect. 7. Finally Sect. 8 concludes the paper.

2   Background

2.1   ITLB (Instruction TLB) Misses

In x86 computing architectures, memory mappings between virtual and physical memory are facilitated by a memory-based page table. For fast virtual-to-physical translations, recently-used portions of the page table are cached in TLB (translation look-aside buffers). There are two types of TLBs: data and instructions, both are of limited sizes.

Since memory access latency is much higher than TLB access latency, address translations that hit TLBs are much faster than missing TLBs. Invariably, the more translation requests that miss the TLBs and have to fall back to page tables (aka, 'page walks'), the slower the instruction executions. iTLB miss rate is a metric to estimate the performance penalty of page walks induced on iTLB (instruction TLB) misses. When the iTLB miss rate is high, a significant proportion of cycles are spent handling the misses, which results in slower execution of the instructions, hence sub-optimal services.

2.2   Huge Pages

Today's computing architecture typically support larger page sizes (2 MB and 1 GB on x86_64, both referred to as huge pages) in addition to the traditional 4 KB pages size. Huge pages reduce number of TLB entries needed to cover the working set of the binary, leading to smaller page tables and reducing the cost of page table walks.

There are two ways of obtaining huge pages on Linux: (1) using THP (transparent huge pages) [5] and (2) reserving huge pages and mounting them as *hugetlbfs* in the application. THP requires minimum changes to the application, however the availability of huge pages is not guaranteed. To reserve huge pages, applying configurations such as *hugepagesz = 2 MB hugepages = 64* (i.e., reserving 64 huge pages of 2 MB each) when booting kernel works.

3 Design

3.1 Overview

When running a service on servers, the corresponding binary needs to be loaded into memory. The binary consists of a set of functions, and they collectively reside in the *text* segment of the binary and are typically loaded during execution using 4 K pages. Each page attempts to occupy an iTLB entry for the virtual-to-physical page translation. Since commodity servers typically have limited number of iTLB entries (e.g., 128 entries for 4 KB pages in *Intel HasWell* architecture [6]), iTLB misses will occur if the text segment is larger than the iTLB entries can cover (e.g., $128 * 4\,KB = 512\,KB$). iTLB misses are counted towards CPU time and are effectively wasted CPU time.

iTLB misses can be reduced by identifying and aggregating frequently accessed instructions into *hot-text* in order to increase spatial locality. By packing hot functions into *hot text*, instruction fetching and prefetching can be more effective and faster, hence a high-performing server and service. Based on our studies with many services, at Facebook more than 90% of the code is *cold* and the remaining is *hot*. By separating hot from cold instructions, expensive micro-architectural resources (iTLB and caches) can more efficiently deal with the hot segment of a binary, resulting in performance improvement.

This benefit can be further enhanced by putting *hot-text* on huge pages for sufficiently large binary (i.e., larger than the regular page size of $4\,KB * iTLB$ entries). By using a single TLB entry, a single 2 MB huge page covers 512 times as much code as a standard 4 K page. More importantly, CPU architectures typically feature some number of TLB entries for huge pages, and they will sit there idle if no huge pages are used. By employing huge pages, those TLB entries can be fully utilized.

3.2 Design Elements and Rationales

The solution consists of three key elements: (a) hot-text optimization, (b) huge page placement, and (3) automated and decoupled pipeline.

The *hot-text* optimization consists of the following steps. First, identifying hot instructions by profiling the running binary. Linux perf tool is used for this purpose. We initially used stack traces, but later switched to LBRs [7] for better data quality and less data footprint. Second, sorting the profiled functions based on access frequencies. We use a tool called HFSort [8,9] to create an optimized order for the hot functions. Finally, a linker script will optimize the function layout in the binary based on the access orders. The result is an optimized binary.

Once the optimized binary with hot-text is obtained, the hot-text region can be further placed on huge pages. We designed an almost-transparent approach which needs little code change for service owners. Specifically, we pre-define a function that remaps the hot-text to huge pages, and all a service owner has to do is calling a pre-defined function early in the *main()* function

Note that *isolating hot-text* and *placing on huge pages* are complementary optimizations, and they can work independently; but combining them achieves best optimization results.

The traditional approach of applying hot-text optimization and huge page placement requires multiple steps, mixes source code and profiled data during linking phase, and involves manual profiling and refreshing, which prevents the solution from being widely deployed. We built a pipeline to automate the entire process, practically making this solution an easy-to-adopt and maintenance-free solution for all applicable services.

The pipeline also decouples the service's profile data from source code, hence allowing smooth and frequent profiling update to accommodate code/usage changes. Specifically, the profiled data are stored in separate storage that is different from source code repository. The advantages of the decoupling is each profiling update becomes part of the linearized code commit history, just like any other source code change. The profiling updates can be treated as source code, enabling easy check-in, review and reverting. Moreover, the profiled data files are stored and retrieved using file handles, hence we don't actually pay the cost of storing these huge almost-not-human-readable files in the source code repository.

In addition to helping reducing iTLB misses, the solution can also help reducing iCache misses. Computing instructions are fetched from memory and executed by CPUs. To expedite the instruction accesses, smaller and faster caches (iCache) are used to hold the instructions. iCache misses can occur when the binary working set is bigger than the iCache size. Caches have multiple levels, and the lowest level iCache is often times much smaller than the binary working set. iCache misses delay the CPU execution due to longer memory access time.

4 Detailed Work Flow

We now present the detailed steps and components of this solution. Note that neither *isolating hot-text* nor *using huge pages* is an invention, and both of them have been tried in several scenarios. However the naive adoption of the solution used to involve multiple manual and tedious steps (e.g., profiling, linking, regularly refreshing the profiles), hence few services have benefited from the solution. To address this issue, we designed an automated framework and data pipelines to remove the manual involvement by wrapping, aggregating and automating each steps. As a result, the solution suite becomes *maintenance free* and requires little code change.

4.1 Diagram and Components

The steps and components of this framework are shown in Fig. 1. Largely it consists of three components of profiling, linking and loading.

- *Profiling.* The profiling component is shown on the top of the diagram. A data-gathering job runs weekly to profile the running service[2]. The job is

---

[2] We observed that most services are relatively stable with regard to hot functions, hence weekly profiling suffices.

using our *Dataswarm* framework [10], a data storage and processing solution developed and used by Facebook. The job profiles running information of the service (e.g., hot functions), and the profiling is carefully controlled to have very light overhead. Profiled data is then sent to a permanent storage called *Everstore* [11], a disk based storage service.

- *Linking.* When building the service package, the linker script retrieves the profiled hot functions from Everstore and reorders functions in the binary based on the profiles.
- *Loading.* When loading the service binary, OS makes best efforts to put hot-text on huge pages. If no huge pages available, then put on regular pages.

4.2   Code Changes

For a new service that would like to apply this optimization, only three places of small changes (boilerplate code) are needed: (a) Dataswarm pipeline creation; (b) Source code (cpp files) change; and (c) Build configuration change.

Storage Pipeline Creation. On top of our data storage framework of Dataswarm, a data processing job regularly refreshes the profiled hot functions

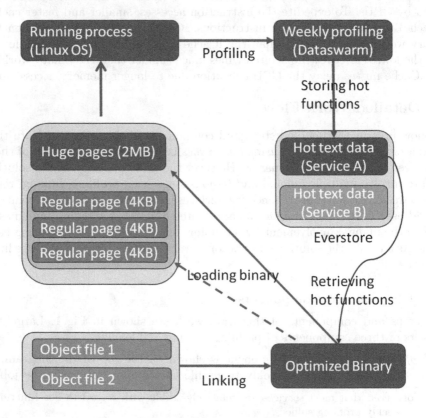

Fig. 1. Diagram of hot text and huge pages

profiles to reflect updates on the service: code changes and usage pattern changes. The data pipeline kicks off a Dataswarm job weekly for each service. When the job kicks off, it profiles the specified service and generates a file containing the hot functions. The hot function file is stored to Everstore. The file is uniquely identified by a file handle and content checksum.

The Dataswarm job also automatically creates a code diff (i.e., code checkin) which updates a meta file containing the newly generated hot-function file handle and checksum, it then automatically lands the diff (i.e., updating the meta file) to the services' source code directory.

Source Code Change. The framework only requires two lines of code change to source code's main cpp file. Specifically, the first line of code change is to include a header file that defines the function that is responsible for putting the

```
0000000000600000 W __hot_start
0000000000600000 0000000000000010 t _ZN4HPHP12InstanceBits7profileEPKNS_10StringDataE
0000000000600010 000000000000000a t _ZN4HPHP11PackedArray11GetValueRefEPKNS_9ArrayDataEl
000000000060001a 0000000000000007 t _ZZN4HPHP20c_AwaitAllWaitHandle6CreateILb0EZNS_31c_A
000000000060001a 0000000000000007 t _ZZN4HPHP20c_AwaitAllWaitHandle6CreateILb0EZNS_31c_A
000000000060001a 0000000000000007 t _ZZN4HPHP20c_AwaitAllWaitHandle6CreateILb0EZNS_32c_A
000000000060001a 0000000000000007 t _ZZN4HPHP20c_AwaitAllWaitHandle6CreateILb0EZNS_34c_A
0000000000600022 000000000000000a t _ZN4HPHP10MixedArray11GetValueRefEPKNS_9ArrayDataEl
```

(a) Hot-text region: starting at 0x600000

```
0000000000d1a000 0000000000000113 W _ZN6brotli20ContextBlockSplitterINS_9HistogramILi256
0000000000d1a113 W __hot_end
0000000000d1a140 0000000000000c6b t _ZN4HPHP12InstanceBits7profileEPKNS_10StringDataE.co
0000000000d1adac 0000000000000010 t _ZN4HPHP3jit14opcodeMayRaiseENS_60pcodeE.cold.0
0000000000d1adc0 0000000000000021 t _ZNSt14_Function_base12_Ref_managerIZN5folly6fibers5
```

(b) Hot-text region: ending at 0xd1a113 (total size: 7.4 MB)

Fig. 2. Verifying the existence of hot-text

```
~]# grep -A 15 "00600000-" /proc/3007136/smaps
00600000-00e00000 r-xp 00000000 00:00 0
Size:               8192 kB
Rss:                8192 kB
Pss:                4096 kB
Shared_Clean:          0 kB
Shared_Dirty:       8192 kB
Private_Clean:         0 kB
Private_Dirty:         0 kB
Referenced:         8192 kB
Anonymous:          8192 kB
LazyFree:              0 kB
AnonHugePages:      8192 kB
ShmemPmdMapped:        0 kB
Shared_Hugetlb:        0 kB
Private_Hugetlb:       0 kB
Swap:                  0 kB
```

Hot-text placed on huge pages (AnonHugePages: 8192KB, or 4 huge pages)

Fig. 3. Verifying the hot-text is deployed on huge pages (host name anonymized)

hot functions to huge pages if possible, and it achieves this by copying the text segment of the binary and using *mmap()* to map the text segment to huge pages.

The second line of code change is to call *hugify_self()* in *main()* function. This function needs to be called in the beginning of the *main()* function for the best result.

Build Configuration Change. The build configuration change allows the profiled data to be retrieved and used during linking. Specifically, it adds a few lines to build TARGETS file. It retrieves the meta file that contains the *hot functions* information of the particular service from *Everstore*. The retrieval is via HTTP, which is supported by *Everstore* and *Buck* [12] using *remote_file* call. To ensure correctness, the meta file is checked by *SHA1* hash.

4.3   Verifying the Optimization Is in Place

To make sure the optimization is in place, two things need to be verified: hot-text is in the binary, and hot-text is placed on huge pages. In the following, we demonstrate the verification steps under Linux.

Hot-text verification. If a binary has the hot-text extracted, the binary should have symbols that indicate the starting/ending address of the hot-text. Specifically, the hot-text region starts with *_hot_start* and ends with *_hot_end*. nm utility [13] can list the symbols from the binary, and by examining the output of the symbols (*nm -S –numeric-sort /proc/pid/exe*, where *pid* is the process id of the running binary), we can verify the existence of hot-text.

Let's examine an example. As it shows in Fig. 2 the hot-text region starts from *0x600000* and ends at *0xd1a113*. The total size is 7446803 bytes, or about 7 MB.

Huge pages verification. To verify the hot-text is stored on huge pages, we can examine the running process by checking the *smaps* file, e.g. *grep -A 20 "600000-" /proc/pid/smaps*. As shown in Fig. 3, the *AnonHugePages* allocated is 8192 KB, or about 4 huge pages (2 MB each), indicating the hot-text is loaded to huge pages. In scenarios where hot-text is not put on huge pages, it will show *AnonHugePages: 0 KB*.

5   Performance Results

5.1   Experiences with Many Services

We applied the *hot_text* and *huge_page* solution to many services and gained deep understanding of the improvement degrees on various types of performance metrics. Based on our experiences, typically the most immediate performance improvement is reduced iTLB miss rate, it can also help on other metrics.

- *iTLB miss rate.* This is the most obvious benefit, we consistently see up to 50% iTLB cache miss drop for almost all the services that adopted this solution.

- *CPU usage.* CPU usage typically drops by 5% to 10% across the services we worked on.
- *Application throughput.* Applications typically enjoys higher throughput, thanks to the reduced cpu usage.
- *Application query latency.* The query latency mostly will drop due to reduced iTLB cache miss and faster execution.

Note that depending on services and workload characteristics, not all of these metrics will improve. In addition, different services see improvement on different set of performance metrics, and the degrees of improvement vary.

5.2   An Example Service

To understand more about the performance metrics and the extent of improvement, we choose a service to elaborate on the detailed results. The particular service is an online one which directly serves the users, hence both application throughput and latencies are important. Moreover, the service fleet's footprint is significant with many servers, and it is desired to reduce CPU usage such that a single host can serve more users and the service fleet can be shrinked.

We will examine both application level and server system level metrics. For application level metrics, we consider both query/call latencies and application throughput (i.e., queries per second). We also consider multiple percentiles of latencies. Overall we observe 15% throughput improvement and 20% of latency reduction.

For system level metrics, we consider host cpu usage (total, user and kernel usages) and iTLB miss rates. The iTLB miss rate is almost halved, and cpu usage is 5% lower. Across the 50+ services we have worked on, applying this solution typically reduces cpu usage by 5% to 10%. We also estimated that about half of such cpu reduction gain comes from *hot-text*, while the other half comes from *huge page*.

Server System Performance. The iTLB miss rate is shown in Fig. 4(a). Before applying the solution, the iTLB miss rate is up to 800 iTLB misses per million instructions during peaks, which is very severe. After the optimization is in place, iTLB miss rate almost drops by half. Specifically, during peaks, the highest iTLB miss rate is about 425 misses per million instructions, or a 49% drop.

As a result of the dropped iTLB miss rate, the CPU usage drops by 5% (i.e., from 32% to 30.5% at their peaks), as shown in Fig. 4(b). The user level cpu drops by 15%, while kernel level cpu increases by about 7%, as shown in Figs. 5(a) and (b), respectively.

Application Level Performance. Application level metrics are shown in Figs. 5(c) and 6. The blue curve is *before optimization* (i.e., data sets of DS1/ DS3/F1), and the yellow curve is *after optimization* (i.e., data sets of

(a) iTLB miss rate (per million instructions)

(b) host cpu usage (%)

Fig. 4. System level performance (iTLB miss rates and host cpu usage)

DS2/DS4/F2). P50 of application query latencies drops by up to 25%, P90 drops by up to 10%, and P99 drops by up to 60%.

The application throughput (qps)increases by up to 15% (i.e., peak throughput increases from 3.6 M qps to 4.1 M qps). It is very delightful to see both throughput and latency improvements at application level.

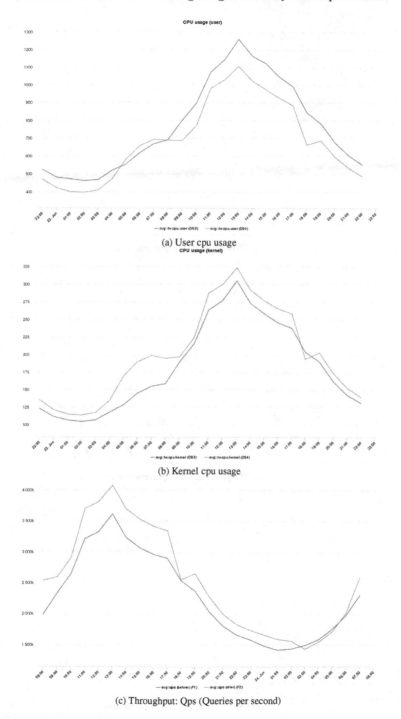

(a) User cpu usage

(b) Kernel cpu usage

(c) Throughput: Qps (Queries per second)

Fig. 5. System (User/kernel CPU) and application level performance (Throughput) (Color figure online)

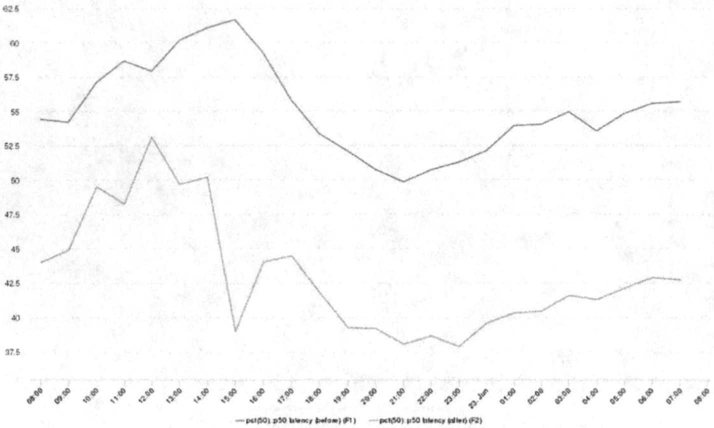

(a) P50 query latency improvement (ms)

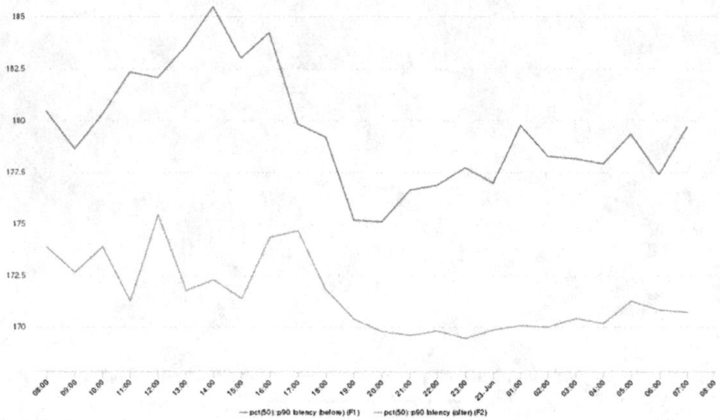

(b) P90 query latency improvement (ms)

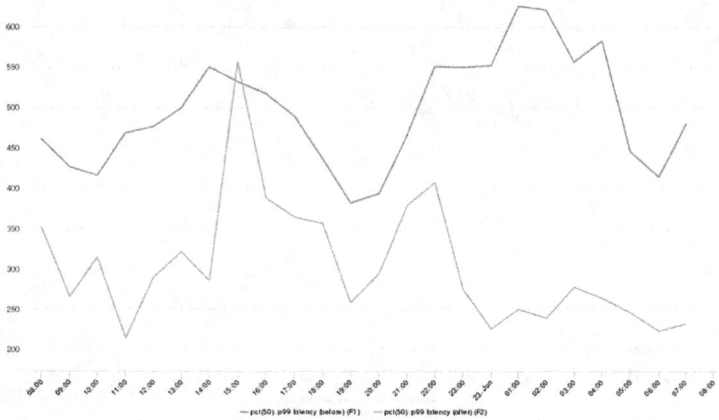

(c) P99 query latency improvement (ms)

Fig. 6. Application level performance (query latency) (Color figure online)

6   Discussions

6.1   Hot-Texts Not Being Placed on Huge Pages

During our performance optimizations with some services, we happened to notice that for some services that already incorporated the solution we propose in this paper, some hosts do not place hot-text on huge pages. We digged into that issue and found it is due to the way the huge pages are handled.

Currently the huge pages are not pre-allocated during OS starts, instead, it is a best-effort. When the binary loads, OS will try to find continuous memory big enough for a huge page to place hot-text. If the memory is sufficiently fragmented and no huge pages can be found, then it will fall back to use regular pages.

To what degree does this issue occur depends on many factors that affect memory fragmentation, including system *up-time* and memory pressure level. For instance, we have found *Haswell* hosts are more likely to have such issue than *Broadwell* hosts, thanks to the former's higher load and memory pressure.

In addition to reserving huge pages, another solution is to *defrag* memory before loading the service binary (e.g., */roc/sys/vm/drop_caches* and */proc/sys/vm/compact_memory*). Memory defragmentation can compact fragmented pages, hence resulting in higher chances of being able to find huge pages when loading the binary.

6.2   Hot Function File Retrieval Failure

Building the binary package with this optimization needs to retrieve the hot function file from *Everstore*. *Everstore* is very reliable based on our experience, and only 1 failure is encountered when loading hot functions in a year. But in the worst scenario where if it fails to retrieve the hot function file, the binary build will fail.

6.3   Downside of This Approach

There is very little downside (e.g., very little performance overhead) about using this approach, thanks to the automatic profiling and diff landing. The major downside is longer binary-building time.

Another concern about using huge pages is the memory waste (i.e., up to 1 page), depending on the way they are used. Reserved huge pages are always paged into memory, and the recommendation is to reserve just-enough pages. THP, on the other hand, is free from this concern. The possible memory waste is when a huge page is not entirely used. When the number of huge pages used is small compared to the total available memory, this concern might be negligible. Based on our experiences, most services only use a few 2 MB huge pages, which is trivial compared to the total available memory (e.g., hundreds of GBs).

7   Related Work

Many works optimize the performance of the binary using various types of techniques during different phases of compiling, linking and post-linking of the binaries.

During compiling time, instrumentation-based schemes have been employed by GCC and Microsoft C/C++. In GCC world, such optimization is called FDO (Feedback-Driven Optimization) [4], while Microsoft refers to it as PGO (Profile-Guided Optimization) [4]. These schemes also effectively re-compile hot code for *speed* and cold code for *size*. As a result, the overall code size is typically reduced by FDO/PGO. GCC's AutoFDO (Automatic Feedback Directed Optimizer, [14]) is another feature that uses run-time feedback mechanism to help compiler, enabling wider range of optimizations. Specifically, LLVM supports AutoFDO framework that easily converts linux *perf* output into LLVM consumable profile file.

During linking time, techniques such as the *hot-text* optimization described in this paper [9] use a linker script and operates on a function-by-function basis. Work [9] elaborates on some of the internal mechanisms to make this optimization happen, and we further build a framework to automate the entire process with an end-to-end pipeline. Safe ICF (Identical Code Folding) [15] takes another approach of detecting functions that contain redundancies and folding/merging functions into a single copy.

There are also post-link optimizers. BOLT (Binary Optimization and Layout Tool) [16,17] is a post-link optimizer developed to improve running performance of non-trivial binaries. It operates on a finer basic block granularity and achieves the goal by optimizing application's code layout based on execution profile gathered by sampling profilers (e.g., Linux *perf*). Specifically for Intel, Ispike [18] is another post-link optimizer.

At system level (i.e., Operating system and hardware), countless works have demonstrated the potentials and shared the experiences of speeding up software running on various types of OS and hardware. Work in [19] evaluates the accuracy of multiple event-based sampling techniques and quantifies the impact of the improvements claimed by many other techniques.

Moving up to application level, even more places can be optimized for better performance, thanks to the heterogeneity of different types of applications and services. At Facebook, we have designed and improved many services and products [11,20]. As an example, RocksDB [21] a persistent key-value store developed by Facebook, has been continuously optimized for many different scenarios [2,22].

8   Conclusion

Facebook, having one of the world's biggest computing infrastructures, treats performance optimizations seriously. During the course of various types of performance improvement efforts, we have accumulated techniques, tools and experiences to speed up our services. One of these approaches is an automated framework to incorporate both *hot-text* and *huge pages* and enable service owners to adopt this optimization with minimum effort. The solution identifies hot-text of the binary and places the binary on huge pages. The solution is further wrapped into an automated framework, enabling service owners to effortlessly adopt it. The framework has been applied to dozens of our services, proved effective and has significantly improved our service efficiencies.

Acknowledgements. The solution presented in this paper involves many peoples' efforts, which include new services or feature enhancements of existing services. In particular, we thank Guilherme Ottoni and Bert Maher for working on HFSort, Mark Williams for implementing hugify_self(), Denis Sheahan and Pallab Bhattacharya for substantiating a generic library, and Mirek Klimos for the support that allows automated refreshing of profiling data.

References

1. Chen, G.J., et al.: Realtime data processing at Facebook. In: Proceedings of the 2016 International Conference on Management of Data, SIGMOD 2016, New York, NY, USA (2016)
2. Dong, S., Callaghan, M., Galanis, L., Borthakur, D., Savor, T., Strum, M.: Optimizing space amplification in RocksDB. In: Proceedings of the 8th Biennial Conference on Innovative Data Systems Research (CIDR 2017). Chaminade, California (2017)
3. Annamalai, M., et al.: Sharding the shards: managing datastore locality at scale with Akkio. In: Proceedings of the 12th USENIX Conference on Operating Systems Design and Implementation, OSDI 2018, Berkeley, CA, USA (2018)
4. Wicht, B., Vitillo, R.A., Chen, D., Levinthal, D.: Hardware counted profile-guided optimization. CoRR, vol. abs/1411.6361 (2014). http://arxiv.org/abs/1411.6361
5. Transparent Hugepage Support. https://www.kernel.org/doc/Documentation/vm/transhuge.txt
6. Intel HasWell Architecture. https://ark.intel.com/content/www/us/en/ark/products/codename/42174/haswell.html
7. Advanced usage of last branch records. https://lwn.net/Articles/680996/
8. HFSort. https://github.com/facebook/hhvm/tree/master/hphp/tools/hfsort
9. Ottoni, G., Maher, B.: Optimizing function placement for large-scale data-center applications. In: Proceedings of the 2017 International Symposium on Code Generation and Optimization, CGO 2017, Piscataway, NJ, USA (2017)
10. Data pipelines at Facebook. https://www.meetup.com/DataCouncil-AI-NewYorkCity-Data-Engineering-Science/events/189614862/
11. Barrigas, H., Barrigas, D., Barata, M., Furtado, P., Bernardino, J.: Overview of Facebook scalable architecture. In: Proceedings of the International Conference on Information Systems and Design of Communication, ISDOC 2014 (2014)
12. Buck: A high-performance build tool. https://buckbuild.com/
13. NM utility. https://sourceware.org/binutils/docs/binutils/nm.html
14. Chen, D., Li, D.X., Moseley, T.: AutoFDO: automatic feedback-directed optimization for warehouse-scale applications. In: Proceedings of the 2016 International Symposium on Code Generation and Optimization, CGO 2016, New York, NY, USA (2016)

15. Tallam, S., Coutant, C., Taylor, I.L., Li, X.D., Demetriou, C.: Safe ICF: pointer safe and unwinding aware identical code folding in gold. In: GCC Developers Summit (2010)
16. Panchenko, M., Auler, R., Nell, B., Ottoni, G.: Bolt: a practical binary optimizer for data centers and beyond. In: Proceedings of the 2019 IEEE/ACM International Symposium on Code Generation and Optimization, CGO 2019, pp. 2–14. IEEE Press, Piscataway (2019)
17. Binary Optimization and Layout Tool. https://github.com/facebookincubator/BOLT
18. Luk, C.-K., Muth, R., Patil, H., Cohn, R., Lowney, G.: Ispike: a post-link optimizer for the Intel Itanium architecture. In: Proceedings of the International Symposium on Code Generation and Optimization: Feedback-directed and Runtime Optimization, CGO 2004, Washington, DC, USA (2004)
19. Nowak, A., Yasin, A., Mendelson, A., Zwaenepoel, W.: Establishing a base of trust with performance counters for enterprise workloads. In: Proceedings of the 2015 USENIX Conference on USENIX Annual Technical Conference, USENIX ATC 2015, Berkeley, CA, USA, pp. 541–548 (2015)
20. Scaling server software at Facebook. In Applicative 2016, Applicative 2016, speaker-Watson, Dave (2016)
21. RocksDB: A persistent key-value store. https://rocksdb.org/
22. Ouaknine, K., Agra, O., Guz, Z.: Optimization of RocksDB for Redis on flash. In: Proceedings of the International Conference on Compute and Data Analysis, ICCDA 2017, New York, NY, USA (2017)

ThunderML: A Toolkit for Enabling AI/ML Models on Cloud for Industry 4.0

Shrey Shrivastava$^{(\boxtimes)}$, Dhaval Patel, Wesley M. Gifford, Stuart Siegel, and Jayant Kalagnanam

IBM Research, 1101 Kitchawan Road, Yorktown Heights, NY, USA
shrey@ibm.com, {pateldha,wmgifford,stus,jayant}@us.ibm.com

Abstract. AI, machine learning, and deep learning tools have now become easily accessible on the cloud. However, the adoption of these cloud-based services for heavy industries has been limited due to the gap between general purpose AI tools and operational requirements for production industries. There are three fundamentals gaps. The first is the lack of purpose built solution pipelines designed for common industrial problem types, the second is the lack of tools for automating the learning from noisy sensor data and the third is the lack of platforms which help practitioners leverage cloud-based environment for building and deploying custom modeling pipelines. In this paper, we present ThunderML, a toolkit that addresses these gaps by providing powerful programming model that allows rapid authoring, training and deployment for Industry 4.0 applications. Importantly, the system also facilitates cloud-based deployments by providing a vendor agnostic pipeline execution and deployment layer.

Keywords: Cognitive computing · IoT sensor data ·
Machine learning · Deep learning · Purpose built AI pipelines

1 Introduction

The single biggest transformation on the horizon for heavy capital, large manufacturing and industrial companies is Industry 4.0 [14]. The promise of this transformation is to provide a digital semantic representation of the physical manufacturing world consisting of the production plant, the heavy capital assets, and the supply chain network (inventory and warehouse systems, and logistics). This representation is continuously replenished with real time sensor data using high bandwidth, low cost networks to provide up-to-date situational awareness of the enterprise. This, in turn, supports improved operational efficiency and production yields, as well as a deeper understanding of the enterprise's effect on the demand-supply dynamics of the manufacturing ecosystem. The key to leveraging the transformation to Industry 4.0 is developing models to utilize the available data to forecast and optimize enterprise operation.

© Springer Nature Switzerland AG 2019
J. Miller et al. (Eds.): ICWS 2019, LNCS 11512, pp. 163–180, 2019.
https://doi.org/10.1007/978-3-030-23499-7_11

Although AI technologies are now mature enough to provide industrial-strength solutions that bring better efficiencies and asset availability [3,5,20], adoption within the heavy industries still lags behind that of several other domains. There are three main obstacles to more widespread adoption of AI. The first is the lack of purpose-built AI solutions designed to improve industrial operations. The second is the lack of tools for automating the construction of AI models over IoT sensor data which are often highly non-linear, contain dynamic state transitions, exhibit lag relationships, and require a great deal of specialized feature extraction before being useful for AI modeling. The third is the lack of toolkits that help AI practitioners leverage cloud-based environments for building and deploying custom modeling pipelines.

The system we have developed, ThunderML, attempts to address these issues. Firstly, it provides pre-built solution templates in industrial domain for expediting the creation of AI models. Next, it aims to provide AI practitioners with a toolkit to translate their industrial problem statements into a well defined and executable pipeline. Lastly, it presents the settings to facilitate cloud-based AI environments including the management of training experiments and model deployment in a vendor agnostic way. In this paper we will focus almost exclusively on the latter two capabilities as we think these are the most broadly applicable.

1.1 Challenges of Using Existing Cloud-Based AI Platforms

While cloud-based AI platforms have done much to facilitate adoption of AI by alleviating many of the infrastructure provisioning and maintenance challenges associated with on-premises enterprise AI initiatives, they have not done enough to abstract away some of the complexity of running AI workflows in vendor agnostic ways. Current platforms expect practitioners to know a given vendor's means and methods of interacting with the computing resources without consideration given to providing a common programming model that makes the job of an AI practitioner easier. Cloud-based AI environments, by their very nature, push users towards batch training modes to facilitate data center resource management via a queued execution model. Such batch training modes are problematic for many data scientists who wish to see errors or results in real or near real time in order to make their modeling workflow more efficient.[1]

Another issue is that cloud-offerings typically approach AI from either a black-box perspective which offers users simplicity at the cost of flexibility or through a more complex runtime environment that requires users maintain code artifacts that often have nothing to do with the actual AI tasks at hand[2]. Even with a diverse set of offerings in the market, we feel a gap remains for the AI practitioner community. Cloud AI offerings should be easy to learn and use and provide the right level of complexity and flexibility AI practitioners need.

---

[1] https://cloud.google.com/blog/topics/research/new-study-the-state-of-ai-in-the-enterprise.

[2] https://aws.amazon.com/blogs/aws/iot-analytics-now-generally-available/.

In order to address these issues, we have developed ThunderML, a Python-based toolkit that makes the creation and deployment of purpose built AI models for industrial applications easier. ThunderML leverages many open source frameworks such as scikit-learn, Tensorflow, and Keras. The extension points are predominantly in terms of how we have built out a series of useful modeling functions and industrial solution templates to expedite the task of building and deploying AI for industrial applications. ThunderML is flexible enough to run on local hardware as well as providing an easier path to using common cloud service provider platforms for enhanced scalability in training and convenient model deployment services.

Before we proceed, it's worth briefly giving a few examples of purpose built industrial solution templates available in ThunderML:

- *Time Series Prediction (TSPred)*: Flexible solution for forecasting time series from historical data in industries.
- *Failure Pattern Analysis (FPA)*: Predicting imminent failures for assets using IoT sensor data and past failure history data;
- *Root Cause Analysis (RCA):* Building interpretable models to assist plant operators track down the root causes for product quality deviances on batch or continuous process lines;
- *Anomaly Analysis:* Building unsupervised/semi-supervised models to identify anomalous behaviors of manufacturing assets;
- *Cognitive Plant Advisor (CPA)*: Combines advanced AI to build a predictive model of one or more key process outputs such as throughput and yield and uses these models within a business objective optimization problem to suggest optimal process settings to plant operators.

In summary, ThunderML can also help alleviate the skills gap issue that has hampered AI adoption in many industries. In our experience, technically adept (but not necessarily experts in AI personnel) can use ThunderML's industry templates and programming interface to enable industry AI models.

1.2 Contribution

Our contribution in this paper is the design and implementation of ThunderML. We elaborately discuss how ThunderML expedites the AI modeling workflow by giving practitioners an easier path for doing advanced modeling work leveraging cloud-based platforms for training and deployment. We then provide a use case to demonstrate the benefits of ThunderML in practice for a very general and widely applicable problem.

Figure 1 shows a high-level schematic representation of ThunderML's component architecture. At the lowest level, "Core AI Toolkits", we leverage common AI frameworks like scikit-learn [17], tensorflow, and keras for building modular AI functions that our purpose built solutions either utilize directly or extend. The next layer, "Pipeline Management", exposes an API that allows users to stitch these modular AI functions and compose multiple path pipelines. This layer also manages the execution metadata like- the choice of target runtimes (e.g., a local machine, a spark cluster, or a remote cloud vendor execution environment), hyperparameter tuning, the maximum allowable training time, and the model scoring metric. In the next layer, "Pipeline Path Decomposer", the large number of possible modeling pipelines and hyperparameter combinations are decomposed to make them trainable in an parallel fashion (e.g., on a cloud vendor elastic compute service which can queue very large numbers of independent user jobs in an asynchronous fashion). In the final layer, "Cloud Vendor Interaction API", decomposed pipeline paths get packaged and transferred in a way suitable for job submission to a cloud-vendor's remote execution service. This layer handles the particulars of a vendor's platform API requirements to liberate users from the laborious task of learning the details of how to interact with a particular vendor's compute and storage services. It submits jobs, monitors progress, retrieves results, selects among the best of these (based on user-supplied metric) and manages the final deployment of models to the vendor deployment services.

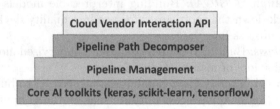

Fig. 1. High-level schematic representation of ThunderML's component architecture.

2   ThunderML: Background

In this section, we establish a few concepts at the abstraction level of activity being performed. ThunderML is based on the foundation of scikit-learn's framework [17] as it is the most commonly used framework in the community, both in academia and industry. We will use one of our purpose built industrial solution templates - **Time Series Prediction (TSPred)** as an example and give concrete examples of the terminology in the context of this problem.

The TSPred is a very pertinent and complex problem in the industry and forms the basis of other time series problems. It provides a good use case for ThunderML for two reasons. Firstly, it demonstrates how a AI problem statements can be converted into a AI pipelines using the ThunderML's unique and flexible programming model (Sect. 2). Secondly, we show how the TSPred benefits from the ThunderML's cloud based execution architectures in a vendor agnostic manner (Sect. 3).

2.1   AI Functions

A **function** is defined as the task surrounding the development of an AI model. This involves transformations on a dataset, training a model on the given dataset, and model performance evaluation. This usually involves the model, and the configuration associated with the modeling activity, like a single set of parameters. Since our focus for ThunderML is it being a toolkit for AI, functions are the fundamental units in higher-level AI tasks. We have created a programming model which allows users to easily define Directed acyclic graphs (DAGs) for controlling the sequence of operation for these AI functions. In the context of TSPred, the AI functions have been defined in four categories- transformers, models, model evaluation, cross-validation.

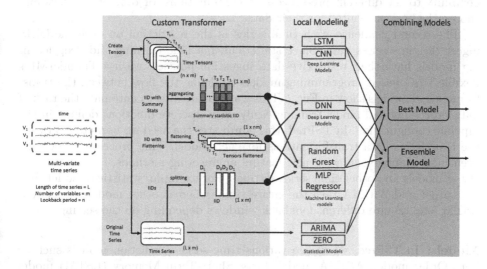

Fig. 2. Architecture of AI pipeline for time series prediction problem.

Custom Transformations: These transformation functions appropriately prepare the data for the modeling activity and it becomes specially important in the TSPred since training time series models requires well-defined time-ordered input and output training data. The time series prediction problem uses a fixed-width sliding window called the **lookback window** and tries to predict the value for future timestamps. For example, in a time series, we can take a sliding window of length n from time t to $t - n + 1$ (inclusive) and predict the value at the future timestamp $t + 1$ for the case of 1-step ahead prediction. In this case, the 3-dimensional vector of multivariate sliding windows is referred to as a **time tensor** and is the input to the model. Whereas the vector consisting of values at $t + 1$ is the output for training purposes. The custom transformer has the job of creation of such input-output pairs for training models in time series prediction problems brings new challenges. The two main challenges which we address are:

1. The temporal nature of the data needs to be retained when creating features from the time series.
2. Different models require different formats of input and output data during modeling.

The Custom Transformer handles the first challenge by considering multiple feature-processing AI functions for time series data. As mentioned above, we have implemented five types of transformer function: identity mapping, time-tensor preparation, window-based feature summary extraction, window-based flattened feature vectors, and time series as-it-is, as shown in Fig. 2. These cover elaborate cases for the use case of time series feature extraction. Depending on the model input, we provide different features to the models. It gives users the flexibility to try different pre-processing combinations for different models and choose the best one suited for their data.

The second challenge with time series is the restriction on each model to ingest the time series data. Since statistical, machine learning and deep learning models have their respective data ingestion policies, we use ThunderML's flexible DAG based programming models to define the flow between the transformers and models show in Fig. 2. This way, we are able to automate the task of data processing and model training easily with discrete functions defined in the pipeline configuration. In TSPred, this eliminates the need for users to deal with the time series data transformations for each model. This process can become even more cumbersome with new feature engineering methods, increasing variety of models and other time series settings. For example, statistical models like zero order and ARIMA take the entire time, whereas other models like CNN, LSTM, etc. require different lookback windows depending on the setting.

Models: In TSPred, we utilize various time series prediction models such as Zero Order model, ARIMA model, Long Short-Term Memory (LSTM) model [9,13], Multilayer Perceptron (MLP) Regressor [18], Random Forest Regressor, Deep Neural Network (DNN), Convolutional neural network (CNN) [12], WaveNet [19] and SeriesNet [11].

Model Evaluation: We also use some AI functions which provide model evaluation capabilities. Our framework leverages scikit-learn's as well as custom model evaluation methods and the pipeline is flexible to use any of them if the models in the pipeline support it.

Cross Validation: We implement the usage of different cross validation (CV) techniques in the form of AI functions. Similar to specifying models and transformers, CV objects can also be provided by the user. CV is critical in the case of time series data as we need to maintain the sequential order. We have implemented several time series CV functions which are illustrated in Fig. 3

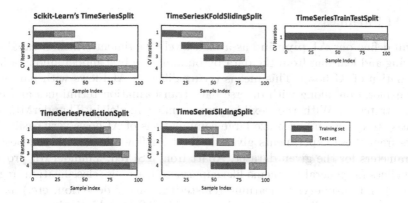

Fig. 3. Comparison of cross validation approaches used for time series models

2.2 AI Flows

An **AI flow** extends the functionality of the AI functions by connecting sequences of tasks like preprocessing the data and post processing the results in 'flows'. Although similar to the machine learning pipelines defined in scikit-learn's framework, AI Flow expands this definition by introducing ThunderML's unique DAG based programming model, providing very high flexibility while defining pipelines. This includes modeling functions, and just like scikit-learn's pipeline, it includes other steps like pre-processing (dimension reduction, scaling, etc.). The AI flow usually consists of multiple sets of parameters for each transformer and estimator, as well as a scoring method (classification-accuracy, ROC, AUC, etc.; regression-r^2, mean absolute error, etc.) based on which the best set of parameters are chosen. Each path from start to end in the Fig. 2 is an example of a AI flow in the context of TSPred.

The process by which the parameters are chosen, or hyperparameter optimization, is conducted by one of the following methods: complete grid search, random grid search and RBFOpt. The parameter grid chosen are model dependent and it consists of values that are known to give better performance. One example of parameter grid specification for ThunderML is described below:

Listing 1.1. Param grid sample

```
keras_param_grid = {'optimizer':[{'adam':{'amsgrad':[False],
                     'beta_1':[0.9],
                     'beta_2':[0.999],
                     'decay':[0.0],
                     'epsilon':[None],
                     'lr': [0.001, 0.01]}}],
                     'kernel_initializer':['glorot_uniform'],
                     'dropout_rate':[0,0.2,0.5],
                     'loss':['mean_squared_error']}
```

2.3   AI Pipelines

We will define our **AI pipeline** as a high-level experiment which is capable of exploring and learning from the data by building the best model among a large combination of AI flows. This means trying different AI Flows with parameter space exploration, along with diverse data transformation techniques and evaluation strategies. With the flexible programming model in ThunderML, it is very easy to define and organize large combinations of AI flows very easily. The results from these experiments gives the best AI flow along with the best set of parameters for the given dataset. Apart from TSPred, ThunderML provides AI pipelines for general problems like supervised learning (classification, regression etc.) and unsupervised learning (clustering, outlier detection, etc.) as well as purpose built pipelines mentioned above. The TSPred AI pipeline consists of three major stages:

1. The **custom transformation** stage
2. In the **local modeling stage** stage, the model for different flows run independent from each other and produce independent scores.
3. In the **model combining** stage, we output the results either by providing the top scoring AI flow or the combination of top AI flows using ensemble techniques.

In summary, there are many different ways to build models for time series prediction problems, and the best method may vary from dataset to dataset. Thus, a tool for automatic discovery of best prediction model is needed, which AI practitioners can easily configure based on their problem statement.

2.4   Practical AI Using ThunderML

The ThunderML toolkit leverages popular machine learning frameworks like scikit-learn, Tensorflow, Keras etc. to allow users to define distinct AI flows and quickly build complex AI pipelines. Along with the pipelines, the users can create AI solution templates by defining other stages surrounding the AI pipelines in a modular fashion. To demonstrate the flexibility and easy of ThunderML, a simple pseudo code for TSPred (Fig. 2) has been provided below:

Listing 1.2. Pseudo code for Fig. 2

```
def  purpose_built_pipeline ():
    Task =  AIPipeline ()

    Task.add_flow (flow_name='temportal'
                [[ TimeTensor ()] , #Transformer AI  Functions
                [LSTM() ,  DNN() ,  CNN()]] #Model AI  Functions
                )
    Task.add_flow (flow_name='iid ',
                [[ IdentityMapping () ,  WindowFeatures () ,
                WindowFlattening ()] ,
```

```
                        [DNN(), RandomForest(), MLP()]]
                      )
    Task.add_flow(flow_name='statistical',
                  [[NoOperation()],
                  [ARIMA(), Zero()]]
                  )

    Task.scoring(['best', 'stacking_ensemble'])
    Task.create_graph()
    return Task

TSPred = purpose_built_pipeline()
TSPred.execute()
```

The next advantage ThunderML provides the user is in terms of the flexibility of execution. Once an AI practitioner pragmatically defines their problem statement in the form of AI Pipelines as shown above, ThunderML provides the flexibility of using local hardware for execution as well as option to going through the cloud route with common cloud service provider platforms for enhanced scalability. These are described in greater detail in the next Section.

3   ThunderML: Cloud-Based Execution Architectures

ThunderML **is one** of the first systems which allows you to interact with enterprise cloud services to perform comprehensive machine learning experiments in a programmatic way. The system **developed** wraps the interfaces between the user and the cloud services API, allowing users to use the cloud services transparently and train models easily.

In any AI tasks, the basic components are the dataset and the AI pipeline definitions. With the introduction of cloud, it adds another requirement for the cloud services. Hence in a cloud based architecture for ThunderML, these are the main components:

- **Cloud Service:**
  - ML training and deployment services: With the addition of cloud platform as the machine learning runtime, the user need to have an account on the respective enterprise cloud offerings and valid 'user-credentials' to access the cloud runtime services.
  - Cloud storage service: Most of the ML services use an internal cloud storage service where the results of the training experiment are stored.
- **Component provided by the user:**
  - AI pipeline definition and configuration: An AI pipeline definition provides details on how to execute the AI flows in the cloud runtime environment. The ThunderML enables users to define a complex AI pipeline in a programmatic manner.
  - User data: This can be provided through local execution environment or it can be uploaded to the cloud storage service depending the cloud ML service specification.

- Credential to cloud services: This is the access key to the cloud service and needs to be provisioned by the user once the services have been created.

The steps for setting up the cloud services (services for training, deployment and storage) are generally very well documented in all enterprise cloud offerings. Once the setup for the above components is done correctly, the user can start defining and executing of their AI pipelines with their data seamlessly with ThunderML's execution architecture. The interaction diagram of how ThunderML leverages enterprise cloud service is shown in Fig. 4.

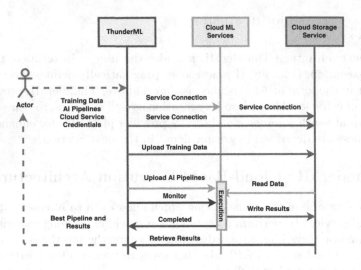

Fig. 4. Interaction diagrams shows how the users can leverage cloud services to run AI pipeline with the help of ThunderML toolkit

The first step in the interaction diagram is providing ThunderML with the training data, AI pipeline and cloud service credentials. ThunderML uses the credentials to connect with the cloud services and creates a client for both the ML and storage services in local execution environment. Using the cloud storage client, ThunderML uploads the user's data to the cloud storage space so that the ML service can use it. Once the data is uploaded, ThunderML configures the AI pipeline to be executed at the ML instance with different settings. There are two architectures proposed here, which provide different execution styles for running AI pipelines. The basic difference between these two architectures are in the following aspects: time, cost, and flexibility. The two execution styles, **coarse** and **fine** execution, are described in greater detail below. ThunderML processes the pipeline configuration before sending them to the ML service. Once the pipeline configuration reaches the ML service, it obtains the data from the storage system and executes the AI pipeline. The training results are generated and stored in the cloud storage. These include the result summary files, log files, trained AI function (for getting trained model weights in the case of deep learning models) and the parameters. Once this process is completed, ThunderML retrieves the training results from the storage service. Lastly, the cleaning of the cloud storage, removal of any temporary files as well as terminating the kernel is handled by ThunderML.

The results of the AI pipeline is returned from the cloud storage and stored locally for the user. The details of the entire process are hidden from the user; they never have to directly interact with the cloud, and the process is essentially the same as running local python code.

3.1 Coarse Execution

Coarse execution refers to executing a AI pipelines in a more traditional way, i.e. **sequentially** on the cloud's processing power. As shown in Fig. 5, the ThunderML takes the pipeline and its configurations and bundles them as a single package at step 3. This package contains the AI pipeline definition along with the supporting configurations.

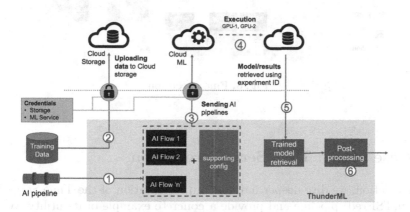

Fig. 5. Coarse execution

Once the AI pipeline definitions reach the ML service, the ThunderML configures the ML service to instantiate a container with on the cloud for executing the pipelines. The container has specific resources allocated to it as defined by the ML service. The pipeline runs in this container and each of the AI flows run one after other in a sequential fashion as shown by the step 4 in Fig. 5.

3.2 Fine Execution

The fine execution architecture leverages the cloud's processing power in a **parallel** manner. ThunderML takes the AI pipeline and splits them into multiple parts, one for each AI flow along with it's associated configurations and creates individual packages for them as shown in step 3 of Fig. 6. Then ThunderML configures the ML service to instantiate multiple containers, one container per AI flow on the cloud. Since each AI flow receives independent resources, the execution process is expedited as shown in step 4 of Fig. 6. The improvement in execution time might come at the cost of less efficient resource management at the enterprise cloud back-end. Although the resource utilization does not differ much due to the fact that number of calculations in the AI pipeline are independent of the type of execution.

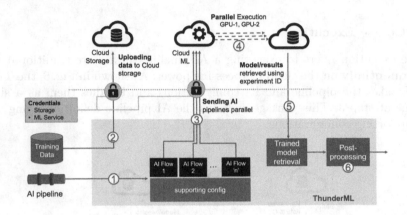

Fig. 6. Fine execution

4   Case Study: Time Series Prediction

In this section, we dive deeper into our implementation of the Time Series Prediction(TSPred) pipeline and provide a concrete example of its utility. We will formally define the time series prediction problem providing some background, then we discuss the different experiments we conducted and the corresponding results.

4.1   Background and Motivation

A time series is a sequence of real valued observations that are captured over a period of time. The time series prediction problem typically takes the form of predicting the future values of some observations over some time horizon, given historical values of those observations. The inputs and outputs may be multivariate or univariate in nature and additional control variables may be present. For simplicity we will focus on the univariate case, but the proposed framework can easily adapt to other settings.

Among all the interesting work on time series analysis such as anomaly detection to root cause analysis, time series prediction (forecasting) is an extremely common problem studied in numerous domains, including weather forecasting, web traffic forecasting, and stock market prediction. With the increasing deployment of IoT sensors for monitoring industrial assets and manufacturing processes, a huge amount of in-operation time series sensor data is now available.

One distinct characteristic of time series data is that they generally do not follow the IID (independent and identically distributed) assumption, i.e., the data points in time series are correlated to each other in the time domain. The non-IID assumption for time series data makes existing off-the-shelf machine learning solutions such as Google's Cloud AutoML[3], Auto-scikit-learn [7], TPOT [16] less applicable, since extra care needs to be taken when performing cross validation and feature engineering for time series data. Thus, there is a need for a framework that specifically supports time series prediction problems.

4.2   Experiment 1: Coarse and Fine Execution

The purpose of the experiment is to analyze the performance of the two cloud based execution architectures discussed in the Sect. 3 on out TSPred pipeline. Since the purpose of this experiment is to compare the two architectures and not evaluate the accuracy, we will apply some constraints to our experiment. We only use 12 models in the pipeline (listed in Table 1), we run this experiment with only two univariate time-series datasets and each model uses default parameters only. Models with '_10' in their name utilize a lookback window of 10 otherwise it is a lookback of 1, which is basically a model which treats the previous day's reading as an IID point discarding the temporal characteristics. The cross-validation strategy used here is $TimeSeriesTrainTestSplit$ (as shown in Fig. 3) with fraction of train, validation and test portions set to 0.8, 0.1, 0.1. The scoring method for evaluating the model performance in the validation set as well as test set is done using Mean Absolute Error. The results of this experiment are provided in the Table 1.

One thing to consider in this experiment is that while using cloud based services, there is an additional cost associated with packaging the AI pipeline and dataset (if the data is not on cloud services initially) and sending these packages to the cloud ML services through rest API calls. The fine execution splits each AI pipeline into a different package as compared to the coarse execution which just sends a single package for the entire pipeline. This means that fine execution has greater time cost associated with managing execution. From our experiments on the three datasets, we have seen that for uploading the package for an AI pipeline with 12 models, the fine execution takes around 80–90 s, whereas the coarse execution takes around 12–14 s which only sends one package. There is a difference of 70–80 s when running 12 models. Similarly, a cost is added while retrieving the results for each AI flow post execution and coarse execution and adding a difference of 70–80 s. This suggests that the fine execution has an overhead of 150 s when compared to coarse execution of AI pipeline with 12 flows. We run this experiment with 2 epoch values for deep learning models - 500 and

---

[3] https://cloud.google.com/automl/.

Table 1. Coarse vs. fine performance results

Univariate dataset 1 (length = 229)				
	Epochs = 500			
Model	Coarse (609 s)		Fine (515 s)	
	MAE	Time (s)	MAE	Time (s)
simple_LSTM_10	0.5	39.35	0.51	38.8
Zero model	**0.91**	0.01	0.91	0.01
mlpregressor	0.56	0.11	0.56	0.12
randomforestregressor	0.57	0.02	0.57	0.05
DNN	0.56	2.91	0.56	2.62
DNN_10	0.55	3.24	0.55	2.66
Wavenet_CNN_10	**0.21**	172.36	0.21	168.36
Simple_CNN_10	0.33	7.05	0.34	4.74
deep_CNN_10	0.23	12.91	0.21	11.75
SeriesNet_CNN_10	0.48	75.61	0.51	72.0
mlpregressor_10	**0.22**	**0.2**	**0.22**	**0.19**
randomforestregressor_10	0.55	0.03	0.55	0.06
Univariate dataset 2 (length = 494)				
	Epochs = 500			
Model	Coarse (770 s)		Fine (696 s)	
	MAE	Time (s)	MAE	Time (s)
simple_LSTM_10	0.44	21.26	0.41	22.16
Zero model	0.52	0.0	0.52	0.0
mlpregressor	0.4	0.1	0.4	0.11
randomforestregressor	1.07	0.03	1.07	0.05
DNN	0.3	2.93	0.31	2.5
DNN_10	0.24	2.89	0.24	2.44
Wavenet_CNN_10	0.28	78.71	0.25	81.62
Simple_CNN_10	0.28	5.61	0.29	4.49
deep_CNN_10	0.36	9.65	0.35	6.44
SeriesNet_CNN_10	0.73	49.46	0.71	49.9
mlpregressor_10	0.23	0.15	0.25	0.17
randomforestregressor_10	0.96	0.03	0.96	0.05

1000 and see if any difference is present. The observations from this experiment are noted below:

- **Model Performance**: The score for a model for a given dataset in both Coarse and Fine execution is similar, suggesting that execution architectures do not affect the accuracy of the models. Sometimes in deep learning models, the scores of a model are drastically different (performing like the baseline model). This can be attributed to random weight initialization in deep learning models.

– **Time of Execution**: The coarse execution take more time than the fine execution in each case. For smallest dataset, the difference between coarse and fine execution (total time) is 80–95 s. With larger datasets this time increase to 90–130 s. Along with the overhead of fine execution, the fine execution is faster than the coarse execution by 220 s–280 s which is one-third of the execution time of the average execution time. This difference will increase with increased data size and larger training run.

4.3   Experiment 2: Univariate Time Series Prediction

In this section we focus on the *univariate time series prediction problem*, where the task is to predict the value of the time series at the next time step. This demonstrates the ability of the ThunderML toolkit to run flexible AI pipelines for a particular learning problem. Since the primary objective is to demonstrate the utility of the pipeline, we will not aggressively search for the best algorithm for the time series prediction problem. Rather, we will demonstrate how multiple models can be explored with the AI pipeline. With proper parameter tuning and training (larger number of epochs for deep learning models), it would be easier to run the same pipeline for surveying which model is the best for the particular problem. We also want to comment on the size of the lookback window which is best for time series prediction for the datasets.

We run this experiment on 15 univariate time-series datasets and 28 models (CNNs, LSTMs, DNNs, Random Forest Regressors, MLP Regressors). Each model is using default parameters and we choose model with either lookback window of 5, 10 or 20 timestamps. Otherwise it is lookback of size 1, which means treating previous day's reading as an IID point and discarding the temporal characteristics. The cross-validation strategy used here is *TimeSeriesTrainTestSplit* (as shown in Fig. 3) with fraction of train, validation and test portions set to 0.8, 0.1, 0.1. The scoring method for evaluating the model performance in the validation set as well as test set is done using Mean Absolute Error (MAE). The summary of the results is provided in the Fig. 7. The _5, _10 and _20 indicate respective lookback window size.

We observed the top five models for each dataset based on the validation score. Since the difference among the top 5 models for each dataset was very small (MAE difference of around 0.01–0.1), we decided to evaluate them on the basis of the top 5 ranking models for a dataset. The observations made from this experiment are intriguing since they allow users to get a deeper understanding of the problem and their data. The main observations that can be made from this experiment are:

Model	Rank-1	Rank-2	Rank-3	Rank-4	Rank-5	Total
Wavenet_CNN_10	3	0	0	3	1	7
Simple_CNN_20	0	2	2	2	1	7
mlpregressor_10	1	0	1	3	2	7
deep_CNN_20	1	2	1	0	2	6
Wavenet_CNN_20	0	1	1	2	2	6
DNN_10	1	1	1	2	0	5
mlpregressor_20	1	3	1	0	0	5
SeriesNet_CNN_20	1	0	1	0	3	5
simple_LSTM_20	3	0	1	0	0	4
simple_LSTM_10	0	1	2	0	1	4
DNN	0	1	2	0	0	3
Wavenet_CNN_5	0	0	1	0	1	2
simple_LSTM_5	0	1	0	0	1	2
mlpregressor	2	0	0	0	0	2
Deep_LSTM_5	0	1	0	1	0	2
Simple_CNN_5	0	2	0	0	0	2
Simple_CNN_10	1	0	0	1	0	2
randomforestregressor_20	0	0	1	0	0	1
randomforestregressor_5	0	0	0	0	1	1
Deep_LSTM_20	0	0	0	1	0	1
SeriesNet_CNN_10	1	0	0	0	0	1
Deep_LSTM_10	0	0	0	0	0	0
randomforestregressor_10	0	0	0	0	0	0
mlpregressor_5	0	0	0	0	0	0
deep_CNN_10	0	0	0	0	0	0
DNN_5	0	0	0	0	0	0
SeriesNet_CNN_5	0	0	0	0	0	0
randomforestregressor	0	0	0	0	0	0

Fig. 7. Results of experiment 2: model-wise occurrence in top-5 ranks from cross-validation score

- Deep learning models outperform traditional machine learning models.
- It is seen that greater historical window size have higher rankings. The top 10 models in the rankings have window size of 20 or 10. The deep learning models with smaller lookback are at the bottom of the table with the reason being overfitting to local trends.
- It can be seen that with sufficient temporal information, even machine learning models can perform better than their IID counterparts.

5   Related Work

In the recent years, there have been many AI and ML frameworks proposed to relieve the pain points of data scientists. Frameworks like Scikit-learn [17], TensorFlow [1], Keras, PyTorch based on Torch [6], Theano [4], etc. provide API to define AI and ML experiments in python. Whereas cloud vendors like IBM [10], Amazon [2], Google [8], and Microsoft [15] provide infrastructure platforms and related APIs to execute machine learning jobs as a service on their respective platforms. These solutions provide many benefits to data scientists, however, they don't bridge the aforementioned gaps that are present for adoption of AI in Industries.

Our Solution, ThunderML, bridges these gaps by providing AI practitioners in the industry with a flexible and easy-to-use framework for defining high-level AI solutions built on top of other widely used open source frameworks like

Sklearn, Tensorflow, etc. It also provides a common interface for executing these AI solutions on different cloud vendors like IBM Cloud, Google Cloud, etc. with relative ease.

6 Conclusion

We have proposed ThunderML, a versatile toolkit for bridging fundamental gaps present in the adoption of AI in heavy industries. ThunderML aims to provide an easy yet flexible programming model which allows data scientists and AI practitioners to convert their unique problem statements into a purpose built and scalable AI pipelines quickly. It also helps practitioners leverage cloud-based environment for enabling AI pipelines with greater control using the two execution architectures. Finally, the case study attempts to provide evidence of the feasibility of ThunderML as a powerful and flexible toolkit which can prove vital in the hands of AI practitioners, as the time series prediction which forms the backbone of many industry solutions.

References

1. Abadi, M., et al.: TensorFlow: a system for large-scale machine learning. In: 12th {USENIX} Symposium on Operating Systems Design and Implementation ({OSDI} 2016), pp. 265–283 (2016)
2. Amazon: Machine Learning on AWS. https://aws.amazon.com/machine-learning/
3. Ardagna, C.A., Bellandi, V., Ceravolo, P., Damiani, E., Bezzi, M., Hébert, C.: A model-driven methodology for big data analytics-as-a-service. In: IEEE International Congress on Big Data, BigData Congress, pp. 105–112 (2017)
4. Bergstra, J., et al.: Theano: a CPU and GPU math compiler in python. In: Proceedings 9th Python in Science Conference, vol. 1, pp. 3–10 (2010)
5. Cheng, Y., Hao, Z., Cai, R., Wen, W.: HPC2-ARS: an architecture for real-time analytic of big data streams. In: IEEE International Conference on Web Services, ICWS, pp. 319–322 (2018)
6. Collobert, R., Bengio, S., Mariéthoz, J.: Torch: a modular machine learning software library. Technical report, Technical report IDIAP-RR 02–46, IDIAP (2002)
7. Feurer, M., Klein, A., Eggensperger, K., Springenberg, J., Blum, M., Hutter, F.: Efficient and robust automated machine learning. In: Cortes, C., Lawrence, N.D., Lee, D.D., Sugiyama, M., Garnett, R. (eds.) Advances in Neural Information Processing Systems 28, pp. 2962–2970 (2015)
8. Google: Cloud AI Products. https://cloud.google.com/products/ai/
9. Hochreiter, S., Schmidhuber, J.: Long short-term memory. Neural Comput. **9**(8), 1735–1780 (1997)
10. IBM: Watson Machine Learning. https://www.ibm.com/cloud/machine-learning
11. Kristpapadopoulos, K.: SeriesNet (2018)
12. Krizhevsky, A., Sutskever, I., Hinton, G.E.: ImageNet classification with deep convolutional neural networks (2012)
13. LeCun, Y., Bengio, Y., Hinton, G.: Deep learning. Nature **521**(7553), 436 (2015)
14. Liao, Y., Deschamps, F., de reitas Rocha Loures, E., Ramos, L.F.P.: Past, present and future of industry 4.0 - a systematic literature review and research agenda proposal. Int. J. Prod. Res. **55**(12), 3609–3629 (2017)

15. Microsoft: Microsoft Azure Machine Learning Studio. https://azure.microsoft.com/en-us/services/machine-learning-studio/
16. Olson, R.S., Bartley, N., Urbanowicz, R.J., Moore, J.H.: Evaluation of a tree-based pipeline optimization tool for automating data science. In: Proceedings of the Genetic and Evolutionary Computation Conference 2016, GECCO 2016, pp. 485–492 (2016)
17. Pedregosa, F., et al.: Scikit-learn: machine learning in Python. J. Mach. Learn. Res. **12**(Oct), 2825–2830 (2011)
18. Srivastava, N., Hinton, G., Krizhevsky, A., Sutskever, I., Salakhutdinov, R.: Dropout: a simple way to prevent neural networks from overfitting. J. Mach. Learn. Res. **15**(1), 1929–1958 (2014)
19. Van Den Oord, A., et al.: WaveNet: a generative model for raw audio. In: SSW, p. 125 (2016)
20. Zhang, P., Wang, H., Ding, B., Shang, S.: Cloud-based framework for scalable and real-time multi-robot SLAM. In: IEEE International Conference on Web Services, ICWS, pp. 147–154 (2018)

Study of Twitter Communications on Cardiovascular Disease by State Health Departments

Aibek Musaev(✉), Rebecca K. Britt, Jameson Hayes, Brian C. Britt,
Jessica Maddox, and Pezhman Sheinidashtegol

The University of Alabama, Tuscaloosa, AL 35487, USA
aibek@cs.ua.edu

Abstract. The present study examines Twitter conversations around cardiovascular health in order to assess the topical foci of these conversations as well as the role of various state departments of health. After scraping tweets containing relevant keywords, Latent Dirichlet Allocation (LDA) was used to identify the most important topics discussed around the issue, while PageRank was used to determine the relative prominence of different users. The results indicate that a small number of state departments of health play an especially significant role in these conversations. Furthermore, irregular events like ebola outbreaks also exert a strong influence over the volume of tweets made in general by state departments of health.

Keywords: Twitter · Cardiovascular disease · LDA · PageRank

1 Introduction

Cardiovascular disease (CVD) is the leading cause of death in the United States [6], with contributing factors including poor health and risk factors such as obesity and diabetes, among others [9]. While prevention is the optimal approach towards reducing CVD, the potential applicability of social media communication remains understudied. Health care professionals have increased their use of social media to engage with the public, to increase health care education, patient compliance, and organizational promotion [22]. To date, social media based health communication research has prioritized studies of theory, message effects, or disseminating interventions to end users [15]. However, state health departments' social media communication can engage with patients to improve their care [23].

Concurrently, research using social media has advanced considerably in recent years. API scrapers [1] enable the rapid collection of data from social media, while data analysis approaches such as time series analysis of user behaviors [14] and topic modeling through Latent Dirichlet Allocation (LDA) [13] allow large textual datasets to be rapidly analyzed in order to draw insights for basic

© Springer Nature Switzerland AG 2019
J. Miller et al. (Eds.): ICWS 2019, LNCS 11512, pp. 181–189, 2019.
https://doi.org/10.1007/978-3-030-23499-7_12

research as well as in applied contexts, such as those related to public health care and associated campaigns [3].

In this study, we analyzed social media activity of state health departments related to cardiovascular disease. The objectives of this study were (1) to determine the most active state health departments on Twitter with respect to cardiovascular disease, and (2) to determine the most important topics that were discussed and the most important terms used in those discussions.

See the next section for an overview of the proposed methodology and related work. Section 3 presents the experimental results using real data and Sect. 4 concludes the paper.

2   Overview and Related Work

In this study, we analyzed both the tweets posted by state departments of health and their Twitter accounts.

In analyzing tweets, we first propose to determine the peaks of public activity by aggregating the tweets posted by all users in the collected dataset for each month under study. To understand the key drivers of those peaks, we then perform a detailed analysis by identifying the most popular topics discussed during those peaks. See Sect. 2.1 for a description of the topic modeling approach used in this study.

For the user analysis, we first examine the total number of messages posted by state health departments since opening Twitter accounts. Then we analyze their communications with respect to cardiovascular disease using an extension of PageRank algorithm. See Sect. 2.2 for a description of the algorithm used to identify the most important users in the collected dataset.

2.1   Towards Understanding the Most Important Topics Discussed by the Public

Topic modeling in machine learning and natural language processing is a popular approach to uncover hidden topics in a collection of documents. Intuitively, given that a document, such as a tweet, is about a particular topic, one would expect certain words to appear more or less frequently than others. For example, words such as 'cardiovascular', 'heart', and 'stroke' will appear more frequently in tweets on cardiovascular disease, 'congress', 'vote', and 'policy' in documents about politics, and 'the', 'a', and 'is' may appear equally in both. Furthermore, a document typically discusses multiple topics in different proportions, e.g., 60% about politics and 40% about cardiovascular disease in a news article about passing a bill on CVD.

Popular topic modeling algorithms include Latent Semantic Analysis (LSA) [5,24], Hierarchical Dirichlet process (HDP) [4,10], and Latent Dirichlet Allocation (LDA) [12,13]. In this project, we use LDA to uncover the most important topics discussed by the public posted by or mentioning state departments of health. The study of alternative topic modeling algorithms will be explored in our future work.

In LDA, each document can be described by a distribution of topics and each topic can be described by a distribution of words [8]. Here topics are introduced as a hidden (i.e., latent) layer connecting documents to words. Note, that the number of topics is a fixed number that can be chosen either as an informed estimate based on a previous analysis or via a simple trial-and-error approach. See Sect. 3 for an application of LDA approach to determine the topics discussed during the peaks of public activity.

2.2 Ranking State Departments of Health by Social Media Influence

With the rise of social media platforms, such as Twitter, identification of the most influential users garnered a huge amount of interest [19]. Different Twitter influence measures have been proposed. Some are based on simple metrics provided by the Twitter API [7,17], while others are based on complex mathematical models [11,16].

In this study, we wanted to rank state departments of health by social media influence. Specifically, we wanted to identify the Twitter accounts whose posts on cardiovascular disease attracted the most amount of attention.

Given the dataset of Twitter users and their tweets, we built a graph where the users serve as nodes. The links between nodes are represented by reply relationships, such that the direction of a link is a directed edge from the author of the reply to the author of the original tweet that was replied to.

Given the directed graph, we can now

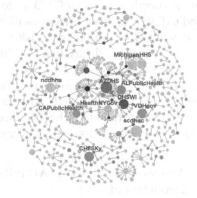

Fig. 1. User ranking based on reply relationships

apply a PageRank algorithm, which is a way of measuring the importance of nodes in a directed graph such as website pages [20]. PageRank works by counting the number and quality of the links pointing to a page to determine a rough estimate of their importance.

See Fig. 1 and the corresponding discussion in Sect. 3 for a visualization of the proposed approach.

3 Evaluation Using Real Data

In this section, we present a pilot study of Twitter communications involving state health departments. We begin by describing the data collection process used in this study in Sect. 3.1. Then we design two sets of experiments as follows. The first set of experiments (Sect. 3.2) analyzes the Twitter activity of all communication involving those departments while the second set (Sect. 3.3) focuses on the communication related to cardiovascular disease.

3.1   Data Collection

In this pilot study, we performed a set of experiments based on real-world data collected from Twitter. For data collection, we used a two-step process. In step 1, we downloaded basic data about tweets containing the keywords that we are interested in. Specifically, we used a JavaScript module called *scrape-twitter*[1]. It allows for querying Twitter for matching tweets based on keywords. In step 2, we used Twitter's statuses/lookup[2] feature that returns a complete set of data for up to 100 tweets at a time.

For keywords, we used the Twitter handles of state departments of health for each state, such as *@ALPublicHealth* for Alabama or *@HealthNYGov* for New York. This allowed us to collect 319k tweets ranging from November 2, 2007 to December 26, 2018 posted by 52.5k users including the 50 state departments of health. This represents a full dataset of all tweets either posted by or mentioning the state health departments.

For the dataset on cardiovascular disease, we filtered the full dataset based on the keywords related to CVD as follows. We included the keywords directly related to CVD, such as 'cardiovascular' and 'CVD.' We also added the keywords related to CVD symptoms and risk factors, including 'heart failure', 'heart disease', 'heart stroke', 'heart failure', 'blood pressure', 'atherosclerosis', 'arrhythmia', 'cardiac', and 'obesity.'

We released both datasets as a contribution to the research community[3]. These are the first published datasets that contain Twitter activity related to all 50 state departments of health covering an 11 year period. The datasets are provided as listings of tweet IDs in accordance with the Twitter policy[4].

3.2   Analysis of Twitter Activity Involving State Health Departments

In this experiment, we analyzed the overall Twitter activity involving state departments of health before focusing on the topic of cardiovascular disease in the next section. Specifically, we aggregated the total number of tweets posted by each department since they opened their Twitter accounts and plotted the results in Fig. 2.

As expected, we observed that the departments that opened their Twitter accounts earlier have a larger number of tweets compared to the departments that joined Twitter at a later date. However, there are recent accounts that managed to generate an unusually high amount of activity despite joining Twitter later, such as the Pennsylvania Department of Health account (*@PAHealthDept*) which joined Twitter on April 28th, 2015.

---

[1] https://www.npmjs.com/package/scrape-twitter.

[2] https://developer.twitter.com/en/docs/tweets/post-and-engage/api-reference/get-statuses-lookup.

[3] http://aibek.cs.ua.edu/files/sdh_all_ids.txt,   http://aibek.cs.ua.edu/files/sdh_cvd_ids.txt.

[4] https://developer.twitter.com/en/developer-terms/agreement-and-policy.

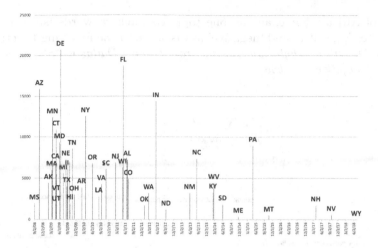

Fig. 2. Total number of tweets since opening accounts by state departments of health

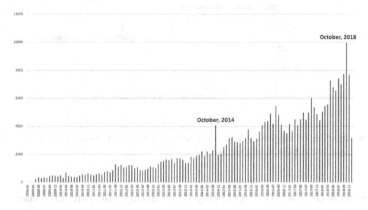

Fig. 3. Monthly Twitter activity involving state health departments, 2009–2018

Next, we analyzed the monthly Twitter activity across all state health departments and plotted the results in a time series graph in Fig. 3. Although we
observed an overall increase of the total number of tweets over time, there are
several peaks with an unusually high amount of activity compared to other
months, such as October, 2014 and October, 2018.

To understand the key drivers of the peak in October, 2014, we analyzed the
topics discussed during that month. Using sklearn [18], we trained an LDA model
based on an arbitrarily chosen number of topics $n\_topics = 10$. For illustration
purposes, we visualized the computed topics and the most important words in
those topics using t-SNE, or t-distributed stochastic neighbor embedding [21].

Based on the visualization shown in Fig. 4, we observed that ebola was an
important topic of discussion during October 2014, which is when ebola spread

outside of Africa[5]. For example, one topic contains keywords, such as 'says', 'dallas', 'test', 'health', and 'negative' as discussed in the following tweet: *JUST IN: Texas Health Presbyterian says test results for a Dallas Co Sheriff's deputy came back negative for ebola.*

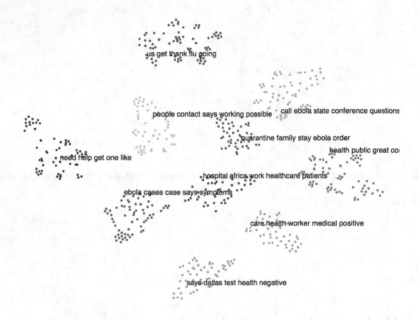

Fig. 4. Visualization of major topics discussed on Twitter involving state health departments in October, 2014 using LDA model

3.3 Analysis of Twitter Activity on Cardiovascular Disease

In this experiment, we analyzed Twitter communication on cardiovascular disease across all state health departments and plotted the results in a time series graph in Fig. 5. We observed that the largest peak of activity occurred in February 2018.

Then, we plotted a diagram of user rankings based on reply relationships in Fig. 1. The diagram was implemented using a JavaScript visualization library D^3 [2]. Each node represents a Twitter user in the dataset, directed edges are based on reply relationships, the color intensity is used to represent the number of tweets containing the search keywords each user has. Lastly, the size of a node is computed based on the PageRank algorithm as described in Sect. 2.2.

For visualization purposes, we added labels to the users with the highest ranking scores. Based on these results, Arizona Department of Health (*@AZDHS*) and South Carolina Department of Public Health (*@scdhec*) are among the most important social media users on cardiovascular disease.

---

[5] https://en.wikipedia.org/w/index.php?title=Ebola_virus_disease&oldid=876053081.

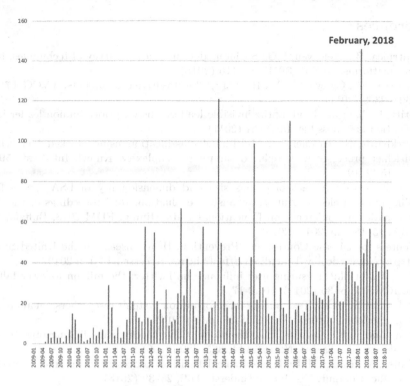

Fig. 5. Monthly Twitter activity on CVD, 2009–2018

4   Conclusion and Future Work

This study demonstrates the increasing Twitter usage of state departments of health and the role of cardiovascular disease and other health-related issues in their communication with the public. It also demonstrates the wide disparity in the Twitter presence of different state departments of health, with a minority of institutions taking an especially central role in conversations about health.

More broadly, this paper demonstrates an approach to mine and analyze social media data in order to draw conclusions about the behaviors and relative importance of various human and institutional actors, as well as the topics that drive conversation and the points in time at which those conversations shift.

Future research should address how individual users' activities affect their influence over time and how prominent actors, in turn, shape the social media conversation. Researchers should also study finer aspects of discourse about cardiovascular disease and other health issues, such as the social structure of conversations among underserved communities, as well as how health-related organizations can influence those conversations to promote healthy behaviors.

References

1. Batrinca, B., Treleaven, P.C.: Social media analytics: a survey of techniques, tools and platforms. AI Soc. **30**(1), 89–116 (2015)
2. Bostock, M., Ogievetsky, V., Heer, J.: D^3 data-driven documents. TVCG **17**(12), 2301–2309 (2011)
3. Britt, B.C., et al.: Finding the invisible leader: when a priori opinion leader identification is impossible. In: NCA (2017)
4. Burkhardt, S., Kramer, S.: Multi-label classification using stacked hierarchical Dirichlet processes with reduced sampling complexity. Knowl. Inf. Syst. **59**(1), 93–115 (2019)
5. Cai, Z., et al.: Impact of corpus size and dimensionality of LSA spaces from Wikipedia articles on AutoTutor answer evaluation. In: Proceedings of the 11th International Conference on Educational Data Mining, EDM 2018, Buffalo, NY, USA, 15–18 July 2018 (2018)
6. Centers for Disease Control and Prevention. Heart disease in the United States. https://www.cdc.gov/heartdisease/facts.htm/. Accessed 14 Jan 2019
7. Cha, M., et al.: Measuring user influence in Twitter: the million follower fallacy. In: ICWSM, p. 30 (2010). 10.10-17
8. Debortoli, S., et al.: Text mining for information systems researchers: an annotated topic modeling tutorial. In: CAIS 39, p. 7 (2016)
9. Van Gaal, L.F., Mertens, I.L., De Block, C.E.: Mechanisms linking obesity with cardiovascular disease. Nature **444**, 875–880 (2006)
10. Kaltsa, V., et al.: Multiple hierarchical Dirichlet processes for anomaly detection in traffic. Comput. Vis. Image Underst. **169**, 28–39 (2018)
11. Katsimpras, G., Vogiatzis, D., Paliouras, G.: Determining influential users with supervised random walks. In: WWW, pp. 787–792 ACM (2015)
12. Kim, D.H., et al.: Multi-co-training for document classification using various document representations: TF-IDF, LDA, and Doc2Vec. Inf. Sci. **477**, 15–29 (2019)
13. Li, C., et al.: Mining dynamics of research topics based on the combined LDA and WordNet. IEEE Access **7**, 6386–6399 (2019)
14. Matei, S.A., Britt, B.C.: Structural Differentiation in Social Media: Adhocracy, Entropy and the "1% Effect". Springer, Heidelberg (2017). https://doi.org/10.1007/978-3-319-64425-7
15. Moorehead, S.A., et al.: A new dimension of health care: systematic review of the uses, benefits, and limitations of social media for health communication. JMIR **15**(4), e85 (2013)
16. More, J.S., Lingam, C.: A gradient-based methodology for optimizing time for influence diffusion in social networks. Soc. Netw. Anal. Min. **9**(1), 5:1–5:10 (2019)
17. Noro, T., et al.: Twitter user rank using keyword search. In: 22nd European-Japanese Conference on Information Modelling and Knowledge Bases (EJC 2012), XXIV, Prague, Czech Republic, 4–9 June 2012, pp. 31–48 (2012)
18. Pedregosa, F., et al.: Scikit-learn: machine learning in Python. JMLR **12**, 2825–2830 (2011)
19. Riquelme, F., González-Cantergiani, P.: Measuring user influence on Twitter: a survey. IPM **52**(5), 949–975 (2016)
20. Sugihara, K.: Using complex numbers in website ranking calculations: a non-ad hoc alternative to Google's PageRank. JSW **14**(2), 58–64 (2019)
21. Van Der Maaten, L.: Accelerating t-SNE using tree-based algorithms. JMLR **15**(1), 3221–3245 (2014)

22. Ventola, C.L.: Social media and health care professionals: benefits, risks, and best practices. P&T **39**, 491–499 (2014)
23. Widmer, R.J., et al.: Social media platforms and heart failure. J. Cardiol. Fail. **23**(11), 809–812 (2017)
24. Yadav, C.S., Sharan, A.: A New LSA and entropy-based approach for automatic text document summarization. Int. J. Semantic Web Inf. Syst. **14**(4), 1–32 (2018)

Author Index

Printed in the United States
By Bookmasters